CAMPEAU

THE BUILDING OF AN EMPIRE

Michael Babad
and
Catherine Mulroney

Doubleday Canada Limited, Toronto

Canadian Cataloguing in Publication Data

Babad, Michael.
　Campeau: the building of an empire

ISBN 0-385-25208-0

1. Campeau, Robert, 1923-　. 2. Campeau Corporation — History.
3. Real estate development — Canada. 4. Consolidation and merger of
corporations. 5. Businessmen — Canada — Biography. 6. Real estate
developers — Canada — Biography. I. Mulroney, Catherine. II. Title.

HC112.5.C35B32 1989　　338.7′4′0924　　C89-094636-1

Typesetting: Southam Business Information
　and Communications Group Inc.
Jacket and photo section design: David Wyman
Front jacket photo: Peter Redman

Printed and bound in the USA by
　R.R. Donnelley and Sons

Published in Canada by
　Doubleday Canada Limited
　105 Bond Street
　Toronto, Ontario
　M5B 1Y3

"My maxim was, *la carrière est ouverte aux talents*
(the road is open to the talented),
without distinction of birth or fortune."

— Napoleon, St. Helena, March 3, 1817

For Jake

CONTENTS

PREFACE

THIS BOOK WAS written without the co-operation of Robert Campeau, who declined to be interviewed unless he could approve sections of the manuscript. The quotes attributed to him throughout the book come from speeches, published reports, interviews conducted prior to the inception of the book and from a single meeting in his Toronto office held to discuss his participation in the project.

In addition to these sources, Campeau's story has been pieced together from interviews with more than seventy people — friends, family members and business associates, as well as arbitrageurs and financial analysts who have followed the ups and downs of Campeau Corp. over the years and of the retailing industry in the United States. Most of the interviews, conducted with people in the Ottawa area, Montreal, the Sudbury region, Toronto, New York, Cincinnati and Columbus, Ohio, were taped. We also drew on thousands of pages of archival materials, among them published newspaper and magazine articles, government records, Campeau Corp. annual reports and documents, court documents, records of securities regulators and various statistical data.

This book could not have been written without the assistance of many people. Thanks to Bill Taylor, who came up with the idea, and Lesley Taylor, who pressed the issue. As well, thanks to our agent Lee Davis Creal, John Pearce and Maggie

Reeves of Doubleday Canada, and our editor, Rick Archbold, whose talents are surpassed only by his patience.

Thanks also to Victoria Gall; Jennifer Lanthier and Mitchell Martin, formerly of United Press International; Heather Clancy of United Press International; Glenn Flanagan; Monroe Greenstein of Bear, Stearns & Co., New York; and Barbara and Don Mulroney.

We also acknowledge the help of the *Financial Post*, the *Financial Times of Canada*, *The Globe and Mail*, the CBC's "Venture" program, Serge Barbe and the Ottawa City Archives, Mary Crocker and the Ontario Securities Commission, Linda Sullivan and the Ontario Municipal Board, and the finance desk of United Press International.

CAMPEAU: THE BUILDING OF AN EMPIRE

PROLOGUE

New York City, April 5, 1988

THE LIMOUSINE PULLED to a stop outside Bloomingdale's just before 8 P.M., and Robert and Ilse Campeau stepped into a cool night filled with the promise of spring. Bob's wavy, thinning gray hair was buffeted lightly by the breeze as Ilse took his arm. They both exuded elegance, wealth and good taste. Bob, trim-figured and ruddy faced, was resplendent in his black dinner jacket. Ilse, who stood a shade taller, wore a red and black lace gown, understated pearl and diamond earrings and a diamond bracelet. A fur stole was draped over her arm and her blonde hair was swept up, accentuating her cool patrician beauty. On this evening, Robert and Ilse Campeau looked every inch the royal couple, the king and queen of Manhattan.

Police barriers held back the large crowd of onlookers craning for a glimpse of the celebrities arriving for the Bloomingdale's Hooray for Hollywood AIDS benefit. Many were teenage girls; most of them had never heard of Robert and Ilse Campeau. They were there to see the Hollywood stars they had heard would be in attendance.

Flashing his dazzling, toothy smile, the new owner of Bloomingdale's and his wife made their way past the crowd and through the entrance of the store into a glamorous fantasy world. They were immediately ushered to the escalators by a phalanx of security men, then whisked upward to the seventh floor for a private glass of champagne with store executives, whose offices were in an area behind the towel department. There they chatted with Marvin Traub, the chairman of Bloomingdale's. Bob, who seldom drank alcohol and was drinking water rather than champagne, turned to his wife at one point and remarked that "New York tap water is the best — that's a known fact." Later as Traub, the experienced retailer, took them on a tour of the store, Campeau, a virtual newcomer to the industry, dominated the conversation, offering his views on running a store in Manhattan. "Macy's is going to 70, 80 percent private label," he said. "We're not going to go that way. If there's a downturn in the economy, down you go."

After the tour, Traub took the couple to the fourth floor to meet some of the hundreds of other guests. Actresses Brooke Shields and Jaclyn Smith were there; so were Douglas Fairbanks, Jr., comedienne Joan Rivers and fashion designers Calvin Klein and Oscar de la Renta. As the glitterati mingled, handsome young men in tuxedos and white gloves served them champagne and hors d'oeuvres from silver platters. Then it was dinner on the third floor, where the tables were adorned with palm fronds and exotic flowers, the tablecloths a silver-spangled black tulle. The evening ended on the fifth floor with after-dinner coffee, a cabaret and dancing. Bob and Ilse stayed late, glorying in their latest success as they rubbed shoulders with the privileged and famous.

Both could remember when things were very different. Ilse could recall her childhood in war-torn Germany; the sometimes lonely years cast in the role of "the other woman," raising Bob's child while he continued to keep up appearances with his first wife, Clauda; the disapproval of Bob's family and most of his friends; her desperation when it seemed he had gone back to Clauda for good.

Bob's memories went back much further — at age sixty-four he was almost seventeen years older than Ilse — to the hardships of growing up in a large French Canadian family in depression-era Sudbury. He could remember the crowded apartment where he and Clauda had struggled to make ends meet while coping with a sick baby. He could recall the heady early days building his first houses in postwar Ottawa, the battles with Mayor Charlotte Whitton, the meteoric growth of his company, the nervous breakdown that seemed like the end of it all. It had been a long, hard climb but on this night the boy from Chelmsford, Ontario, must have felt it was all worth it.

Bob Campeau is a complex man who is loved and hated, admired and feared. He is a tyrant in business who can ride roughshod over lesser egos. He has a famous temper, is quick with a threat when it suits him and is not afraid to wield money as a weapon. He is obsessed with winning, often selfish and vain. Yet he can be kind, generous, warm and loyal, eager to help a friend or relative in need. He can be a tender family man, and despite his sins he has always seemed to believe he can charm his way into Heaven.

On this April evening in 1988, New York City was still not sure what to make of the new boy on the block, the French Canadian developer with the audacity to buy a U.S. institution like Bloomingdale's, the grande dame of American department stores. Just six days earlier, he had emerged the victor in a bitter struggle for control of the parent company of Bloomingdale's, Federated Department Stores, the fifth-largest take-over in U.S. history.

Since the takeover, Bob Campeau's story has been told time and again. His name is constantly in the news, whether on the business pages, in society columns or on *Chatelaine* magazine's list of the ten sexiest men in Canada. His casual quips have been known to send share prices spinning. But the real Bob Campeau remains an elusive figure.

It seems as though everybody who has known him has a Robert Campeau story to tell. Many of these tales either are untrue or are exaggerations based on a nugget of truth. "A lot of things that have been said about Bob Campeau are almost a myth," says a former close associate. "A lot of the things that have been written and said about Bob have become a myth. A lot of it is not true."

But the truth, both good and bad, makes a remarkable success story.

PART I

Un Canadien Errant

1 / The Boy From Chelmsford

*"I thought any house with indoor plumbing
was a palace and I hated the people who
lived there."*
— Robert Campeau

JOSEPH AND LUCIE Campeau watched constantly over their
four-month-old son Robert during the bitter winter of
1923 – 24, certain a chest inflammation he had developed when
barely a few months old would kill him. The older children,
Beatrice, Ovila, Lionel and Gilbert, looked on as Lucie
administered camphor and hot compresses, just as she did for
them whenever they had chest colds. At first they did not even
consider calling the doctor. Robert's sickness did not seem
serious enough to warrant the trouble or expense. But Lucie's
ministrations failed to ease the baby's difficult breathing or
stop the crying that lasted as much as twenty hours a day. As
the days became weeks, the young couple grew increasingly
desperate; they had already lost three infant children. Finally
they turned to the only doctor in the tiny community of
Chelmsford, Ontario, near Sudbury. Dr. Rudolph Tanguay,
who had delivered Robert in this same cramped apartment,
was new in town and fresh from his medical training in
Montreal. He was young and inexperienced, but full of new
ideas.

As Lucie and Joseph watched anxiously, Dr. Tanguay
examined their failing child. Then he delivered his verdict. Yes,
indeed, there was a good chance little Robert would die of the
infection. But there was also a chance that a radical new
treatment would work: ice compresses instead of the tradition-

3

al hot ones. This prospect was too much for Lucie, who ran from the room in tears and waited upstairs, leaving her husband to talk to the doctor alone.

When Joseph called her a few minutes later, Lucie had calmed down somewhat. But the doctor had failed to convince her husband.

"Lucie, what are we going to do?" he asked.

"Do whatever you want," she replied. "We have nothing to lose anyway. I hate the thought of him in ice, but I'm willing to try it."

Joseph reluctantly agreed, and they instructed the doctor to proceed.

Tanguay packed the child in ice, and Robert remained that way for the next several days, steadily improving, although he would stay *chétif* — frail — for many months.

This early brush with death came to symbolize for other members of the family just what a fighter Robert Joseph Campeau was to be. "When he wants something, he doesn't let go," recalls his brother Lionel, who was nine years old when Robert was ill. "As a baby, he was quite a fighter. He didn't want to die, and he didn't die."

Illness was nothing new to the Campeau family; of the fourteen children Lucie bore, only seven survived past infancy. After Robert was born, Lucie, then thirty years old, herself fell ill for almost two weeks, during which Beatrice, at eleven the eldest child, cared for the baby while the oldest boy, Ovila, ten, tended their mother. A baby was born prematurely about ten months after Robert, and Lucie almost died during that labor. Only two of the six children born after Robert lived past young childhood.

Campeau's official curriculum vitae, distributed by the New York public relations firm he hired in 1988, gives his birthdate as 1924. But members of his family as well as legal documents say he was born on August 3, 1923. His first home was a two-room apartment annexed to a boarding house on the northeast corner of what is now Errington and Main in Chelmsford. Some of the family slept upstairs and some on the ground floor. St. Joseph's Roman Catholic Church, where the

Campeaus worshipped, still sits across the street. Other than that, Robert Campeau would likely find little to remind him of the tiny village of his birth. Chelmsford was then a settlement of unpaved roads and small houses. Now the roads are paved and the houses more modern. But it is still home to many of the men who worked in the mines of the Sudbury basin, an area of mountainous snowdrifts and bone-chilling winters.

Joseph Campeau's roots can be traced to Étienne Campeau, who sailed from France in the 1660s during the mass migration to New France and settled in the Montreal area. Joseph was born in Quebec in 1893, and around the turn of the century his family settled in Hanmer, another small satellite to Sudbury. There are still Campeaus living in and around Hanmer. There Joseph met Lucie Ranger, who had arrived from Quebec, and they were married in early 1911. Beatrice, their first child, was born that November.

Joseph was a restless sort, unable to settle in one spot for long. He moved his family from town to town as he went from venture to venture, working at such diverse jobs as lumberjack, farmer, blacksmith and auto mechanic in pursuit of the financial success that would raise his family above a marginal existence. During the First World War, he moved briefly to Montreal to work on the Grand Trunk Railway. But he kept returning to the Sudbury area, where his parents and many of his relatives had settled.

In 1923, just before Robert was born, Joseph, who like his wife was then thirty years old, moved the family to Chelmsford and opened his own combination garage–blacksmith shop. Most of the work in the small community was smithing, though there were about ten car owners who required a mechanic.

The oldest son, Ovila, now a retired diocesan priest, remembers his father as a man of imagination and determination, someone who believed in his stars. Yet his constantly shifting sights often led to trouble, usually of a monetary nature. Ovila's brother Lionel agrees.

Father Ovila Campeau, now a frail man in his mid-seventies, has retired to Chelmsford, and he lives at the rectory of St. Joseph's Church across the street from where Robert was born.

He clearly remembers his father's struggles for success. "You would think that whatever he undertook he would have had the necessary money to finance," he says. "He didn't make an awful lot of money always, but he spent money, spent money, spent money. Then the revenues were not as large as he thought they would be. And when he worked in the garage especially, he was too soft. Of course, he was not learned. He could hardly sign his name. Somebody would come and say he wanted his car fixed but did not have any money and would ask my father to please mark it down, and he would do something in the book. I think that 75 or 80 percent of those who had something on credit there never paid him."

Robert Campeau inherited both his father's generosity and his drive. He also inherited his father's way with machines and his determination to master every challenge. Joseph always had to understand how something worked. In 1920, his career as a blacksmith threatened by a changing world, Joseph taught himself mechanics by dismantling the engine of a Chevrolet 490 and reassembling it piece by piece. Though the experience taught him how to fix cars, Joseph did not yet grasp how an internal combustion engine worked. He fretted and worried the problem constantly, needing to understand the mechanics of it. One morning, much later, Joseph simply woke up and, turning to Lucie, said abruptly, "I understand it now."

Lucie Campeau, who was less than a year younger than her husband, was "a very simple woman," Father Ovila remembers. "She did not believe in wealth and big things. She believed very much in the farm, enjoying watching things grow, which you plant yourself, and earning your own living with that. And you pay your homage to God because it's so wonderful, all the things that come from the earth just for the living of man. She was very religious at heart, and she was very faithful, she was very honest, she was a very hard worker. She believed in work and simplicity. She did not believe in hard poverty, but she believed in enjoying life as God made it and gave it to us."

Like most French Canadian women of her era, Lucie was a faithful Roman Catholic. For her, worship was a pleasure, not an obligation. She enjoyed a life of hard work centered on her family and felt that even the simplest product of her garden glorified God.

Joseph, too, was a devout Roman Catholic and devoted family man. Each night when he returned from work he would immediately ask, "Where is the little one?" and he always reserved a place at his side at the dinner table for young Robert. He was generally a quiet man but when angry had a fierce temper.

Within a year of Robert's birth, Joseph abandoned his business and moved his family into Sudbury, to a house on Notre Dame Street in a French section of the city known as Moulin de Fleur. Here the family lived for the next seven or eight years. Joseph at first went to work as a blacksmith for a cartage firm – this was a time when most heavy vehicles were still pulled by horses. But the introduction of trucks soon revolutionized the industry, and Joseph became the company mechanic. Then he decided to open a garage in Sudbury in partnership with another French Canadian. When Robert was older, he would join his brothers helping out in the shop.

The Campeaus were a close family and spent many evenings together singing and dancing. (Bob enjoys singing and has been known to entertain more than one senior executive with lusty renderings of both traditional and salty French Canadian songs.) Every Sunday, they would drive to the country to visit uncles and aunts on their farms. They lived a simple life. Meals often included food from Lucie's garden. At Christmas, the toys were more often homemade than store bought. And the Campeaus were bonded by the shared experience of sorrow so deep it would be burned on their minds forever.

In the winter of 1930, when Robert was seven years old, his infant brother Gerard died. No one can now recall what caused the baby's death, but the memories of that time remain vivid. One of the rooms in the Sudbury home was draped in white, and the family held vigil by the little corpse for two days and two nights, speaking always in whispers. It was customary that someone always stay with the body, so each member of the family took his or her turn. Robert's uncles came to help, each staying for a few hours at a time so Joseph, Lucie and the children could sleep.

The funeral in Hanmer was a lonely and somber affair. Joseph drove the bad, frozen roads from Sudbury, with the children crowded in the back seat holding the four-foot casket on their knees. They were the only ones at the service at their old church. Then they took the casket to the cemetery and placed it in the *chaumière*, the small building where it would remain until the ground thawed in the spring. The cold was bitter, and when they returned home to Sudbury, the fire was out and the house freezing. Lucie went and sat in the rocking chair in the living room, wrapped in her coat, not speaking, as Joseph tried to get the fire going again.

What sort of child was Robert Joseph Campeau? His older brothers and sisters, who helped raise him, describe a cute, headstrong little boy with a flair for mischief. His oldest sister, Beatrice, now in her late seventies and still living in Hanmer, recalls that once, when Bob was about eight years old, on his way home from school in Sudbury he came upon a team of dogs harnessed to a cart and tied to a fire hydrant. Dogs and boy took to each other instantly and Robert and the dogs arrived home shortly before the police. When his father asked where the dogs came from, Robert boldly replied, "A man gave them to me." But the owner had promptly reported the dogs missing, and Joseph, on learning the truth, promised swift punishment, noting, "He took them, but believe me he'll pay for it."

Campeau early on revealed his knack for making a profit, bringing an entrepreneurial spirit to the classic childhood job of paperboy. The story is now part of the Campeau legend, one he and his family recount often, and like all such legends has probably been embellished over time, though there seems little doubt of its essential truth. After school during his days in Sudbury, Robert would race to be among the first to pick up his copies of the *Sudbury Star* and then would fight off older boys to protect the most profitable corner in town, Elm and Durham, near the post office in the heart of the city. But he was not content with just that. He saw a way to profit from his early arrival at the printing plant: he offered, for a percentage, to pick up papers for the other boys. Campeau recalls simply, "That's the way we sold newspapers in those days."

Father Ovila sees it differently: "He was very, very daring sometimes, bold, selling the *Sudbury Star*. He always looked for some way of making money when he was very young. That's an indication that it's always been in his mind to make a few dollars here and there."

When Robert was a child, Ovila was his hero and role model, and the two have remained close throughout their lives. Almost as soon as he could walk, Robert was following his older brother around the house. Later, when the family was living on a farm in Hanmer, whenever Ovila was home on vacation from Sacred Heart College in Sudbury, Robert was constantly at his heels, suggesting, "Why don't we do this, why don't we do that?" Ovila enjoyed lending a hand around the house, washing clothes and dishes or preparing meals. Robert insisted on helping him with these chores and was always hunting for new things for them to do. The boy particularly enjoyed outings to pick blueberries for their mother to preserve or bake into pies. Younger sister Gerarda recalls that on these expeditions Robert would never let Ovila out of his sight and would always pick just as many blueberries as his brother.

Ovila enjoyed carving toys for his little brother, but Robert soon outshone him, demonstrating at an early age an innate talent with his hands. During one summer vacation, when Robert was about twelve, Ovila attempted to build a small cupboard in the basement of the Campeau home. Sawing the wood, Ovila cut a good straight line crosswise, but his cut top-to-bottom was crooked.

"Don't you know how to cut a board the right way?" young Robert asked. "It has to be a right angle this way and the other way."

He took the saw and demonstrated the proper cut, handing the board to Ovila.

"See, *that's* straight," he said.

In later years, Ovila became his brother's spiritual counselor in times of crisis. At one time, when Robert was overwhelmed by a personal crisis involving the women in his life, it was his older brother who suggested he once again turn to working with his hands to help him think through his problems.

The Sudbury area, where the Campeau family lived for most of Robert's childhood, was the world the boy first explored. The Sudbury Basin in the late 1920s had a population of about 37,000 people. The region's primary industry was mining, and its largest employer was International Nickel (now Inco, the largest nickel miner in the non-communist world). The huge smelting operations that processed the raw ore belched clouds of pollution that stripped vegetation for miles around and caused serious erosion of the bleak basin of Precambrian rock in which Sudbury lies. When Robert Campeau was old enough to notice his surroundings, the Sudbury area resembled a blackened moonscape whose major physical feature was the mountains of spent slag from the smelters. (The landscape is so barren that the Apollo XI astronauts rehearsed their 1969 moon mission there.) International Nickel employed many people from families such as the Campeaus, French Canadians lured west along the CPR line from Montreal by the prospect of work. Today, French Canadians make up about one-third of the city's population.

The French community in Sudbury in the late twenties and thirties was tight-knit; though the Campeaus all learned to speak English, they spoke French at home, attended primarily French parochial schools and socialized mainly among *la francophonie*. Sudbury had its own French districts, notably Moulin de Fleur and Frenchtown, where the Campeaus later lived. The region was one of several Francophone pockets in a province then known for its staid Anglo foundations. The French and English got on well enough, partly because Sudbury lacked the linguistic class lines that could be found in such cities as Montreal, where the English elite laid claim to the exclusive neighborhoods and controlled the levers of economic power, and partly because Sudbury was already home to a great mix of cultures.

"French people in Sudbury had to fight for two things,"

Campeau once remarked. "One was to preserve our French culture and traditions. The other was to get ahead in the world. In Sudbury, life was easier for Finns and Ukrainians, who were prepared to assimilate. Everyone resented us because we wouldn't give up our language. That was why we had more trouble getting ahead in the mines and other places."

Campeau recalls a scuffle during a Dominion Day parade with some schoolboys bearing a Union Jack, the British flag which was then Canada's flag. Robert held high a flag emblazoned with a maple leaf and waved it proudly through the streets. "I was brought up in the separate school system with a Francophone background, and I'm proud of it," he said in a speech many years later. "On May 24 Victoria Day, we used to go out at night amid the fireworks and tear down as many Union Jacks as we could. Not because we hated England. We certainly didn't want a French flag. We wanted a Canadian flag and wanted to be recognized as Canadians. We wanted Canada to be a country, not subjected to any special ties with anybody, including England."

Robert was just six when the Great Depression hit, and when he recalls his childhood he tells of his father losing everything during the Dirty Thirties. However, Father Ovila and Lionel remember things differently, saying that throughout the thirties Joseph and the family lived on a farm on Dominion Drive in Hanmer. Lucie raised fruit and vegetables in a big garden. They kept a few head of cattle, some pigs and a few hens. The produce of the farm combined with Joseph's wages and his government relief payments, supplemented by the few dollars he could earn hauling gravel with his team of horses, meant the family did not suffer unduly by the standards of the day. Indeed, the Campeaus were among the few families in the Hanmer area who owned a car. They were poor but not destitute. Nonetheless, their living conditions were primitive. "When I was growing up, I thought any house with indoor plumbing was a palace and I hated the people who lived there," Bob Campeau later recalled.

His formative years were shaped as much by the Catholic Church as by the bilingual culture of Sudbury and the rigors of the depression. The Church — the revolutions of Vatican II decades away — was an institution whose believers never questioned its authority on morality and, indeed, life in general. These were the days when young Catholics were warned of the evils of *les danses dangereuses et les baisers prolongés* — slow dancing and prolonged kissing. Priests urged their congregations to pray *plus vite et plus fort* — faster and louder. Most of the French Catholic clergy in Ontario had been educated in Quebec, and they brought with them a strong sense of French Canadian nationalism, preaching "one language, one faith, one school." And since French Catholic children generally attended parochial schools, these teachings became part of their everyday thinking. Robert Campeau, a student at French Catholic schools, was no exception.

Grade 8 was as far as Robert got in his formal education, the end of an unremarkable academic career. He did not skip much school, but, like most boys his age, he was far from a devoted student — though he was always the leader of his group of friends. His cousin Antonio (Tony) Campeau, who lived near the farm in Hanmer, remembers Joseph once bringing Robert to school and issuing a stern warning to stay there. About five minutes after Joseph left, Robert was gone for the day. "He couldn't stay quiet," Tony recalls. "He's got to be on the move."

Robert was fourteen when he quit school for good in 1937 and started to work full time. His first job was with Smith and Travers, a research company that drilled exploratory mine shafts. After a few months there, he got a job with International Nickel as a general laborer, even though Ontario's Mining Act at the time prevented youths under the age of eighteen from working underground in the mines and those under sixteen from employment in aboveground operations. Campeau simply lied his way into the job with the unwitting help of the Catholic Church. One of Robert's brothers, René, had died at about the age of three, roughly a year before Robert was born. René's baptismal certificate was in the hands of the pastor of St. Jacques Church in Hanmer. So Robert went to see the pastor and asked for his dead brother's certificate. The priest obliged, and Robert was in possession of proof that he was eighteen years old. The certificate read only "R. Campeau," and International Nickel registered Robert's birthdate as June 18, 1919.

He started work in the maintenance shop at International Nickel, sweeping floors for 55 cents an hour. It was a giant open-pit mine where large trucks worked on a merry-go-round system, continuously carrying ore from the crusher to the smelter. Campeau made his name there one afternoon when various problems had sidelined all but two trucks, and then the engine of one of the remaining pair began to knock, threatening to cripple the entire operation.

Robert approached the maintenance shop's master mechanic as he stood discussing the problem with other workers.

"You know, I think I can fix your truck," Robert said.

"What do you mean?" asked the mechanic.

"Well, we're going to take the pan off, I'm going to take the emery wheel and I'm going to grind the crankshaft and fix what's causing the knock. It could work for the time it'll take to finish repairing another truck, and then we can bring this one back in and do a proper job on it."

The master mechanic mulled it over for a few minutes before replying, "You might just be able to do that."

So Robert worked through the night, and the truck was put back in the system long enough for another to come out of the shop.

Many such stories are told about the years in which Robert Campeau grew to manhood. He was good with his hands and was never afraid to assert himself when the opportunity presented itself. Although some undoubtedly resented this brashness, his native charm seems to have smoothed the way and generally won the day.

He continued to work for International Nickel until the spring of 1940, still as a general laborer. He put in extra hours without pay to try to rise above that status, spending as much time as he could learning the machines. In less than two years, he was referring to himself as an expert machinist.

In May of 1940, the Campeau family, including uncles

and aunts and cousins from the Sudbury area, traveled the seventy-five miles to North Bay for Ovila's ordination into the priesthood. The Campeaus sat in their pews in the crowded cathedral, watching with pride as Ovila, with five others, went through the ceremony. When the service was over, the family knelt at the communion rail and Father Ovila, laying his hands on their heads, blessed each one in turn. It was a very solemn moment for all involved, particularly Joseph and Lucie, who, now forty-seven years old, would remember the day to their graves.

Not all their children would go as far as their eldest son, though the ones who were out in the world were doing well for themselves. (Their youngest, Gerarda and Thérèse, were still living at home.) Beatrice had married a Falconbridge mine worker, Matte Larivière, a good man, and the couple was leading a stable life in Hanmer. Lionel, just after completing high school in 1937, had married Rolande Prevost and now worked for International Nickel. He had two children. Lionel was also active in French Canadian politics, his latent nationalism stirred by the threat of conscription. Gilbert, now working at International Nickel, was about to marry Blanche Laframboise. Then there was Robert, still living at home and still with International Nickel, but a lively and self-confident seventeen-year-old who was determined to succeed.

The coming of war brought new economic opportunities for Joseph Campeau, who, around the time of Ovila's ordination, moved to the town of Nobel, Ontario, near Parry Sound, so he could work at a munitions plant. The Second World War was nine months old, and munitions factories were springing up throughout central Canada to supply the Allied effort. Robert and Lionel followed their parents to Nobel and lived with them while working at the same plant as their father. In 1941 the family packed up again and moved to Valleyfield, Quebec, southwest of Montreal, to work in another war plant. In 1942 they returned to the Sudbury area, to a farm near the town of Blezard Valley, and Robert rejoined International Nickel's maintenance department.

It was in Blezard Valley that he met a brash teenager, Maurice Bisaillon, known as Bidou, who ran a pool hall in town and had a definite eye for pretty girls. So did their friend Côme Belisle, who later married Robert's youngest sister, Thérèse. The three young men spent much of their spare time playing pool and talking about girls. In the summer they went swimming together and in winter dog-sledding.

"His family was on a farm a mile away," Bidou recalls. "In those days a mile was nothing, and we'd walk halfway, we'd meet at the same beach or wherever. I had a poolroom. Pool was really the only thing to do for boys our age. We were big boys then. We'd lift 150 pounds, and we were all right."

Robert soon began dating Bidou's seventeen-year-old sister Carmen. She was a striking girl, tall and slim with dark hair and brown eyes and a lively sense of humor. But the relationship perturbed Carmen's father, who did not like the way Campeau styled his long hair — puffed at the front and slicked back — or that he combed it so often. He asked frequently, "Why the hell doesn't he cut it?" He also frowned upon Robert's late arrivals at Mass and Lionel's expanding political activities. And he feared that because the Campeaus moved so often, his daughter might leave Blezard Valley. He warned Carmen that if she married she would become *un oiseau sur une branche* — a bird on a branch — flitting from place to place. But to Carmen, eighteen-year-old Bobby, with his "cute little mustache," was "my kind of man."

Campeau was exempt from home conscription, introduced in the summer of 1940 by Mackenzie King's Liberal government, because he had worked at the Valleyfield munitions plant, a vital industry. But some of his friends were not. This was a time of worsening tension between French and English. English Canadians, referring to home conscripts as mostly French "zombies" while the enlisted soldiers overseas were primarily English, were pushing for full conscription while the French were opposed. King's government, pulled in two directions, held a plebiscite in the spring of 1942 to determine whether Canadians were prepared to release Ottawa from its pledge of no conscription for overseas service. The country voted 80 percent in favor of the resolution, while Quebec voted more than 70 percent against.

Bidou was among those who feared they would be called. So in 1942, when Campeau was preparing to head off to Cornwall, Ontario, to work in another munitions factory, Bidou decided to go with him.

One night before they left Blezard Valley, Campeau proposed to Carmen as they sat on the sofa in her parents' living room. "I remember it well," Carmen says. "We were sitting in the living room and every time Dad would go by we'd probably be in each other's arms and that."

Carmen did not come right out and say no, but she did say she was too young to marry. They continued to date for a while, until Carmen's father told her one day that she must end her relationship with Bob. He never explained why, and she still does not know. But he was not to be disobeyed, and when Bob came to pick her up one evening to take her to a birthday party, Carmen remained upstairs. She had left him a note saying her father had forbidden her to go to the party or to see him again. She has seen Bob only once since, in an elevator in an Ottawa hospital about fifteen years ago. He appeared not to recognize her, and she did not speak to him.

Still, when Robert left for Cornwall, his family expected he would marry Bidou's sister eventually. Thus they were shocked when he phoned home just a few months later to announce his engagement to another woman.

2 / Clauda

"That's Bob, the way he is — he wants the best."

— Bidou Bisaillon

IT WAS THE FIRST time Bob and Bidou had lived away from their families, but Cornwall was not an especially alien environment. The population then as now was about 25 percent French-speaking, and many Quebeckers commuted from across the nearby provincial border to work in the town's industries. So Bob and Bidou fit easily into the large French Canadian community. They were among many young people attracted by the jobs in the new plants that had opened since the war began. And there was no chance they would be without company: Bob's brother Lionel, his wife Rolande and their two daughters moved with them to Cornwall.

Bob's connections landed him, Bidou and Lionel jobs at the new Dominion Industries munitions plant. Their boss was Jack Pace, whom Campeau had first worked for in Valleyfield. In fact, Pace so admired the young man who seemed able to master any manual skill, from carpentering to mechanics, that when he retired years later he gave Bob his custom-designed toolbox and tools.

The three young men worked at first as carpenters, then as millwrights, maintaining machinery. Campeau was an old hand at this kind of work, but Bidou was more familiar with a pool cue than a wrench and recalls with fondness how Campeau, who was senior to him in the plant, helped him along. Bidou describes Campeau as a perfectionist who worked six days a

17

week and put in extra hours to ensure the work was flawless. "He showed me the trade and he was very good. If he made a mistake, he wouldn't tell anybody. He would work an hour extra and repair it. Couldn't be a mistake. That's the way he was."

Though there was not much time for a social life, Bob and Bidou were two nineteen-year-olds on the prowl, and they found the pace at their rooming house too slow. But it was not long before they stumbled on something much better. One evening they were chatting with Mme Boileau, the wife of the owner of a restaurant the boys frequented, two doors down from where they were staying.

"Do you know anybody who has a room?" they asked her.

Mme Boileau sized up Bob and Bidou and decided she liked what she saw. "I think I might know somebody," she replied, revealing nothing. "Come back tomorrow evening."

The next evening, Bob and Bidou dutifully showed up at the Boileaus' restaurant and were informed by Mme Boileau that she herself ran a boarding house and would make space so the boys could share a room. Already in the restaurant that evening were three of her five female boarders, who had come to check out their future housemates. The three young women sat in the booth opposite Bob and Bidou and ogled. There was much giggling and whispering before the two groups were formally introduced by Mme Boileau. By the end of the evening all five were sitting together, talking like old friends.

One of the three girls was a beautiful seventeen-year-old named Clauda Leroux. Bidou remembers her as easily the nicest and most attractive of the group, and it was soon obvious that Campeau agreed. As Bidou escorted her from the restaurant, Bob, who was farther back with the other two women, moved up and maneuvered his friend out of the way so he could accompany Clauda home to Mme Boileau's rooming house.

"I used to like them good-looking myself, but in the other places I used to get them first," Bidou recalls. "And I didn't suspect that he was going to work so fast because he never did before. He was so goddamn slow in the past that he really tripped me on that one."

Nonetheless, as Bob's relationship with Carmen had shown, he definitely had an eye for a pretty woman. "Bob always wanted the better-looking girls," Bidou says. "And he always wanted the best. If he bought a truck, for instance, it was new and shiny. And his clothes would be flashy. He didn't buy much, but that's Bob, the way he is. He wants the best."

As Bob's brother Lionel remembers her, Clauda Leroux was a young woman of warmth and charm with lovely blue-green eyes. "She had special eyes, very expressive eyes," he says. "They were *auréole*, as we say in French. It was a kind of shade around her blue eyes."

Slim and athletic, Clauda in her youth had been something of a tomboy who enjoyed playing baseball in the schoolyard with the boys. Now she had developed a kind of beauty that prompted people to remark that she could be a model.

Campeau may have moved fast that first evening, but over the next several weeks it was Bidou who became friends with Clauda. While Campeau would remain at home Saturday nights to plot the following week's work, Bidou, Clauda and a couple of the other women would go out for the evening to bowl or have a drink. So it came as a surprise when Campeau made his next play. Bidou recalls it was a Saturday about five weeks after he and Bob had moved into the Boileau rooming house. Campeau had left work early and come home to find Bidou, Clauda and another couple preparing to leave for a weekend in Montreal. Bob approached the car.

"Clauda, come on out, I want to speak to you," he said.

Clauda got out and spent several minutes talking to Bob before returning to Bidou in the car.

"Bob says he wants to marry me if I don't go to Montreal with you," she told her weekend date.

"Well, what do you want to do, get married or go to Montreal?" Bidou replied. "I'm going to Montreal. You want to get married? Go and get married."

At that, Clauda left the car without another word. Bidou, faced with a weekend without female companionship, went back inside the house to ask one of the other women to go with him. He remembers only that she was a schoolteacher whose entire wardrobe seemed to consist of two black dresses, one of which she was wearing.

"I went upstairs and I got the schoolteacher," he says, with a wry smile and a gleam in his eye. " 'Come on, we're on our way,' I said. She said she didn't have anything to wear. I said, 'Well, wear the other black dress.'"

Robert Campeau was nineteen and Clauda Leroux only seventeen. Her older sister Laura, who was also her best friend, remembers Clauda visiting her in Ottawa in September of 1942, not long after the engagement, and showing off the photograph of Bob she carried with her.

"She was so much in love with him," Laura recalls. "There was nothing else."

It was only now that they had become engaged that the young couple began to get to know each other well. They had much in common — their mother tongue, their Roman Catholicism — but Clauda's life had already been marked by great tragedy. When she was seven years old, her father, a cheesemaker, had died in a car accident, leaving the family with his pension and a small insurance policy. Her mother used the insurance money to buy a small house in Alfred, Ontario, just east of Ottawa, and raised her five daughters as best she could, selling her knitting and the vegetables she grew in her garden to supplement her meager income. When Bob told her of his own family, she could more than relate to their struggle to make ends meet.

Soon after the war began, when Clauda was sixteen, she and Laura left home to work, packing bullets in a munitions plant near Lachute, Quebec. Six months later, Clauda left for Cornwall, hoping to make more money there. When Campeau met her, she was working full-time in a textile mill and part-time as a waitress. Bob understood what her life was like. He had started work at fourteen and he too had been moving from job to job and town to town ever since.

Bob's proposal to Clauda may have been an impetuous act, but the two were soon deeply in love. At work, he spoke often to his brother Lionel of Clauda, the angel he had met. Before long, Lionel and Rolande were introduced to Clauda, and they too fell in love with her. One Saturday evening, Lionel and his wife hosted a small dinner party for the couple, inviting Bidou as well. Bob brought a case of beer. Rolande cooked a simple dinner. They talked about the progress of the war, Mackenzie King's betrayal with conscription, the conditions at the factory. After dinner they danced, waltzing and foxtrotting, singing along with Lionel's recordings of Tino Rossi, an Italian who sang in French, Maurice Chevalier, Rita Care and Ray Ventura.

A few days later, Campeau borrowed $235 from Bidou to order a wedding band and modest diamond ring from the People's Credit Jewellers catalogue. When the package arrived by train from Montreal, Campeau, as always, was at work, so Clauda was the one to pick up her own ring at the train station.

Bob and Clauda set the date for late December 1942. The place would be Alfred, Ontario, where Clauda's mother still lived. A few weeks before the wedding, Campeau hopped a bus to Ottawa, where he would for the first time meet Clauda's beloved sister Laura. Laura would then take Bob home to meet his future mother-in-law, also for the first time, and discuss plans for the wedding. Laura remembers quite clearly the Friday night when she met Bob Campeau for the first time. He appeared at the restaurant they had agreed on, sporting a big grin and lugging a battered old green suitcase borrowed from Bidou. One of the first things that struck Laura about her future brother-in-law was his appetite — he ate at least three hamburgers, possibly four, she cannot remember for sure. And she, like so many, was taken by his charm. Before they parted, Bob promised to meet her the next day at the bus station on Albert Street to catch the 1:30 bus to Alfred.

The following afternoon, Laura and a girlfriend arrived in good time and waited on the bus.

But they soon became concerned. Departure was only a few minutes away and still there was no sign of Bob. She had not asked him where he'd planned to sleep, and had no idea where he was. At the very last moment, he suddenly came racing down the street, carrying the old suitcase. Just as he was about to board the bus, the handle broke off and the suitcase fell to the ground, spilling clothes across the road.

"I don't know if it was embarrassing for him," Laura says. "He's not embarrassed very easily. I was. In front of my friend, I was more embarrassed than him. I think he was laughing."

Campeau and Clauda were married on December 28, 1942, in a quiet ceremony at St. Victor's Catholic Church in Alfred. Campeau called Bidou as his witness. Clauda's mother, Azilda, and sister Laura attended, as did Alban Cadieux, Laura's fiancé. But none of Campeau's family could make it. It was winter and too far to travel from Sudbury. After the service, the wedding party of about fifteen people returned to the Leroux home for wine and a small meal before Clauda and Bob left for a brief honeymoon at the Lord Elgin Hotel in Ottawa.

Bidou went off to join the Royal Canadian Air Force, deciding that was infinitely preferable to the life of an army conscript. He was never called to fight overseas and spent the remainder of the war in a construction maintenance unit in Ottawa. After he left the air force, he joined an Ottawa construction company.

Bidou, who is happily married with several grandchildren, is now retired and living in Sudbury. He still remembers, however, his disappointment when Clauda agreed to marry his best friend. "We stayed friends, and that was it," Bidou says. "There was no fighting or anything like that. I was disappointed, really. I was disappointed that it happened that way, but there are always other days."

Bidou remained friends with Bob and Clauda during the next several years, although he would visit them only occasionally.

For the first half of 1943, Bob continued to work at the Dominion munitions plant in Cornwall, and he and Clauda moved into a large apartment. Life was happy for the young couple. Sometimes they would go to dances or parties thrown by friends. On several occasions they joined Lionel and his wife Rolande on weekend trips to Montreal to hear a new singer at a nightclub and enjoy the bright lights of the big city. During this time, they also saw a lot of Laura and her beau, Alban, who often traveled to Cornwall to visit Bob and Clauda. The Campeaus frequently returned the visits.

Alban Cadieux was a quiet man who at age twenty seemed years older than the nineteen-year-old Clauda had just married. Alban's father and mother ran the general store in Alfred, where he and his three brothers and two sisters had spent many childhood Saturdays and afternoons after school helping out. When Bob and Clauda married, Alban was in school studying to become a veterinarian, but soon abandoned his studies. Laura and Alban today own and operate a golf course just outside Montreal.

Bob and Alban became friends, and their relationship would eventually develop into a business partnership that would be the first but certainly not the last time Bob Campeau would mix business and family. For a good part of his life, though, Alban would live in his brother-in-law's shadow.

Laura remembers the young Bob Campeau as headstrong and just as persuasive as he is today. That winter, Bob and Clauda, in Alfred for a weekend visit, suggested that Laura and Alban accompany them on the forty-mile cab ride back to Cornwall. The trouble was that a heavy snowstorm had been raging since morning, and the deep snow had made the roads virtually impassable. But Campeau insisted that he and Clauda return home that night, despite the protests of Clauda's mother.

"You can't go," said Mme Leroux. "The storm's not over and there are no cars on the road."

Campeau persevered, finally coaxing Clauda, Laura and Alban into a taxi, which set off into the blizzard. They got only about four miles beyond town before they were forced to stop. The cab could not make it any farther and it could not go back. The two young couples, in danger of freezing in the storm, approached the nearest farm, whose owner knew Alban's family and would gladly have let them stay the night. Instead, Bob persuaded the reluctant farmer to let them use his horses and sled to return to Alfred.

"Bob was so convincing," Laura recalls. "When he wants something, he *wants* it."

Work at the war plants was often short-term, a matter of installing machinery for a few months. Then, machinists would either stay on to maintain the equipment or move on to another project. In the summer of 1943, when the job in Cornwall was finished, Bob and Clauda moved with Lionel and his family to Sarnia, Ontario, where the two men did a similar job at another munitions plant. After only a few months, they returned to Sudbury, Campeau to work for the last time in International Nickel's maintenance department. Bob and Clauda moved into the Campeau family home, where Clauda befriended Bob's two younger sisters, Gerarda and Thérèse, often helping them clean the house and finding that work fun.

Lionel also returned to Sudbury and threw himself back into politics. He became deeply involved in the formation of a new political party, the Bloc populaire Canadien. He had worked for the "No" campaign during the plebiscite over conscription, and the Bloc, a Quebec-based group, led the battle against full conscription. In 1943, this battle was escalating to the point where it would soon explode in fights between English and French schoolchildren and between soldiers and so-called zoot-suiters — as the English called French draft dodgers — on the streets of Montreal. As tension mounted between the English and French communities, the Bloc grew quickly.

Bob and Clauda lived generally on the fringe of Lionel's political activities, which at times could involve four or five meetings in the space of one weekend in various towns all over northern Ontario. But sometimes they would accompany him. "He was quite a speaker, Lionel, and they would come home at night and talk about what had happened," recalls Campeau's younger sister Gerarda. "He had a special talent for that, Lionel." Thus, through Lionel, Campeau became exposed to the deep political feelings of his French brethren.

The most involved Campeau got in politics at this time was during the visit of Camillien Houde to northern Ontario in the fall of 1944, part of his campaign to rouse French Canadian feeling inside and outside Quebec. Houde, a large man with a prominent nose who smoked foul-smelling cigars, had just been released from prison and re-elected mayor of Montreal in the summer of 1944. He had been interned for advising his constituents not to take part in the national registration mandated under the National Resources Mobilization Act in 1940. His incarceration had made him into a French Canadian martyr, and Bob was fascinated. He wanted to meet this charismatic figure. "Robert had not shown very much interest in the plebiscite or the Bloc populaire campaign before that, but Camillien Houde interested him," says Lionel.

It is safe to assume that Bob was attracted more to the man than to his ideas. Houde was famous, he had a large and passionate following, he could shape people's opinions and affect the course of history. Perhaps one day Bob could be as powerful and influential.

Since Lionel was accompanying Houde on part of the swing through northern Ontario, it was easy enough to arrange for Bob Campeau to become Camillien Houde's chauffeur. Bob borrowed his uncle's Studebaker and drove with Lionel to North Bay, where they met Houde and his daughter, who were arriving by plane from a meeting the night before in Quebec City.

After a short meeting in North Bay, the entourage headed back toward Sudbury, stopping about halfway for a speaking engagement in Sturgeon Falls. Then, on to such places as St. Charles, Noelville, Chelmsford and Sudbury, spreading their political gospel to the transplanted French in Ontario. Everywhere, Houde was greeted by cheering crowds. In the outlying areas, the meetings, held in parish halls, lasted about forty-five minutes. At each meeting, Houde was the main speaker, and after he left the podium Lionel would take his turn. During the long rides between towns, Houde talked, between puffs on one of his pungent Tueros cigars, of internment, the war, Mussolini (whom he admired), and of his belief that the structure of governing in Canada was changing and that the federal government would grow rapidly as it became involved in more areas of society. With the growth of the government, Houde predicted, the city of Ottawa also would grow.

Houde had had a tiring, busy day by the time they stopped for dinner, and he was annoyed with Lionel for planning so many speaking engagements in one day. He did not want to go to the event planned for Chelmsford, but rather on to Sudbury to finish off this leg of the tour. Bob convinced Houde, however, to stop in his hometown, and when they arrived the parish picnic grounds were filled with townsfolk and farmers from the surrounding area. Houde stayed for about two hours, and Lionel had to go on ahead to Sudbury to start the meeting there because the star attraction would be late.

After the gathering in Chelmsford, Bob bundled Houde into the Studebaker and raced to Sudbury, arriving at about 10 P.M. Not only were the two floors of the Ste. Anne parish hall packed but the street outside was filled with people waiting to listen to the great man's speech through loudspeakers. Bob Campeau must have been impressed.

Despite the efforts of Houde and the Bloc populaire, conscription was inevitable, though its introduction late in 1944 caused a political crisis in the King government, and French Canada withdrew its support of the Liberals. Nonetheless, in the first election after the war ended, Lionel Campeau, running for the Bloc populaire, was unable to unseat the Liberal in Nipissing riding. King's Liberals were returned to power with a reduced majority. "I even lost my deposit," Lionel recalls.

Bob Campeau took no part in his brother's campaign. As usual, he was too busy working and looking for every opportunity to better himself. As he would later disclose to Alban Cadieux and Lionel, ever since he had worked at his father's garage as a boy he had dreamed of building his own machine shop in Sudbury. The shop would sell to International Nickel and Falconbridge, the two big mining concerns in the area, and he would become rich. This dream never materialized, but it is indicative of his restless desire to get ahead.

He finally quit International Nickel in late 1945 to take a job as a millwright at a pulp mill opening just west of Sudbury. After only about two weeks, Lionel recalls, Bob was named foreman. There was something about this cocky twenty-two-year-old, a know-it-all who actually had the knowledge and skills to back up his bravado. He had been at the pulp mill for about a year when the company decided to shut it down and lay off the workers.

By now, Bob Campeau was getting tired of working for others.

Then, one day in 1946 when he and Clauda were visiting Laura and Alban, who had recently married and were now living in the Ottawa suburb of Orleans, restlessness turned to resolution. Alban was complaining about his job in a nearby cheddar cheese factory. He had slashed his forefinger, developed blood poisoning and could no longer keep his hands under water for long periods — something the work required.

"Why don't you come with me?" Campeau said. "We'll go to Cornwall and we'll do something, I don't know what."

So began one of the longest business associations of Campeau's career.

Alban quit his job and the two couples set off for Cornwall. Bob, Clauda, Alban and Laura and their infant daughter, Nicole, all moved into one half of a duplex. The two families worked together and shared the kitchen and the dinner table in the two-bedroom home.

"Bob Campeau had nothing," Laura recalls. "We had a kitchen set and we had a bedroom set. In the living room we had just a chair. And we split the bedroom set. We gave him a dresser and he bought a bed. That's all he had back then."

But Bob and Alban were young, strong and eager to try anything. In one of their first joint ventures, they bought three five-ton haulage trucks, one of them a new 1946 Dodge. These they used for whatever jobs they could find: hauling building materials for a new silk-manufacturing plant; buying lumber up north and selling it in Cornwall; even removing snow by the hour. The first winter, Alban worked with one truck, hauling logs from the bush near Montebello, Quebec, to a sawmill not far from Alfred. During the week he stayed with his parents, returning to his wife and baby daughter only on weekends. Meanwhile, Campeau hauled snow all day in Cornwall. Several times a week, Bob would quit work at about five in the afternoon and drive the new Dodge seventy-five miles to meet Alban at the mill. There they loaded the truck by hand with fresh two-by-fours that Bob would take back to Cornwall that night.

One night, the platform they had built to hold the heavy lumber broke loose under the load, and the planks tumbled off with Alban on top. He was uninjured, but it was near midnight and he wanted to pack it in for the day. Bob insisted the job be finished.

"Let's quit," protested Alban. "I'm tired. I spent all day in the bush picking up logs. Let's quit."

"No. Let's load it again and then we'll go," Bob insisted.

"Come on, that's enough," returned Alban.

"No," said Bob again.

Alban relented, and they loaded the truck by about 3 A.M., then headed to Alfred. After two or three hours of sleep Bob drove the truck back to Cornwall.

Alban remembers those days as filthy, hard work, but he felt an obvious sense of accomplishment. "We had *will*," he says. "We wanted to do something, we *did* something." Often bone-weary and hungry, they would not eat in restaurants, believing their overalls were too dirty and their beards too long. But for the first time in their lives they had no boss save themselves.

Clauda and Bob's first child, Rachelle, was born on January 18, 1947. Clauda was sick throughout her pregnancy and the labor was long and painful. She later underwent a partial hysterectomy, which left her unable to bear more children. To make matters worse, baby Rachelle was suffering from a serious digestive problem that did not allow the infant to keep much in her stomach. She cried constantly and put on little weight. Bob and Clauda were terribly worried because she was so thin. "They were lucky they saved her," Laura says. "After three months they found a good doctor, but she was so thin and she was sick and crying all the time."

That spring, the two families gave up on the trucking venture, leased a shop in Cornwall and opened a grocery store. Campeau and Alban worked the shop with one of the two women while the other stayed home to care for Nicole and Rachelle. It was a small store with a large stock, some of which they had purchased from Alban's father. It was a big investment, requiring much of their savings and the proceeds from the sale of the trucks. Alban remembers his partner at the time as a man with "guts and willpower."

In those days of food rationing, meat was difficult to obtain for the store, so Campeau bought direct from the farmers, once or twice a week driving out to the farms and returning with a freshly slaughtered cow or pig in the back of his old car. The two once ordered an entire railcar of potatoes from New Brunswick and sold and delivered the full load — more than 500 seventy-five-pound bags — in three days. They took orders and sold some of the potatoes directly from the rail siding, shouting to passersby, "Who needs potatoes?" While the women ran the grocery, Campeau and Alban, with a car and small trailer, delivered the rest of the potatoes around Cornwall, often dropping the heavy bags into their customers' basements through small windows. "We wanted to make money — not steal any money, but work," Alban says.

But they found no real money in the grocery store business and they quit the venture in late 1947, about nine months after it started. Alban returned to Alfred to open a soft-drink business with his brother. And Bob Campeau was again looking for the right opportunity.

Rachelle was still sickly, so Bob and Clauda decided to move to Ottawa, where the baby could receive better medical care. They rented a rundown house at 412 Rideau Street, in an older section of the city near the downtown shopping district, and moved in with their scanty worldly possessions. After more than a year of the entrepreneurial life, Bob Campeau had little to show for it.

It is tempting to speculate that another reason for the move was Camillien Houde's rosy predictions about Ottawa's future. But there is no evidence that this was the case. Robert Campeau was simply a young father worried about the health of his baby daughter and in need of a steady job.

The job he found was as a millwright at a Canadian International Paper mill in the Gatineau Hills, across the Ottawa River. After only about two or three weeks there, Campeau was named foreman — by now a familiar pattern. This naturally led to some complaints from older men who had been passed over, but the complaints came to nothing. Bob Campeau had lost none of his charm — or drive. And he would not long be satisfied as somebody else's foreman.

But Bob's prospects must have looked bleak in April of 1948 when he returned home to Sudbury for his father's funeral. Joseph had died of a cerebral hemorrhage after a large road grader tipped and crushed him at a Sudbury lumberyard. At such a time of reflection and introspection, Robert Campeau may have wondered whether he would, like his father, spend his working life in the vain pursuit of that elusive pot of gold.

PART II

The Irresistible Rise

3 / The Builder

*"Even the bad contractors made good
money — I figured I could make a fortune."*
— Robert Campeau

ROBERT CAMPEAU GOT the idea of going into the construction business from his cousin Tony, with whom he had gone to school when the family lived on the Hanmer farm in the 1930s. By 1949, Tony, who like Bob had held various jobs all over — including a stint as a Sudbury police officer — was back in Sudbury and trying his hand at building houses. He started small, building his first house for $1,600 and selling it to his brother for $3,200, for a profit of 100 percent. Bob, visiting his widowed mother in Sudbury, was duly impressed with Tony's success, which he immediately saw as the opportunity he was waiting for. He persuaded Tony to join him in Ottawa, where they would form a partnership. Tony agreed. "I packed my tools and I remember that he quit his holidays," Tony recalls. "And I forget how many days after, but we were building shortly after."

It was the first on Campeau's long list of successful business ventures. He immediately saw the potential for a housebuilder in the postwar boom. The number of housing starts nationwide was approaching 90,000 the year the two cousins entered the business. The entire population of Ottawa-Carleton County, which included several surrounding towns and villages, grew from 206,367 to 287,246 — an increase of almost 50 percent — between 1941 and 1956. The federal bureaucracy was also growing: the number of civil servants had hit more than 334,000

by the mid-fifties. "Even the bad contractors made good
money," Campeau later said. "I figured I could make a
fortune." The success that had eluded his father was not going
to elude him.

Tony recalls that Bob had an impressive $4,000 in cash to
contribute to their venture; he himself had $2,000 in equity, a
truck and some tools, to put toward what would become
Campeau Construction, a 50 – 50 partnership. The pair bought
a lot on Guy Street, near an area of northeast Ottawa known as
Eastview. They hired men and, in the summer of 1949, began
work on their first house – a modest three-bedroom,
one-and-a-half storey detached stucco home that took about a
month to build.

Tony lived with Bob, Clauda and Rachelle in the rented
house on Rideau Street. He supervised construction during the
day while Bob continued to work at the mill. In the evenings
they would discuss how the work was going, make plans and
dream. It was a good arrangement. Tony had a bit of experience
and Bob had a bit of money. But they were both neophytes and
relied heavily on the people they hired to do the job right. Tony
recalls one of the carpenters wanting to show him how to build
a set of stairs. "Look, I don't want to learn how to build stairs,"
Tony told him. "We hired you to build stairs – you build
them."

Tony simply wanted the job done, apparently not wishing
to be bothered by details. Bob would adopt a different
approach, becoming so conscious of quality that he had to know
every facet of the business. However, such differences in
approach caused no serious friction.

It cost Bob and Tony about $5,000 to build that first house,
and it sold for about $7,300.

By this time, Bob and his cousin had two or three other
homes under construction in the same area. The sale of these
gave them enough capital to put up five houses on Edgehill
Street, several blocks south. And so it went, the profits from
each successful project helping to fund the next. Each of these
simple dwellings took about one month to build. At this point
the two men had no grand scheme of developing vast

subdivisions of hundreds of houses. They simply started building, and one thing led to another.

That first year, Bob and Tony built about a dozen more homes on Laperriere Avenue, well to the west of where they had started. Campeau Construction was on the move.

Tony continued to supervise the construction and Bob handled the administration: he dealt with the city and the lenders, bought the lots and kept the books. By early 1950 their venture was becoming so successful and growing so fast that they decided they needed another partner to help with the increasing workload. Bob naturally turned to Alban Cadieux, whose abilities and talents he knew and who he felt sure would see the potential. Alban, showing his trust in Bob and in his leadership, promptly sold his soft drink business in Alfred along with one of his two trucks, contributing the other to the new venture. Alban was given 20 percent of the company; Bob and Tony each kept 40 percent. Laura remained in Alfred until her husband could find them a home, and Alban temporarily moved into Bob's already crowded Rideau Street house. Laura arrived in Ottawa several months later.

Among the first loans the young builders arranged was $50,000 from the Bank of Nova Scotia branch at Rideau and Williams. The branch manager, Thomas Boyles, a cultivated Englishman who could not have been more different from these earthy French Canadians, saw something in Robert Campeau. The result was a business relationship that would last for decades.

"Tom Boyles is probably the main reason that Bob has been as successful as he has been," says a former Campeau Corp. board member. "Tom was manager here at a branch where Bob was dealing and eventually became chairman of the board of the Bank of Nova Scotia. So that's the relationship all the way through. I've always felt that Tom probably through Bob saw a way of doing a lot of the things that he couldn't do on his own because he was caught in the bank set-up."

Campeau would later appoint Boyles to his own board of directors, returning the support the banker had given him during the struggle of those early days.

The bank loans allowed the young builders to carry on the day-to-day business. The purchasing of land and the construction of the homes, including the first house on Guy Street, was partly funded by Central Mortgage and Housing Corp. (CMHC), a government agency that oversaw matters pertaining to housing and promoted the residential building industry. In those days, CMHC provided to builders loans that covered a percentage of the selling price of a house. Up to about 80 percent of the loan could be drawn in stages as a house was being built. The remainder was paid once the builders found a buyer, who had to be approved by CMHC and who, after a down payment, assumed the builders' loan in the form of a long-term mortgage.

In 1950, just before the three partners launched their first major project, Campeau was confident enough of success to quit his job at Canadian International Paper and assume a full-time role in the company. The three men had no titles at this point; they worked together as friends and equals. The project in question, a subdivision in an area known as Billings Bridge, began with the purchase of about 60 acres from a 250-acre farm on the east side of the Rideau River in Ottawa.

Ottawa at the time was still very much a small city bounded on two sides by water — the Ottawa and Rideau rivers. The much broader Ottawa River, which separates the city from Quebec, prevented expansion to the north. But Billings Bridge, east of the Rideau, seemed a logical choice, given its nearness to downtown and the reasonable cost of the land. Campeau was anticipating the city's expansion to the east, which was inevitable, thanks to the postwar boom.

They arranged financing through CMHC, obtained building permits and began work on the subdivision in the spring of 1950. Because they were working on virgin land that was too far away from existing development to be linked up to city sewer and water systems, the young developers were limited to building only on every second lot in order to allow enough space to ensure that wells would not be contaminated by the septic tanks on each property. As well as digging wells and installing septic tanks, they had to construct their own concrete roads. Over the course of the project they would employ as many as 150 men.

Working days at Billings Bridge were long and arduous. For the first six months, there was no secretary in the cramped little shack that served as their office, and the three partners did almost everything themselves. Alban took over the books from Bob and supervised the purchasing of materials. Bob continued to handle paperwork and arrange loans, and Tony continued to supervise construction. Still, jobs tended to overlap. Bob and Alban often worked alongside the men in the field as they toiled in the mud digging the septic tanks.

"If you're well organized, it's not difficult," says Alban. "The worst thing to do is to get the land and get the services in and start to build the first one. And after that it goes. We didn't know much but we learned fast. We built some good houses. We were selling houses, working in the bush, working in the project and seeing the customers, selling houses at night. We'd sell at night and start over again in the morning."

As Billings Bridge progressed, Campeau learned about some of the ways in which the building industry was inefficient, and set about to improve what he could and speed up the on-site work. He convinced a supplier to ship windows already installed in their frames; it took too long to put them together on-site. He then convinced the company supplying material for stairs to assemble the stairs in the shop before shipping them.

Campeau soon set up what was to become a rigid inspection system to maintain standards. He often conducted inspections himself, sometimes following on the heels of his own inspectors. Jean-Marc Prud'Homme, a young carpenter on the Billings Bridge project, can still picture an angry Bob Campeau arriving unannounced at a site on Kilborn Avenue for one of his infamous snap inspections in 1951. As the plastering contractor watched, Campeau surveyed the job, taking particular note of the bottom of one wall. Suddenly he snatched up a board, checked that it was straight, then placed it against the wall. As he had suspected, the plaster was uneven.

"It's all full of bumps," Campeau said. "You're going to fix that."

"We can do that," the plasterer assured him.

"I'm going to make sure you do it." Campeau replied. He then grabbed an ax and smashed about twenty holes in the wall. "Jesus Christ," he shouted, "ça ne vaut pas le cul" — that work is not worth an asshole.

It was about 3 P.M., ninety minutes from quitting time, and Prud'Homme watched in amazement as his boss chopped apart the bottom of the wall. Christ, he thought, what kind of man is this? Later, as he packed his tools to head home, several carpenters from nearby sites walked over to find out what had happened.

"Campeau was here — look what he did to the wall."

"Our work had better be good or he's going to do the same to us," one of the startled carpenters replied.

Campeau later learned that shining a flashlight along a wall in the dark quickly revealed any defects, so evening and night inspections were not uncommon. His eye for detail helped establish his name in Ottawa — even today classified advertisements in the local papers describe resale homes as Campeau-built. Not surprisingly, this very attention to detail helped establish Campeau's reputation as a difficult and demanding boss.

"When I was a youngster, my mother always told me that if I did things I should do them well," Campeau said years later. "On top of that, when we got into housing we were aware that buying a home is probably the biggest transaction most people make in their life. So we felt we owed them the responsibility of giving them quality for their money. That was basically at the bottom of our decision. But I also felt that, if we built quality then we would go much further, much longer. And we did, so it was a good decision."

In his quest for perfection, Campeau responded to complaints personally, something he continued to do even after his company had become quite large. "I remember he built our first house, and when I had a complaint, he came himself to take care of it," recalls Gittel Tatz, who bought a Campeau home in the 1950s. "I had a complaint with something in my garage that wasn't right. And he came — it was something that they couldn't correct — so he told me that it was impossible to correct it and that they were wrong, and he offered to do something else to make up for it. And they did. They sodded my whole yard. And I had a huge yard. It was like a small park. I remember him then, when he was just one of the guys. He dressed like the workmen and he was on the job all the time."

But although Campeau realized the importance of satisfied customers, he did have his limits. One particularly annoying purchaser, who bought one of the later homes in Billings Bridge, simply could not be satisfied. He complained about the paint on the walls and about small cracks, which were impossible to avoid, in the hardwood floors. He bothered workers at the field office almost daily and bickered with the general superintendent, complaining about these and other imperfections. Finally, he went to the main office and demanded action. So Campeau phoned the field office to find out what was happening.

"He's not happy with his house," the superintendent told him. "The foreman has been there, I've been there, other people have been there, and we just can't please that guy."

Campeau checked with the foreman, whose assessment of the situation was the same. So he decided to go to the site himself the next day. To no one's surprise, he found the man's complaints to be unfounded.

"Mister, you're asking just too much," Campeau told him. "There's only one thing to do, give you back your money."

At this, the customer blanched, realizing he had gone too far.

"Where will I go?" he asked.

"You'll go wherever you want, but I'm not giving you an inch anymore." Campeau was shouting now. "Nothing. That's it."

There was never another complaint from this buyer.

Homes in Billings Bridge were one and a half storeys and sold for about $9,700. They were selling before they were completed; young couples began calling, saying they knew other people who had purchased some of the original Campeau homes and they wanted to get in on a good thing. During the next few years, the company's reputation made advertising almost unnecessary. In the years when Campeau was still primarily a housebuilder, more than half of a proposed development was often snapped up before the homes were even under construction.

But this did not mean that the three partners quickly became rich. "We made a lot of money but we didn't touch the money," Alban remembers. "The money stayed in the company, and the company grew. Supposing we had $50,000 in the bank. We didn't own that. That was owned by the company. We had a small salary, a small expense account."

By mid-1951, after about fifty homes in Billings Bridge had been built and most of them sold, it looked as though the young company was invincible. But there was a crack in the foundation. Tony was growing more and more uncomfortable with the swift pace. He and Bob got along well, but he was feeling overworked and increasingly distressed by his cousin's relentless drive. Tony could see that his cousin would never be satisfied — he would always want more, bigger, faster; he wanted to be on top. "Bob was doing his job and I was doing my job and everything went fine," Tony recalls. "But I'm not Bob. My constitution is not his. It was growing too fast. My dream is not that dream."

So Tony made the difficult decision to quit, and he sold his share of the company to Bob and Alban, leaving him free to strike out on his own and work at a pace he liked. He formed his own company, which at first was called ATC Construction Co. and then Castle Construction Co., and continued building in Ottawa, enjoying reasonable success. He went on to build about 2,000 units before he stopped construction in 1956.

When Tony left, Bob and Alban decided to bring in Bob's brother Lionel as a replacement. Other projects were about to get under way, and they already had their hands full with Billings Bridge. They needed someone they could trust. So they made Bob's older brother an offer he couldn't refuse: 10 percent ownership of the company for one dollar. Bob and Alban split the remainder on a 60 – 40 basis. Lionel's dollar's worth – later increased to 15 percent – would soon become very valuable indeed.

Bob soon opened a small office at 523 Bank Street in downtown Ottawa. Lionel was named general superintendent in charge of projects in the field. For the first three years, he also did the survey work.

Lionel is now in his seventies, his wife Rolande is dead and, although his years at Campeau Construction left him a wealthy man, after his wife's death he lived alone in a cramped apartment in Ottawa until late 1988, when he moved to a seniors' home. Somewhat wistfully he recalls those early days when he and his brother were still getting along and it seemed that they could do no wrong. "Robert took a son-of-a-gun chance" in bringing him in, he says. "I wasn't a good carpenter, I wasn't a good millwright. They felt that I was a good organizer." Certainly he had proved his organizing skills in his political work for the Bloc populaire. And for the first few years things worked out well.

When Lionel arrived, the Billings Bridge project was not even half finished. It would take about two years to build the 200 homes in the subdivision. The young company had also just won a contract with the Department of National Defence to build eighty-four housing units for the air force at Uplands Airport in Ottawa. And Bob had just bought some land in the west end of the city to put up eleven six-unit buildings known as the Tillbury apartments, Campeau Construction's first such project.

The growth of the company in the early 1950s soon necessitated transfusions of new blood. This turned out to be an area in which Bob Campeau excelled and which undoubtedly had a lot to do with his subsequent success. He knew how to recognize talent, cultivate it and capitalize on it.

One of the first newcomers was Ray Larocque, a friend of Alban's from Alfred. In the beginning Larocque handled everything from accounting to purchasing and selling houses. He, Alban and Bob frequently worked nights, planning purchasing and production. Larocque soon recruited seven-teen-year-old Marcel Lalande, another friend from Alfred, then employed as a bank teller in Hull, Quebec, to work as a bookkeeper. Alban, Larocque and Lalande, together with a couple of others from Alfred who would come later, became known within the company as the Alfred Boys. (Lalande hired a draftsman and accountant from Alfred, and Clauda's uncle and her brother-in-law soon joined the company.) Other senior executives who were to arrive over the next several years would join Alban, Larocque and Lalande to form a core group that was passionately devoted to both Campeau Construction and Bob. "It wasn't a job to me — it was like a religion," says one member of the original group. "That was the case for most of the people who were there. Absolute devotion. Because it was our company. We made it."

But even as new people were coming into the organization, trouble was brewing among the three principals. Bob was good friends with Alban, but was starting to have hard times with his brother. Former employees recall Bob complaining that Lionel, apparently unwilling or unable to make decisions on his own, was constantly consulting him. Alban disliked Lionel, who admits he enjoyed arguing for the sake of argument, and the two did not get along. But for the time being, this problem was only a minor irritant.

Campeau was quick to promote talent among his staff — and this usually paid off. Jean-Marc Prud'Homme, the carpenter who had watched in amazement as Campeau took an ax to a plaster wall, rose fast within the ranks and soon entered the inner circle. So did his friend Eugène Lavigne, another carpenter who had worked on some of the first Campeau homes with a subcontractor and joined the company at Billings Bridge. (Prud'Homme had joined Campeau Construction in the fall of 1951 to work on an apartment project.) Together these two quiet, unassuming men were responsible for many innovations in Campeau construction methods.

Lavigne and Prud'Homme searched constantly for ways of producing better homes more cheaply while making the job easier. In 1951, Marcel Chaput, a Campeau superintendent on the apartment project on which they were both working, overheard Lavigne and Prud'Homme — whom the older carpenters saw as young know-it-alls — discussing the possibility of prebuilding soffits, the overhangs of roofs, on the ground. No one in the organization had ever seen such a thing done. The system then in use required elaborate scaffolding and was awkward because soffits had to be constructed on the building, several storeys up. Lavigne and Prud'Homme were proposing to dispense with scaffolding; the soffits would be hung from atop the building after being constructed on the ground. Not only would this take far less time, it would be less costly than the traditional method.

Chaput liked their idea and took it to Campeau, who ordered it done immediately. Campeau never held back on innovation, and this was one of many times when his willingness to try a new idea paid off.

Later, the two young carpenters devised an improved method of handling framing panels, which form the frame of the walls. Under the existing system, suppliers simply dumped materials at a site, leaving carpenters to cut wood with handsaws. Why not set up a small mill at the site of the Uplands Airport housing project? the two men asked. The panels needed for these six-unit buildings had to be uniform, so precutting made sense. There would be less waste, less room for error and greater speed.

Once again, Campeau did what they proposed. At Uplands, he installed a small mill to house a radial saw and a couple of Skilsaws. Suppliers then delivered materials to the mill, where panels and two-by-fours were precut and distributed to each site. Precutting was done primarily during winter months. "We tried to do prefabrication like that during the winter because in those days you didn't pour foundations during the winter," Lavigne recalls. "So in order to keep some of our better carpenters — and laborers, for that matter — we would premanufacture our panels during the winter and stack them neatly there so that we would have access to the panels in the summer."

With ideas such as these, Prud'Homme and Lavigne helped

create for Campeau Construction a system of prefabrication that the company developed to the level of an art. Prefabrication itself was not new, although it was not yet as sophisticated as it would become. Campeau was the first Ottawa builder to use prefabrication on a mass scale. By the early 1960s, Campeau's prefab system would be refined to an intricate in-house assembly line operation. Prefabrication led to higher standards because the shop offered a better working environment and quality was easier to control. "We were always thinking of innovation of some type to have a better job, in a sense, and also to be able to do it faster and with less manpower because there was always difficulty in obtaining enough workers," says Lavigne.

The prefabrication system eventually became extremely elaborate, allowing the company to phase out various suppliers. In the early days, other companies supplied such components as windows, countertops, stairs and cupboards. In 1956, Campeau Construction would begin making its own building components at a plant on the corner of Smyth and Russel roads. Initially, the company produced its own stairs and cupboards and some specialty items. Later, sashless window frames were added, and they installed a small planing mill to make casings and baseboards.

As his company grew, Campeau himself constantly searched for better building techniques. In the late 1950s, he traveled to Germany and France to investigate methods of prefabricating highrise apartments, but found that these were too expensive to duplicate in Canada. The power crane — a huge piece of machinery that could be operated from within the shell of a building, then in use in Europe but not in Canada — particularly caught his eye. He brought the first such crane to Canada from France and wanted Campeau Construction to seek North American distribution rights for the equipment. But his colleagues talked him out of it — a rare occurrence. Campeau virtually always got his way because he did not ask — he demanded. You could not tell him something couldn't be done. In this case, he should have demanded. The power crane is now widely used in North America.

In the early days, Campeau Construction abounded in a team spirit. The hard, often dirty work of building was made easier because most of those in the core group were good friends, and Bob and Alban led a small, happy band. "He was the boss but also at the same time a co-worker," says Lavigne. "The original group, even though we had different titles here and there, were all equal as far as we were concerned. We had to work together to develop what we had. We had pride in the amount of houses that we were building, the quality we were giving, because it was well known that a Campeau home was quality." It should be noted that these were modest, functional homes, not the three-bathroom models with big kitchens and large family rooms that fill today's real estate pages.

Early in 1952, Lionel moved the field office from the Billings Bridge project to the Uplands site so he could keep closer tabs on both the Uplands housing units and the Tillbury apartments, which were starting up simultaneously. That year the company put up sixty-six units at Tillbury and eighty-four at Uplands. And with Larocque, one of the first Alfred Boys, on board, Bob and Alban set their sights still higher. By the end of the year they had completed the excavations and put in foundations for twenty-five six-unit apartment buildings on Kirkwood Avenue, west of downtown. These squat, undistinguished brown brick buildings, with center stairways and no ornamentation, still line Kirkwood today.

Campeau Construction entered 1953 with its attention divided between apartment projects — those on Kirkwood and new buildings on Riverdale Avenue — and a major housing project called Meadowvale Terrace, off Fisher Avenue, a few minutes' drive from downtown. Kirkwood would eventually include 150 apartments and Riverdale twenty-four, while Meadowvale would consist of 200 homes. Demand for apartment buildings, however, paled beside the growing civil service's desire for single-family homes. So by the end of the year, the company's focus returned to houses, with thirty roofs up on Larose Street, just a few blocks north of the Kirkwood apartments. And, of course, Billings Bridge continued.

The business was burgeoning, perhaps faster than anyone

had expected — but not fast enough to satisfy Bob. Still more people were needed, especially someone to shoulder some of the day-to-day administration. In 1954, Campeau snatched from CMHC the head of the agency's Ottawa branch, Jean Charles Paradis. Paradis, an intelligent and refined man, became secretary of Campeau Construction, releasing Campeau from the time-consuming task of handling mortgages. One of the few things they had in common was that they were both French Canadian. Paradis was impressed by the rough-hewn character he believed would become a force in the building industry. The two soon became close friends.

"I joined on a hunch," Paradis said years later. "Campeau seemed so confident and a comer. Although he was not all that polished, he was a hell of a pusher and very aggressive and dynamic. If things did not go his way, he would get very mad. His English was fairly limited, but his aggressiveness did not deter him from speaking it. In the early days of the company, he was its heart and soul."

Paradis was a good foil to his new boss. Whereas Bob was often rash, Paradis always took time to weigh matters. When Bob blew his stack, Paradis would calm him down. He often picked up the pieces and soothed the bruised egos that Bob left in his wake. In time, he helped polish both Bob and Campeau Construction. One of the company's early competitors says of the duo: "He made Jean, and Jean made him." In her book *Men of Property*, Susan Goldenberg writes that Paradis was "credited by many as having been Campeau's Professor Higgins, who, as in George Bernard Shaw's *Pygmalion*, has been responsible for giving Campeau polish and cooling down his flareups at public meetings."

About this time, Bob and Alban decided that they needed to be freed from handling most of the sales themselves. There were no real estate agents. Having failed to teach the site foremen to sell houses as well as supervise construction, they decided to hire an experienced salesman who, in turn, hired two more.

The salesmen were needed. In 1954, Campeau started a second subdivision in the Billings Bridge area that would be known as Applewood Acres. He bought a nearby apple orchard from two sisters of the Billings family, after whom the area was named, and that spring began work on the project, which would comprise 240 homes. Lionel recalls that the excavation of the Applewood site was the most difficult to date. Some of the rock had to be blasted away with dynamite, and the proximity of a clay quarry meant that rainfall turned the area to slop.

Campeau soon bought more farmland, purchasing hundreds of acres on the east side of the Rideau River for a huge development to be called Elmvale Acres, which became the company's biggest housing project ever, with a total of 1,600 homes. Work began in the summer of 1955 and stretched over several years. Because of the project's size, Campeau personally recruited workers from the Maritimes, traveling to New Brunswick to hire men himself. He was changing the shape of Ottawa: thanks to Bob Campeau, the city was now spreading farther from the Rideau River, growing eastward.

What had begun as a small ad hoc family effort had by the mid-fifties taken on far grander proportions. Campeau Construction Co., the heart of the business, had assets of more than $500,000 and annual sales of more than $1.4 million. Bob was president, Alban treasurer, Lionel general superintendent and Jean Paradis secretary. Alban also became president of Allied Building Supply (Ottawa), a subsidiary that was to supply the Campeau construction business and later market components and materials to other companies.

The companies' profits were impressive, and there was enough money to pay the principals handsome salaries. Bob Campeau and his partners were getting rich quick.

4 / Nouveau Riche

*"He was quite a rough diamond and then he
got much more sophisticated."*
— Bill Teron

ALTHOUGH BOB CAMPEAU'S success was mounting, he had yet to
acquire his later veneer of sophistication. And so it was with
Ottawa of the early to mid-fifties. It was still in many ways a
small town. There was little to do in the capital in those years,
and Bob, Clauda, Alban and Laura were seldom far apart,
especially after they moved into the growing new Billings
Bridge subdivision. (Bob and Clauda moved into 270 Chever-
ton Avenue; Alban moved his family into 1236 Livingston
Avenue, one street over.) These modest homes the two families
occupied were the first new houses they had owned. These did
not look like the homes of wealthy men.

The families spent many weekends and holidays together,
the highlight of each year being the Christmas season, which
soon took on far grander proportions as Bob and Alban began
to throw large parties for employees, contractors, businessmen
and politicians. The first staff Christmas party was held in
1951 in one of the empty homes in Billings Bridge and was a
fairly simple affair. But the following Christmas, Bob and
Alban rented the elegant Hunt Club near Uplands Airport and
invited not only their employees but business associates,
prominent civic and federal politicians, personal friends and
their parish priest. The hall, Lionel recalls, was decorated in red
and green ribbons, and a large Christmas tree lit up its center.
Bob, Clauda, Alban and Laura formed a receiving line and then

sat at the head table while the guests were served turkey and wine.

After dinner, Bob Campeau rose slowly from his place. Clauda and their little daughter Rachelle also rose, looking on proudly — it was Bob and Clauda's tenth wedding anniversary. "After my wedding day, this is the best day of my life," Campeau told the cheering crowd. Then he spoke of the houses and apartments the company had built that year, and of the triumph of Campeau Construction.

He thanked his employees, various municipal leaders and Tom Boyles of the Bank of Nova Scotia. One of the local politicians present, city councilor Paul Tardif, then remarked to the crowd that never before in Ottawa's history had any company built so many apartment units in one year.

After the speeches, Alban organized a darts tournament while others polkaed to "Roll Out the Barrel" and sang in French and English. The French sang English songs, but, says Lionel, the English did not like to sing French songs, unless it was "Alouette," which they "loved to make into gibberish in every imaginable way."

Clauda, who delighted in singing, led the assembly in "Maître Pierre," which seemed to sum up the spirit of the evening:

> *Qu'il fait bon, chez-vous, maître Pierre,*
> *Qu'il fait bon dans votre moulin.*
> *Le froment vole dans la lumière,*
> *Et partout ça sent bon le grain.*
> *J'avais six ans et j'étais haut comme trois pommes;*
> *En me voyant, on me disait d'un air bonhomme,*
> *Voyez-moi ce sacre p'tit drôle,*
> *Le métier lui semble à son goût.*
> *Il prend ce sac, le met sur l'épaule,*
> *Maître Pierre, qu'il fait bon chez-vous.*
> *Hardi, hardi, petit gars,*
> *Bonnet sur l'oeil, sourire aux lèvres,*
> *Hardi, tant qu'il a deux bras,*
> *Un bon meunier ne s'arrête pas.*

Things are good with you, master Pierre,
Things are good in your mill.
The wheat flies in the light,
And you can smell grain everywhere.
I was six years old and as tall as three apples;
When they saw me they said I was a jolly fellow,
Now you see me, a proper little clown,
The trade seems to be to his taste.
He takes the bag and hoists it onto his shoulder,
Master Pierre, things are good with you.
Brave, brave little boy,
Your cap over your eyes, a smile on your lips,
Go to it as long as you have two arms,
A good miller never stops.

Several days later, Alban and Bob decided to throw an impromptu party for the people who had bought Campeau homes, an unusual move and one that no other developer in the city would copy. They delivered the invitations personally, going door to door in the Billings Bridge project. That night, many dropped by the Campeau house.

This Christmas party for homebuyers became an established tradition and evolved into a lavish affair. Bob always assumed the role of *le patron* — the master of the feast; Alban, by nature quiet, unassuming and somewhat humorless, gladly ceded the limelight. When these celebrations are noted now in media profiles of Campeau, they are referred to as having been given by Bob and Clauda. There is no mention of Alban and Laura.

Eventually, Bob and Alban began to throw these annual parties at the 7,000-seat Ottawa auditorium. After one such event in the early sixties, the morality squad of the city police — in an example of the self-righteousness typical of a country where the biggest department store, Eaton's, still draped its display windows on Sunday — considered charging the company with running a lottery. The grounds? Children at the Christmas fete had received prizes from a draw. About 5,000 people, homeowners and their children, were given the draw tickets free, and the prizes, which included a $500 scholarship, were obviously gifts. In the end, charges were not laid.

Not everything was rosy, however. It wasn't long after the first company party that Alban returned home late one winter night to find his daughter Nicole ill and wanting to sleep in the same bed with him. That day he and Bob had been negotiating for hours with CMHC over a contract for apartment units, and Alban was exhausted. "No, I'm tired, Nicole, I want to sleep," Alban told her. "Please leave me alone."

He soon regretted his words. Nicole's condition steadily worsened, and the following afternoon the child was rushed to hospital. "Bob and I were at Civic Hospital," Alban says, "We were walking together, trying to find a solution, getting all the doctors that he knew, that I knew." Nicole was two months shy of her eighth birthday. She died three days later of meningitis.

The tragedy brought the two couples even closer together. Several weeks later, in early 1953, the families left for a month's vacation in Miami. The business was running smoothly and making money, and Bob and Alban decided that they could afford the time away and needed the holiday to try to get over their grief.

The vacations Bob and Clauda took with Alban and Laura were to become more exotic: one year it was Mexico, another Puerto Rico. As Bob Campeau got richer, he learned how to reap the benefits of success, teaching himself about the finer things in life. Considerably later, on a family vacation to Europe, Bob had his Lincoln Continental shipped over for the six-week holiday.

At home in Ottawa, the two couples enjoyed many nights out on the town. The real action was across the river in Hull, Quebec, where they frequented places like Madame Berger's — the area's best restaurant — and Standish Hall and the Gatineau Club, which featured the big names in music, from the Ink Spots and Tommy Dorsey to the Andrews Sisters.

In 1953, Bob and Alban moved into new two-storey, plain brick semi-detached houses at 898 and 900 Kirkwood, handy to the site of the Kirkwood apartments project. Now next-door neighbors, the two couples spent many weekends socializing, playing ping-pong in Bob's games room, or singing and dancing to Clauda's records. Often some of Bob's employees were invited over. And Father Ovila would frequently travel to Ottawa to visit. Bob was a devout Roman Catholic who never missed Sunday Mass and was proud whenever his brother the priest came to Ottawa.

Since his father's death in 1948, Bob had come to assume the role of head of the extended Campeau family, even though he was the youngest son. His brothers and sisters often turned to him for advice and help, and he was always discreet; they knew that the problems they took to Bobby would go no further.

It became customary for most of the Campeau clan to gather for a reunion at least once a year. On the Dominion Day long weekend in July 1953, the annual get-together was at a group of rented cottages on the French River near the village of Alban in northern Ontario, the parish where Father Ovila was then stationed. The family's widowed mother, Lucie, was now looking after the priest's rectory.

Everyone had been concerned about Thérèse, the baby of the family, who had married Côme Belisle, Bob's buddy from their teenage years in Blezard Valley. Less than three years earlier, Côme had been shot and killed in a hunting accident, and Thérèse had been on the move ever since, searching for a new foundation. She had moved in at first with Gerarda, then returned to work as a hospital receptionist in Sudbury, then moved in with Côme's sister in Montreal for a few months. Finally she had arrived at the rectory in Alban, contemplating becoming a nun.

Despite the worries about Thérèse, it was a happy family gathering. Everyone now looked up to Bob because of the success he had brought not only to himself but also to Lionel. But, Bob being Bob, he could not simply relax and enjoy a couple of days off — not when there was a chance of doing some business. Another family, the Lahaies, who owned a sawmill in the village, had also been invited for the weekend. After Mass on Sunday, the whole crowd gathered at Gilbert and Blanche's cottage for a lunch of freshly caught fish, and Bob and Alban spent a lot of time with the Lahaies trying to negotiate a sales contract for their lumber.

That evening, while the others played bridge, sang and danced at Bob's and Alban's cottage, Bob continued bargaining with M. Lahaie. By the time the party broke up he had negotiated a three-year contract to buy the annual output of the Lahaie sawmill.

Family was terribly important to Robert Campeau. So it was a major source of frustration and heartache that he and Clauda could have no more children. In 1954, when their daughter Rachelle was seven, they adopted a fifteen-month-old boy, named Jacques, from a Montreal orphanage. At last, a son to share in the love and the riches. Lionel became his godfather, an indication that Bob and his older brother, though they had differences at work, remained close.

In 1955, with a growing family and more money at his disposal, Bob Campeau built a house on Applewood Crescent in the new Applewood Acres project. The home, at 2134 Applewood, was a classic fifties bungalow, much larger than his previous homes, with a stone front, two huge picture windows, a fireplace and a two-car garage, all built on a large lot at the cozy bend of the crescent.

A portrait of Bob Campeau during this period would not be complete without a scene showing him and his family socializing with the families of his senior employees, still an exclusively French Canadian group. In 1955, Campeau Construction began treating its key people and their wives to long weekends every summer at a resort. At these retreats Bob, Alban and Lionel were joined by Jean Paradis, Marcel Lalande, Ray Larocque, Eugène Lavigne and Jean-Marc Prud'Homme. The couples played golf, swam and sang. Although Bob, Alban and Lionel were the others' bosses, job titles were forgotten at these friendly gatherings. Participants remember Bob, at dinner, waving his fork and knife in his hands, singing between mouthfuls of fish.

"Bob is like most of us, Bob loved to party," recalls one. "He

used to have a great voice. He loves to sing French songs, dirty
songs. Oh, loves it. I don't know what you'd call dirty songs.
You've got to put it in the context, I guess, of what might have
been considered a dirty song thirty-five years ago in the
Catholic Church. And Bob used to swear like a lumberjack. He
wouldn't swear now."

In the mid-fifties, Bob and Alban built cottages on Lake
Deschênes, a basin of the Ottawa River about five miles upriver
from Aylmer on the Quebec side. The cottages became a
popular spot on summer weekends for Bob and Clauda and
their family, who went swimming, boating and sunbathing.
Senior staff and friends would gather here to talk business or
shoot the breeze when they weren't catering to Bob's
competitive spirit, which constantly spilled over into games,
swimming contests and boat races. Bob loved this place. Ever
conscious of maintaining his physique, he found it an ideal
locale to indulge in one of his favorite pastimes, swimming. He
was even known to brave the chill of the Ottawa River in
November.

Back in the city, Bob Campeau's life demanded increasing
refinement. Friends advised him to stop swearing and to
change his style of dress. So he traded his flannel lumberjack
shirts first for a suede vest and later for flashy suits. Whereas in
the early days he was content to drive his one-ton truck for
personal use, he was soon behind the wheel of a two-toned
hardtop sedan with white-walls. Bob Campeau was gaining a
name and he was determined to fit the image. "He was quite a
rough diamond to begin with, quite rough," recalls rival builder
Bill Teron. "I mean, he started as a truck driver, all the rest of
it. He was pretty rough. And then he got much more
sophisticated."

One of the signs of refinement was golfing at the better
Ottawa clubs. And, as in anything Bob Campeau tackles, he
was determined to be the best. His efforts are the stuff of many
stories told by friends and business associates. Paul Tardif, his
main ally on city council and a good friend, remembers one
particular outing when Bob was growing frustrated with his

game. He had missed several shots, and Tardif was ribbing him, implying that he was doctoring his score.

"Listen, Bob, I'm counting those damn strokes, so don't shave any," Tardif joked.

Bob was unamused by Tardif's jollity. He appeared somewhat nervous, taking the game far more seriously than his friend. He swung again and missed.

"That's another," Tardif prodded.

Furious, Bob swung his golf club as if it were a baseball bat, wrapping it around a nearby tree. His caddy was so frightened that he dropped the bag and ran.

"As a golfer, he wanted to be Number One," Tardif now says. "So he went to the driving range every night in summer, and he drives and he does this and he practices. To do what? To be Number One. Bob was more angry at imperfection in himself than in anybody else. To say he didn't like to lose is not the right term — he always wanted to win. He always wanted to win at anything. He's driven now? He was driven like that then. He wanted to be Number One. He wanted to build more houses than anybody else in town. He wanted to have fewer people complaining about anything that he built than anybody else in town."

Golf became a popular game in the Campeau circle, played on weekends and at company tournaments, and Bob was known among friends and associates for occasionally cheating when he was not playing well. He took the game so seriously that he sometimes stormed off the course if he missed too many shots. And he could grow so impatient with other golfers that he would breach golf etiquette with his overly aggressive style.

"God, he would not finish every game because he'd lose his temper," recalls Andrew Perrier, who joined the Campeau organization as a salesman in the late 1950s. "He became obsessed with it. And he needed to have the longest drive, you know, and he wasn't averse to sometimes dropping a ball, and we all knew that. It would go off in the bush somewhere and he'd have one in his pocket and he'd drop it and say, 'Oh, I have it,' rather than lose a couple of strokes. But I wouldn't want to tarnish his wonderful image with a little story like that. All golfers do that occasionally."

Learning golf was easier than becoming a member of the Royal Ottawa Golf Club, Ottawa's exclusive establishment club. But he could play there as a guest of his friend Joe O'Brien, an executive of Royal Trustco in Ottawa, who would later join Campeau Corp. After one of their games together, there were complaints about Bob's behavior on the course. It was clear that the rich young builder was not welcome. While freely acknowledging his friend's fiercely competitive nature, O'Brien says the problems at the Royal Ottawa stemmed from the English establishment's dislike of the French Canadian outsider himself, rather than his behavior.

"I ended up getting censured on two occasions – a letter from the board — because of Bob's behavior on the course," says O'Brien. "He wouldn't have to do very much to where there would either be somebody in front of us or somebody behind us who didn't like Bob Campeau anyway, and didn't like him being there and wondered why the hell he was there. And it wouldn't take much for me to get a letter."

While Campeau wanted to win every contest, he was not unable to view this streak in himself with a sense of humor. Perrier recalls one picnic for subcontractors and some employees at the Campeau cottage. In the afternoon, they decided on a tug-of-war, and Bob handpicked his team, which included all the big men at the picnic, including Gilles Archambault. Archambault stood six-foot-two, weighed 245 pounds and played tackle for the Ottawa Rough Riders. The other side jokingly complained when Campeau's side won the first match with no effort.

"It's that team, Bob," they said.

"All right, I'll switch teams," Campeau replied.

He switched sides, went to the back of his new team and, unseen by the other side, tied the rope to a post.

By the late 1950s, Bob was clearly changing, enjoying what money could buy. But Clauda remained relatively untouched by the trappings of wealth. She still chopped her own wood, was not embarrassed to be seen in old slacks with her hair tied up in a kerchief and continued to do her own housework. Bob offered more than once to hire a maid to help out, but his wife refused.

"She was fantastic, let me tell you," recalls Bob's younger sister Gerarda, who knew her well. "She was lots of fun. That woman never had somebody to clean her house, and she could have. But she would wash her ceiling, her walls, just like I do. She would wash everything herself. And she was an excellent cook, she was a good wife, she was a good mother."

Bob and Clauda still wanted more children, and in 1959 adopted a second son, Daniel, from the same orphanage that had given them Jacques. Rachelle was eleven and Jacques almost seven. Those who remember Clauda in this period recall a vibrant woman who loved being a mother and enjoyed being the wife of Bob Campeau. There was no sign that this domestic tranquility was soon to be shattered.

5 / Subdivide and Conquer

"Get out of the way."

— Robert Campeau

THE LATTER HALF of the 1950s was an exciting time for Robert Campeau. His company was growing by leaps and bounds, and the competition in the Ottawa area was also becoming fierce. Irving Greenberg's Minto Construction came on the scene about 1955, and soon after William Teron entered the fray with Teron Construction. Both companies went into housebuilding in a big way, but their approaches were quite different. Greenberg's Minto very much followed Campeau's lead, building solid, repeat dwellings. Teron had an entirely different attitude. A high school dropout who had trained as a draftsman, he viewed construction with a designer's eye, figuring he would give Campeau and Minto a run for their money by building better-designed houses. The government and the city were growing, and there was plenty of business to keep all three companies busy.

"There was a big void to fill," Teron says. "Campeau came along and really built a lot of housing, and Minto came along too. You could see what was happening. And they were more alike. I think our own role was very, very different in that in '55 there was criticism that these guys were turning up little berry boxes."

Lionel recalls that when Minto started construction, Greenberg and his partners would come early in the day to stand for hours across the road from a Campeau site, watching and absorbing everything, not really caring that the Campeau men found this funny. When Minto's men began building near a Campeau site, Lorry Greenberg, one of the principals, brought his clients to a Campeau model home, saying he could offer the equivalent. Whenever the Campeau sales manager was asked if he was at all perturbed by this, he would reply that "the poor guys don't realize they're helping to sell Campeau homes." Recalls the sales manager: "They were showing my wares."

Both Minto and Teron grew fast. "There was Bob Campeau, Irving Greenberg and Bill Teron, and we were the three guys in one small town," recalls Teron. "We did a lot for each other in that the competition between the three of us was so intense that to survive with the other two you had to improve yourself."

Developers of the time say the industry was very different then, the quality control better. Many new homes do not have the quality of a Campeau, Minto or Teron home of the 1950s. Nor could the smaller developers of that era match them. The big three had well-trained service people for follow-ups; they would remove their shoes before they walked into a customer's home. To compete, each developer had to come up with something better than the next. Homebuyers were getting into comparative shopping, and each competitor sought to outdo the others in quality and design. Where Campeau may have built a street of similar red brick houses, Teron designed a street with homes in different styles.

But neither Minto nor Teron could catch up with Campeau. His head start and the sheer pace at which he worked kept him on top. Minto was second and Teron third, a pecking order that remained firmly established until Campeau and Teron quit Ottawa years later. Teron is now a Toronto builder and Minto is now the dominant developer in the capital.

Although Campeau continued to lead the pack in house-building, he and Alban began to focus once again on apartments. In about 1956, they put up an eight-storey, eighty-unit structure at the corner of King Edward and Stewart in the Sandy Hill area near Lower Town. Far grander apartment buildings soon followed. Their first real highrise — also Ottawa's first — was Colonel By Towers: twelve storeys containing 142 apartments in a section of Ottawa known as the Glebe, near Carleton University. That building also held two floors of office space, which they leased to the federal government — their first such deal.

In 1956, Elmvale Acres was reaching its peak of construction, about 400 houses a year. Having laid claim to much of the available farmland in the east, Bob now made haste to gobble up land to the west of the city. Early that year, he began building Bel-Air Park, just north of Baseline Road and east of Woodroffe, an area where there was as yet little development. Bob planned to put up about 115 houses a year for three years on this eighty-acre property. Next he purchased what was known as the Arkell farm, farther to the west, just north of the Queensway highway. This would become the Queensway Terrace North development. Soon thereafter, he bought a farm on the other side of the highway, which became Queensway Terrace South. Together, the Queensway Terrace developments were to include 900 houses and solidify Campeau's hold on the west end of Ottawa, which he in large part created.

He was now operating on a large scale at both ends of Ottawa, with Eugène Lavigne in charge of Elmvale Acres and the other properties to the east, and Jean-Marc Prud'Homme heading up the Bel-Air site and the properties to the west. It was no longer a matter of sporadic building, of one thing leading to another. Campeau was buying up land primarily on the perimeter of the city, and the city followed him as his subdivisions began to dot the map and farms disappeared.

Working on farmland in undeveloped territory was often trying, and the delays could be grave. Lionel recalls four days of torrential rains that filled up the trenches and buried in mud the virgin roads of the portion of Elmvale Acres under construction in the spring of 1956. It took days to repair the damage.

Delays are extremely costly to developers building with borrowed money. This was true even in the 1950s, when interest rates were much lower than today. Deluges such as those that washed out Elmvale Acres could be disastrous, as could April snowstorms. Suppliers could also create dilemmas. Lumber, for example, might be riddled with termite holes, or gnarled, or not sufficiently dry to prevent warping.

The company had now reached a size that demanded further expansion of the management structure. As usual, when new blood was needed, Campeau turned first to family. Bob was intensely loyal to his relatives, besides which bringing in family also meant that he had eyes and ears in all his various operations. His older brother Gilbert, thirty-nine years old at the time and an eighteen-year veteran of International Nickel, joined Allied Building Supply in 1957 as yard foreman, responsible for supervising delivery of materials to the subdivisions. Gilbert's son René was also to be recruited to the Allied Building Supply operation. Bob and Alban gave Gilbert and his wife Blanche the money to buy their first Ottawa house, which was in Billings Bridge. Bob also offered his sister Beatrice's husband, Matte, a job in Ottawa, but he declined.

The Campeau organization increasingly attracted English Canadians. The real change began with the hiring of Joe Johnston, a friend of Paradis's from CMHC, as sales manager. Despite his name, Johnston was French, but he was to hire many English sales agents. Alan Jones joined the company as an engineer in heavy construction. Max Ballantyne, a technical school graduate who would later become head of heavy construction, joined soon after.

More French Canadians were coming in as well, notably Clem Cadieux, a Lower Town Ottawa boy who was no relation to Alban. He joined in 1958 and was to become chief financial officer, responsible for many of the Campeau business deals.

Of the English Canadians who joined the company at this time, only Max Ballantyne ultimately entered the inner circle, which eventually became known as the Twelve: Bob, Alban, Lionel, Gilbert, Ballantyne, Jean Paradis, Ray Larocque, Marcel Lalande, Jean-Marc Prud'Homme, Eugène Lavigne, Clem Cadieux and Joe Johnston.

Meanwhile, Bob's strife with his brother Lionel was coming to a head. The two exploded at each other almost daily. They both had fierce tempers; colleagues who worked with both use the phrase "Well, he's a Campeau" in trying to explain. Former employees recall telephone battles of up to an hour — Campeau in the office and Lionel in the field. During one of these, Bob smashed a glass on his desk in his fury. Part of the trouble seems to have been Lionel's habit of checking with Bob whenever there were problems to be solved. According to Eugène Lavigne, "Lionel was always consulting Robert and having arguments, terrible arguments, about almost anything." Bob was very much a hands-on manager, but he expected his executives to solve their problems themselves.

Despite the brothers' fights, former employees say that much of the Campeau reputation for quality was Lionel's doing because he was in the field, supervising the early projects. Even those who disliked him agree that Lionel was obsessed with the quality of Campeau work.

The overall picture at Campeau Construction remained rosy. By 1958, it was a large and profitable company indeed. It had almost $9 million in assets (up from $563,426 in 1953) and more than 1,000 acres of land held for development, and was bringing in almost $11.5 million a year from house sales and rental income (compared with just $1.4 million in 1953). Campeau sold 575 houses in 1958, an astounding improvement over the 155 sold just five years earlier.

In relation to what was happening nationwide throughout the second half of the 1950s, Campeau was a player of moderate scope. He was certainly building on a large scale and beginning to assemble a land bank for future development, but had not yet branched out from housing and apartment units to far grander projects. By contrast, developer William Zeckendorf, who in 1960 would form Trizec, began work in 1958 on Montreal's Place Ville Marie office-commercial development. But Campeau was far ahead of Cadillac Development Corp., which later would merge with two other companies to form the giant Cadillac-Fairview and which, in 1958, was building small apartment projects in Toronto.

By the early 1960s, Campeau had a components plant operating on Baseline Road that produced moldings, roof parts, panels, trusses, windows, stairs, flooring, countertops and struts for his own projects and for other builders. There were two assembly lines just for trusses — which form the supporting framework of a roof — and panels. And even that became too small. A second shop was built just to meet the demand for more than 2,000 sets of trusses a year.

Prud'Homme remembers clearly the Saturday afternoon in 1958 when Bob took him, Alban and Lionel for lunch in nearby Bell's Corners and then drove them to see the land he had just bought for the components plant. What did they think of the idea? he wondered. He needn't have asked. Excavation began within a week.

The Baseline Road complex ultimately grew into a twenty-one-acre site that housed 30,000 square feet of office and retail space, 98,000 square feet of manufacturing space and 50,000 square feet of warehouse space. The office and manufacturing complex was the result of the company's galloping expansion throughout the 1950s. Many building products developed here — including roof truss connectors that became a major part of the Campeau components business — were sold across the continent and, to some extent, overseas.

At about the same time, a new subsidiary, Queensview Construction and Development, was formed to handle heavy construction. Then Campeau began producing prefabricated housing and cottage units to be sold through distributors in eastern Canada.

Throughout the company's expansion in the late 1950s, Bob remained a stickler for quality control. He continued to make snap inspections on all his building projects. If a wall was out of line, he would smash it to pieces. If defective lumber was delivered to a site, he flew into a rage. Prud'Homme recalls his boss once kicking a twisted two-by-four across the floor, shouting, "I'm going to call the supplier and tell him to stick the goddamn thing wherever he wants to. That's no good. That's not what we bought." You had to deal carefully with Bob Campeau.

Two employees recall an incident on a weekend retreat at a resort north of Montreal. A supplier of hardwood flooring who had somehow cheated the company happened to be in the same dining room, sitting a number of tables away. Campeau did not recognize him at first, but he knew the man's face was familiar. As he ate his meal, he kept trying to remember where he had seen him. Suddenly it struck him, and he swung around in his chair and bellowed across the dining room, "You won't fool me anymore."

As the target of this outburst sprang from his chair, Campeau rose as well, strode over, grabbed the man by the throat and pushed him up against a stone fireplace. The fight was quickly broken up, but presumably this man never again messed with Campeau Construction.

Campeau soon devised a system of fines levied against any subcontractor whose men either failed to work fast enough or in some other way delayed production. "When a person put his trust in us and bought a home, we told him exactly what he was going to get and considered it our responsibility to make sure that he got it," Campeau said many years later. "We paid the workers, we paid the subcontractors, so I felt it was our responsibility as managers to insist that they both provide good quality and good workmanship."

Former Campeau employees recall that his inspectors would issue "tickets," fines that would be deducted from the bill when the time came to pay the subcontractor. If work was not completed in time, and another subcontractor was delayed in starting his part, the offender was fined a set amount per day. But the system worked only to a point.

"I know that we paid for that down the road," says a former senior executive. "Of course the next year the contractor increased his price accordingly. In the end, who is kidding who?"

Even in the late 1950s, when Campeau was running a large company and delegating a great deal of authority, he still generally insisted on direct involvement in all major negotiations. The truth is that he loved to haggle, enjoyed the game, whether the stakes were high or low. His executives remember one occasion on which he was selling eleven of his original small apartment buildings to a group of investors represented by

Mike Greenberg, a prominent Ottawa real estate lawyer who
was no relation to the Greenbergs of Minto Construction. At
about $600,000, it was a major sale, but what the discussion
came down to, in the end, was the fate of an old lawn mower.
When they were closing the deal, Campeau insisted that the
mower was not included in the sale. Greenberg maintained that
it was, and so it went.

"Here are these two guys closing a huge deal, Bob and Mike
Greenberg, and they started arguing about a lawn mower, who
was going to own the lawn mower, was the lawn mower part of
the deal or not part of the deal," recalls an observer. "And
neither one of them was going to lose. The lawn mower was with
the buildings and Bob was trying to say that he hadn't sold the
lawn mower with the buildings, so they ended up tossing a coin.
I forget who won. But Bob wouldn't give up and Mike wouldn't
give up, and the lawn mower became more important than the
$600,000 deal. Bob had to win. Here are these two guys arguing
about the damn lawn mower, which was probably worth 50
bucks, and Bob wasn't going to lose."

One of Campeau's few bad deals in this period came when
Queensview Construction bid for the contract to build the
$5-million Britannia filtration plant just below the Deschênes
Rapids on the Ottawa River. It was Campeau's first major
non-housing project and the first time he had hired himself out
as a general contractor in industrial construction. It appears to
have been a case of ego interfering with good business sense.

"Bob wanted to build that goddamn plant because he
wanted to show that he was not just a small housebuilder, that
he could also build a filtration plant," recalls a former top
executive. "So we put in a bid. We had no experience at all in
that field, and I recall that, at the last minute, Bob dropped the
price by half a million bucks just to make sure we got it. And we
got it by more than $700,000, so it's as if he left half a million on
the table. We lost our shirts on that job."

This was winning at all costs. Campeau would later develop
it to an art in his takeover battles of the late 1980s.

Things went from bad to worse. The purification plant,
which was supposed to have been completed by September 15,

1960, was delayed by spring flooding from the Ottawa River. Then electricians at the site walked out on strike, and work was stalled when the bricklayers and carpenters refused to cross the picket lines. Campeau seethed, railing against this show of worker solidarity, claiming that the refusal to cross amounted to an illegal strike because of no-strike clauses in the workers' contracts. But he was powerless.

Campeau realized that unions were a fact of life and that he had to coexist with organized labor. His own production employees at Baseline Road were unionized, as were the subtrades on the sites. However, "he didn't like unions for what they represented, and it wouldn't take much for him to get into a fight with the union," says then company salesman Andrew Perrier. "If there was a strike that caused a stoppage of work, he'd get pretty upset."

One of Campeau's more dramatic showdowns with the unions came on a cold January morning in 1962. The Wood, Wire and Metal Lathers Union and the Plasterers and Cement Masons Union had been picketing the site of the fourteen-storey Champlain Towers apartment project to protest a subcontractor's use of non-union plasterers and lathers on the job. The thirty or so pickets on the line that morning had not tried to stop the job superintendent from entering, but they planned on halting Campeau. He first noticed them as he neared the project just after 8 A.M. Undaunted, he leaned on the horn of his new Chrysler and proceeded at about five miles an hour.

"Get out of the way," he shouted through the open car window at the men who stood blocking the vehicle. Few moved, and Campeau did not stop.

Elphage Chainex, a thirty-four-year-old union member, was pushed about three feet, and another picket was brushed by the fender of Campeau's car. At this point, Campeau stepped on the brakes, leaped out and furiously demanded that Chainex be taken to hospital and examined. It turned out that he had a minor bruise on his hip.

The next day, Campeau applied for an interim injunction to halt picketing, alleging that the unions had thrown kegs of roofing nails and a tree trunk in the roadway. County Court Judge Peter Macdonald granted the injunction, which later was left in force, prohibiting any obstructive picketing.

Campeau's antipathy toward the union movement did not diminish with the years. He once grew so irate during a bricklayers' strike that he proposed that the construction industry unite in province-wide lockouts in contract talks the following year. "The pendulum has swung, and labor is now more powerful than management," he told the Ottawa Institute of Association Executives. "I don't think a lot of members in the general contracting industry are strong enough to meet labor in 1971, but I would love to take a leading role in getting ready for it." And he once told guests at his company's Christmas dinner that President Richard Nixon's economic policies were dead on because "any politician who puts his name on the line against labor has to have guts."

In the late 1950s, however, Bob was more worried about his brother Lionel than about occasional labor disputes. Their clashes were growing in both number and ferocity, creating an increasing strain. It was certainly not all Lionel's fault – the two brothers were an explosive combination – but those who were company insiders at this time agree that Lionel was becoming more of a liability than an asset. Office employees were complaining to Bob that Lionel was interfering in aspects of the business outside his turf. For example, Lionel would often phone the purchasing division and scream that his men had run short of supplies. Even in his own domain, as general superintendent, Lionel's problems were mounting. René Arvisais, a carpentry contractor, once insisted that if Lionel did not steer clear of a certain project, he would quit. Reluctantly, Bob and Alban chose to let Arvisais leave.

By this time, Lionel was relying heavily on his two lieutenants, Lavigne and Prud'Homme. The two carpenters had a technical mastery of the construction business that he would never achieve. But he did make some decisions on his own. And, like his brother, he was usually immovable once his mind was made up. Prud'Homme, who was also bull-headed, would argue with him, trying to change his mind, but to no avail. Lavigne took a more subtle approach, reasoning calmly with his boss and occasionally talking him out of an entrenched position.

Lionel's temperament often resulted in problems in the field. One episode Lavigne remembers particularly vividly occurred in late July of 1959 at the site of the Queensway Terrace North project. Lionel's men were preparing the site for the installation of storm and sanitary sewers, a separate contract let by the city but for which Campeau Construction was required to pay 80 percent of the cost.

One warm summer afternoon, as Star Construction Co. was finishing the sewer excavation work under the direction of part-owner John Susin, Lionel and Lavigne arrived on the scene. Lionel took one look at the work Susin's men were doing and decided that it did not meet city specifications. So he marched over to Susin — who could be every bit as ferocious as the Campeaus and, at six feet tall, towered over Lionel — and launched into a tirade. He insisted, among other things, that Susin remove a number of large rocks still on the site. The two crossed swords until, finally, Lionel roared, "If you're not happy, you can just fuck off the project."

"What did you say?" asked Susin.

"I said, if you're not happy, just fuck off the project."

Suddenly, Susin punched Lionel in the face, knocking him to the ground. Dazed and dumbfounded, Lionel got up and sprang into his car.

"Come on," he shouted to Lavigne, and the two raced to the field office, where Lionel phoned his younger brother.

"I've been attacked by John Susin," he told Bob, who immediately left his office, picked up Lavigne and headed back to the site for a showdown. When he got there, he leaped out of the car and rushed at the offending contractor.

"You hit my brother. Now you're gonna hit me." Bob stared down Susin, who towered above him as he had above Lionel.

Susin removed his sunglasses and searched for a spot to put them as Bob tore off his jacket, ready for a fight. But when he realized that the cocky Campeau meant business, he decided to back off.

"I knew he wasn't going to hit me when he started looking for somewhere to put his glasses," Bob told Lavigne as they were leaving the site. "I could have hit him right then."

But the war was not over. About a day later, Susin was on the project filling a trench with sand that he apparently insisted was the property of Star Construction. Lionel disagreed and another row ensued.

"That's not your material — it's mine," Lionel shouted. "You're not going to touch that."

When Susin refused to listen, Lionel sent two of his men in bulldozers — one a fifteen-ton D7 — to reclaim the sand. Susin, fuming, mounted a far bigger forty-ton D9 to turn back the assault. He charged with his blade raised, and one of Campeau's men swung his bulldozer around to meet him. The scene now briefly took on the air of a Grade B gladiator film, but after an initial round in the sandy arena, the cable holding the blade on Susin's bulldozer caught and broke, leaving him weaponless. Unfazed, he swung the huge machine around and backed up into one of the Campeau bulldozers, almost tipping it over. He then broke away and prepared for another rear assault, but the terrified Campeau employee disengaged his machine and fled.

The final act of this melodrama was played out in the courts. In the end, Star Construction was forced to pay $263.61 for damage inflicted on the Campeau bulldozer.

The battle of the bulldozers seems emblematic of Lionel's problems as the sixties began: much ado about very little. He himself must have been aware that the situation could not go on forever. When he finally did leave, it was, he says, over a matter of principle. In 1961, Bob and Alban decided to change the way Lionel's carpenters were paid. Several years earlier, Lionel had been instrumental in changing the carpenters' pay system from an hourly rate to piecework, believing that this would weed out those who could not — or would not — meet the pace demanded. He also instituted a bonus system for foremen.

He was extremely protective of his men in the field but wanted no bad carpenters in the bunch. As Lionel recalls it, Bob and Alban elected to return to an hourly-rate system that he believed would necessitate clock-watchers "spying" on his men. When it became clear that Bob and Alban were determined to make this change, Lionel quit.

But this was really a pretext, a convenient out for both sides. Virtually all the other senior people in the company at this time say that Lionel left primarily because of his constant clashes with his younger brother.

"It had been building and building for years," recalls a former senior executive who had been close to Bob. "It was vicious. The battles between these two guys were just unbelievable. I mean, you could hear them from almost a mile away. My recollection is that Bob reached a point where he said it's not worth it. See, Lionel never had the vision that Bob had, and he'd never live long enough to have that vision."

Perhaps Lionel had other reasons. Eugène Lavigne says that Lionel was afraid the company was headed for bankruptcy because it was growing too fast. Lionel was heard to say more than once that Robert "has gone crazy, he's going to run the company bankrupt." Maybe he decided to get out while his 15 percent stake was still worth something. Bob and Alban bought him out for about $750,000 in the summer of 1961 — not a bad profit for a one-dollar investment. At a banquet marking both Lionel's forty-seventh birthday and his resignation, he also got a watch from the company. He retired and invested his money in the stock market.

Bob appointed Eugène Lavigne as Lionel's successor, naming him general superintendent. Prud'Homme became Lavigne's assistant. Taking his cue from Lionel, Lavigne began phoning Bob to ask for advice and check many decisions. Finally Bob was frank.

"Listen, Eugène," he told Lavigne. "I put you in charge to look after my projects and you're going to make the decisions. You'll make some mistakes — just try not to make too many. I have other things to do, I can't be answering the phone for every decision that you have to make. You make your own decisions."

By the early 1960s, Campeau's head office housed about thirty people. There were four architects, and the company used almost thirty contractors and hundreds of men on the sites. Campeau Construction was now a very large concern, and for Campeau, plotting its strategy began to take on the aura of a military campaign like those in the history books he began to devour in increasing numbers. Above all, he was captivated by great men. He had a particular fascination with history's conquerors; former employees recall that business conversations often contained allusions to such great generals as Napoleon. Of his passion for studying the past, Campeau says: "History is very helpful in anything I do."

"Bob would read everything he could read about those kinds of people in history," recalls a former employee and friend. "It's an obsession with him. Not money, it's power. Bob read everything he could about the great men, the great conquerors of history."

By the beginning of the 1960s, Campeau's success and belief in himself seemed boundless. His friend Paul Tardif, the city councilor, remembers a conversation from this period that seems to sum up Campeau's attitude.

"Bob, you have lots of money," Tardif told him. "Why do you give yourself all that trouble?"

"I don't really want a lot of money, Paul," Campeau responded. "I want power."

"What are you going to do with power?" Tardif asked. He thought that by power Campeau meant the ability to control and dominate others.

In fact, Campeau saw himself in terms reminiscent of a feudal lord. For him the idea of power was combined with a strong sense of responsibility. "I keep 400 families living well, eating well, being well dressed, sending their kids to school," he told Tardif. "I want to have the power to do that for thousands of families. I'm not working for money only."

6 / The Taming of the Shrew

*"I was her friend, her enemy, everything but
her lover, and maybe even that — not
physically, in that way."*
— Robert Campeau

LIONEL'S DEPARTURE WAS not the only strain on Bob Campeau
as the 1960s commenced. He was also engaged in an ongoing
battle with Ottawa's feisty mayor, Charlotte Whitton, who was
re-elected in 1960 after a four-year absence from municipal
politics. Her victory raised the curtain on the second act of one
of the most famous running feuds in Ottawa.

They had first locked horns back in 1952 when both were
just starting out — Whitton in her first full term as mayor and
Campeau as the confident young developer on the rise. He was
a brash twenty-nine years old, determined to conquer the
world, and she was fifty-six but no less full of fire. No petty
politician was going to stand in his way. No crass young French
Canadian builder was going to take over her city.

No one can recall just what sparked the feud, or even
whether it was the result of a single incident. But soon after she
became mayor, there was trouble between them at a Board of
Control meeting to discuss a Campeau housing project. The
four-member Board of Control was chaired by the mayor and
acted as the city's executive committee. There is no record of
what Whitton and Campeau said; minutes of the Board of
Control meetings of that year are sketchy. At issue was
Campeau's bid for a thirteen-acre subdivision site owned by the
city. His sealed offer of $75,000 had been accepted. Now he
wanted to revise it downward by $20,000 because of a

72

miscalculation in the amount of landfill the site would need. In addition, the area of the land was considerably less than the thirteen acres advertised. But Whitton and her colleagues said no. So Campeau walked away from the deal and forfeited his $500 deposit.

There is no record of Campeau's reaction, but it is certain that he seethed. The $500 was beside the point. Whitton and company had prevented him from getting his way. And what Bob Campeau wanted was good for everybody. He did not like this woman mayor, and there were often harsh words between them.

"When I look at his houses, I think perhaps nuclear bombardment might not be such a terrible thing after all," Whitton said once, early in their feud.

"Every time she opens her mouth, nonsense pours out," responded Campeau. "At the rate she talks, you'd think speech was going to be banned tomorrow."

Friends and former employees say Campeau *never* forgets once someone has crossed him, and perhaps this incident continued to irk him for several years. He was always emotional in his dealings with Whitton and city hall. In *Men of Property*, Susan Goldenberg wrote that "in his younger days it was not unusual for Campeau to jump up and down at zoning hearings with deputy chairman Jean Paradis . . . tugging at him to sit down and be quiet." Once, in 1960, when the city revoked a building permit on an apartment building, Campeau vowed to press ahead with the project anyway, saying that "just because council wants to withdraw a permit doesn't mean it's withdrawn." And though he would back down later, Campeau waved in reporters' faces the registered letter he had received from the city revoking the permit, railing that "this letter is illegal, this council motion is illegal." His encounters with Whitton were peppered with such remarks.

Charlotte Whitton was a pioneering feminist who had made her name as a social worker and crusading journalist. She had entered politics on a dare, responding to a challenge issued in an *Ottawa Journal* editorial after she complained in a speech to a women's club about the shortage of women in public life. Never one to shy away from a challenge — her mother once told her that she did not have to fight but "if someone wants a scrap it's your Christian duty to meet them half way" — Whitton ran in the next election and won a seat on the Board of Control. When Mayor Grenville Goodwin died ten months later, she suddenly found herself the first woman mayor in Canada. She soon became renowned for her volcanic temper.

From 1952 to 1956 Mayor Whitton did everything in her power to make Campeau's life miserable, throwing roadblocks in his path, impeding his projects and speaking out at every opportunity in opposition to the French Canadian developer and his grand plans. Fighting city hall became a constant ordeal. If Campeau was not pushing for a bylaw change or new sewer route, he was pressing to pay less in various city charges or win approval to build penthouse apartments on buildings not zoned for them. Always, Mayor Whitton was there to stand in his way, hurling insults and challenging his every move.

But early on, Campeau found an ally and protector at city hall in the form of city councilor Paul Tardif, who saw only good in what the developer was doing for Ottawa. Tardif usually discovered a way to help Campeau get what he wanted despite the mayor's opposition. Nonetheless, Campeau must have heaved a great sigh of relief when Whitton dropped out of municipal politics in 1956, supposedly for good. But she soon learned that she could not bear to be away from the fray. In 1960, after a futile attempt to win a federal seat for the Tories in the Liberal stronghold of Ottawa West, she again ran for mayor and won.

Although she had been pretty in her youth, by the time of her re-election in 1960 Charlotte Elizabeth Hezeltyne Whitton had become a dumpy and unattractive woman. Her five-foot frame had thickened, her face grown haggard. When not decked out in the finery of her office, she wore frumpy clothes and, occasionally, hairnets to work. But these things did not seem to bother her. She once recounted to city council the story of a train ride to Toronto, when she had trouble sleeping in the upper berth because of a noisy drunk below her. Fed up, she jiggled the curtains on the bunk as a hint for him to be quiet. A voice boomed from below in response, "No thanks, lady, I saw you when you got on the train."

There have been few politicians in Canada to compare to Charlotte Whitton. She would say anything to anyone. Once, when the Lord Mayor of London was traveling across Canada, Whitton hosted a formal civic banquet which the Lord Mayor attended in all his finery: buckled shoes, silk stockings, his robe and beloved chain of office. Whitton wore her mayoral robes, adorned with a corsage.

"Madam, if I smell your rose, will you blush?" the Lord Mayor, leaning over during dinner, inquired in a whisper.

"Sir, if I pull your chain, will you flush?" Whitton retorted.

Whitton and Campeau shared certain characteristics — notably fierce determination and a hot temper. But although she was just as feisty and just as stubborn as he, they were otherwise quite different. Both Campeau's parents were Roman Catholic. Whitton was the child of an Irish Catholic mother and a Protestant father. Campeau had been educated on the street. Whitton had entered Queen's University with scholarships in six subjects. And no one would have accused Bob Campeau of being a supporter of feminist causes.

Now *she* was back.

Just before the 1960 election, Campeau had gone to the Board of Control to discuss proposals for a low-cost housing development at Baseline and Pinecrest roads. But the old board had deferred the matter until after the election, and early in the new year Campeau received a letter asking him to appear at a meeting on January 10, 1961. On the appointed day, he dutifully showed up and sat patiently, biding his time. And sat. And sat — through two hours and thirty minutes of tedious city business. There was no way Whitton could have failed to notice her long-time foe. When she finally called for a motion to adjourn the meeting, Controller Tardif objected. What about the scheduled appearance of Mr. Campeau?

"This is the first I've heard of it," the mayor snapped. "It isn't fair to me to be faced with a delegation on a matter I am not familiar with."

To be fair, Whitton had only been in office a few days. But given past history it's a safe bet that she was only using this as an excuse to annoy Campeau. Campeau, in an uncharacteristic show of patience, held his fire, agreeing to return two days later and so allow the mayor time to become familiar with the matter. Perhaps he was deliberately trying a new tactic against his old enemy, attempting to restart their relationship on a different note. If so, this resolve did not last long.

Soon the walls of city hall shook once more with their Olympian screaming matches. Of their tempestuous relationship, Campeau later observed: "I was her friend, her enemy, everything but her lover and maybe even that — not physically, in that way, you know."

Less than three weeks after Whitton refused to hear Campeau's low-cost housing proposal, she accused him of having improperly gained knowledge of the municpality's 1961 capital budget, which had not yet gone to city council. Her case was based on a letter Campeau sent to a closed Board of Control meeting arguing the necessity of the city providing a sewer link for one of his subdivisions at a cost of $18,000. Since this money was not in the new budget, Whitton found the timing of the letter more than suspicious.

"It's an absolute and utter mystery how Mr. Campeau knows about the contents of the capital budget when it has not yet been made public," Whitton told reporters after the meeting.

Campeau, who had by then presold 100 of the 300 homes planned for the development, subject to beginning construction that year, responded by way of the media: "It is true that on January 26 I wrote the mayor and Board of Control with regard to proposed services for the Munro Farm subdivision. It is untrue that this letter was the outcome of any information passed on to me in relation to the contents of the 1961 capital budget. I have not, nor have I had, any such information. I respectfully suggest that Mayor Whitton forget her personal phobia with regard to myself, that she forego histrionics in favor of business principles designed to allow Ottawa to live up to the motto she is so fond of quoting: Advance."

This seeming tempest in a teapot was all too typical of their stormy relationship. Moreover, the issue of a sewer link was not a minor one to a builder. Without it, construction of the new development would be delayed indefinitely. Tardif, still Campeau's best friend on council, complained to his colleagues that the cost to the city would be minor when compared with the tax revenue that would result. He cannot now remember whether on this occasion he won the day. But more often than not he did, a fact that further fueled Whitton's ire.

Campeau's relationship with Tardif must have appeared to many a little too cozy. Tardif always took Campeau's side against the mayor; he insulted and baited her every chance he got. When Whitton said no, Tardif said yes. If Bob Campeau wanted it, it had to be good. Whitton once got so furious with Tardif during a closed-door meeting of Board of Control that she kicked and punched him. Another time, she threatened to shoot Tardif and turned up the next day with a toy gun. At least the mayor retained her sense of humor, however offbeat.

Tardif, a heavy man with a gap-tooth smile, had much in common with his friend Bob Campeau. Like Campeau, he was a French Canadian born to a large Roman Catholic family, who had set off early to make his way in the world and had made something of himself despite the odds. They were natural allies and theirs was a lasting relationship stretching from the early 1950s until Campeau quit Ottawa. They golfed and hunted together. They socialized together at parties. They even lived two doors apart on Applewood Crescent and shared neighboring cottages on the Ottawa River. Tardif had bought both his properties from Campeau.

Tardif and his wife became good friends of the Campeau family, and he is adamant that he got no special favors for his support. If anything, he argues, he received tougher treatment because he was a friend. After Tardif purchased his house, Campeau told him that he owed the company more money.

"You know, that window in front of your house cost $360," Campeau said.

"So?" replied Tardif.

"Well, you owe me $360 more."

"Like hell I do."

"Yes, you do."

"Have a look at this." Tardif handed Campeau the papers on the house. "See that. I had it specified and you signed it."

"Jesus, how did I sign that?"

"I don't know, but you signed it."

At one point, Campeau tried to lure the city councilor away from politics and into his company, telling him he had "too damn much brains" and offering to double his salary. Tardif declined. "To do that, I would have had to quit my political life, which I did for fun," he says. "It didn't pay at that time — it does now — but it was fun. You were a small fish in a big pond, but you were a small fish and a lot of other people weren't. So that flatters your ego and, unfortunately, I suffer from that too, maybe not to a degree where it shows."

Campeau and Tardif obviously saw nothing wrong in their relationship. Tardif says he backed Campeau because the developer never proposed a project that could not be supported. As well, the politician saw the young builder as a doer who was fulfilling a desperate need for housing in the capital. He says Campeau never received anything from the city that he did not deserve or that was not fairly negotiated. There were, he recalls, discussions about Campeau virtually every day, with Whitton constantly trying to slow down the developer's expansion.

"She wanted to stop him dead in his tracks at the beginning of the line," Tardif says. "She was trying to arouse them against Campeau, the people that bought Campeau houses, or anybody else, to prevent them from buying Campeau houses. Because he got to a point where you'd have to shoot him — you couldn't make rules that would stop him. You could make rules that would give him a hell of a lot of trouble, but not stop him. And the hell of a lot of trouble, *I* prevented that."

With these three headstrong personalities at work, city meetings could be raucous affairs. At one such meeting in June 1961, Whitton accused Campeau of conniving to obtain sewer services for one of his subdivisions, Queensway Terrace South, by bypassing a group of city residents. Whitton claimed that Campeau had persuaded a junior member of the Planning and Works Department to draw up, on Campeau's instructions, a new set of blueprints that excluded sewer service for the residents who had not signed the required petition. Campeau claimed that he had merely approached the bureaucrat in question for an opinion, and that no such blueprints existed. Whitton claimed that she had seen the offending documents.

"I object violently to this attack on my integrity," Campeau screamed at the meeting.

Whitton pounded the table, threatening to throw Campeau out of the meeting room.

"You try to make it look like I connived to get the sewer routes changed," Campeau said.

"That's just what I had in mind," Whitton responded.

"Well, you're wrong. I didn't. I value my honesty, my integrity, as much as you do."

"Go back and get the signatures from the remaining property owners," Whitton told him. "And I intend to call an immediate inquiry."

At this, Tardif jumped in. "I'm fed up with you and your inquiries," he told the mayor. "Why don't you stop persecuting this fellow and get along with developments that will bring more taxes into the city treasury? You and your inquiries make me sick."

Despite her failure to produce the sinister blueprints, Whitton stuck to her story. Later, when the meeting calmed down, Campeau apologized for his outburst.

"I have a temper as bad as yours," he told the mayor.

"No matter how you feel about me," Whitton responded, "I am the presiding officer and you have no right to disrupt proceedings as you did. Come back with the full petition. And I shall see there will be a proper hearing on the junior executive and his role."

It wasn't just the big things — sewer lines, subdivisions and such — that caused problems between the mayor and the developer. Even the little things did not escape Lottie Whitton's eye. About a month after their run-in over the blueprints, Whitton complained that the builder had no legal right to put up a thirty-by-twelve-foot sign at the corner of Pinecrest and Baseline roads advertising the Queensway Terrace South subdivision. "The sign committee did agree to it, but had no idea the sign would be as big as a billboard," the mayor said. "It was even put up before final approval was given."

Her colleagues did not back her, and the sign stood.

That summer, city council passed a new policy under which builders would be charged $1,500 an acre to help defray the costs of new sewage disposal and water filtration plants. Campeau told the Ottawa media the new policy was the "straw that broke the camel's back." The new charge would increase the retail price of homes in new subdivisions by about $500, he claimed. The city, he warned, seemed bent on driving developers to the outlying areas.

He was fed up enough to contemplate going into politics himself. "I am very seriously considering running for mayor because it's obvious that a businessman is needed to end inefficiency and foolishness at city hall," he said. "And let me stress it is not only the present administration but previous administrations too that have been guilty of foolish decisions and inefficient work."

Why did Whitton oppose Campeau every step of the way? Although many of her colleagues believed she was anti-development, Bill Teron, Campeau's competitor, says he and Irving Greenberg of Minto Construction never had the same trouble with Charlotte Whitton that Bob did. Teron and Greenberg were building mostly in Nepean, outside the city limits, and thus were far less involved with Ottawa city hall. Yet they occasionally had to deal with her and, says Teron, she was always straightforward.

Teron suspects that Whitton was annoyed by Campeau's close relationship with Tardif. Tom Kerr, a journalist who covered many of the Campeau-Whitton battles for the *Ottawa Journal* in the early 1960s, agrees that the mayor had a problem with Campeau's closeness to Tardif and other city councilors. She was a very suspicious person, and appeared to be suspicious of every developer — but especially of Bob Campeau.

Once, during a council meeting discussion of a Campeau project, Whitton accused Tardif of accepting his $6,000 controller's salary to represent Ottawa residents while acting as "Campeau's advocate at this table." It sometimes appeared that way. And certainly the obvious closeness of such a relationship would not be as readily accepted today, when voters and the media expect an arm's-length relationship between politicians and those who do business with government. But all this took place in a much more innocent time.

Tardif, like many others, believes that part of the problem was that Whitton was anti-French. Some believe that her Protestant-Irish Catholic roots produced in her a definite bias against French Canadians. Tardif maintains that the mayor once said in his presence, "If we don't stop these Frenchmen they'll take the town over, and that's the last thing we want to happen."

Still others feel that she was vainly trying to stifle the growth of a city that, because of its position, could not stop growing — that she was a small-town girl of the old school, who refused to keep up with the times. By 1961, the federal civil service had come to comprise about 350,000 people and the population of Ottawa had reached 268,000. The county's total population had surpassed 358,000. The best Whitton could do was guide the city's growth. And that meant dealing with the city's largest developer.

And he was big. Eugène Lavigne, who now oversaw all construction and development, was supervising fifteen foremen and three housing inspectors. There was even a housing project starting up at Pointe Claire, near Montreal. The Baseline complex now included the head office of Campeau Construction, which housed Bob as president, Alban as first vice-president, Jean Paradis as second vice-president and Marcel Lalande as treasurer. Ray Larocque and Gilbert Campeau were running Allied Building Supply.

By the end of 1962, Campeau had built 6,000 houses in Ottawa and hundreds of apartments, and he held almost 3,500 acres of land still to be developed. And he was known for being tough. One newspaper journalist recalls watching Campeau emerge with several of his foremen from a building under construction on Kent Street. Campeau stepped onto the sidewalk, turned suddenly to face his men and, throwing his hardhat to the ground with a crack, said, "Well, *you goddamn will*," in response to whatever had taken place inside. It was a vignette typical of the period.

Bob Campeau *was* becoming powerful, changing the face of Charlotte Whitton's city. And she resented the fact that, despite the power of the mayor's office, she could not control him. "A lot of it was power," says Peter Jackman, who covered many of their colossal clashes for the *Ottawa Journal* in the late 1950s and early 1960s. "People say that she was anti-French, which she was, but Charlotte was anti-everything. And I think she just liked to fight."

Whatever it was that motivated the mayor to fight Campeau, there is no question that she did everything she could to hamper his progress. Yet she was, in the end, just one woman. Hers was but one vote among many on city council. Although she could cause Campeau trouble, she could not stop his forward march. But, since developers cannot build without all sorts of permits and approvals from the city, Whitton could cause major delays that cost Campeau huge amounts of money.

Once a piece of land is bought, a detailed plan for the proposed subdivision must be approved by the city — exactly where homes will be built, what land will be set aside for schools and how parking demands will be met. Then the city must agree to provide the necessary services — everything from sewers to hydro — and the required building permits must be issued. All this takes time, and, as Tardif recalls, Whitton regularly questioned every stage.

"I was the chairman of the planning board at one time," Tardif says. "So she would say he can't have something because he's going to be needing schools. I would say that he's only going to need schools if there are children. You're not going to have schools just to have schools. And it's going to increase the traffic, she would say, and people are going to park on that street. I would say that the people from that street are going to be allowed to park on the other streets too. And I was the chairman of the thing, and I passed it."

Developers were required to give 5 percent of subdivision land to the city for recreational purposes. So it was not too difficult for Whitton to delay Campeau's proposals by constantly questioning the quality of the land he was donating, how his projects would be laid out or where he proposed to put schools.

In the spring of 1962, for example, city council had ordered a planning board review of the recreation land proposed at Campeau's Riverside Park South subdivision after one alderman raised questions about adequate drainage provisions in the subdivision agreement. At the planning board meeting, Whitton accused Campeau of giving the city swampland for recreation purposes. She told the board she had visited the site and had seen dried bullrushes and pockets of water in the designated area. "That's a swamp or was a swamp," Whitton declared.

Controller Don Reid, then the chairman of the planning board, disagreed. "I went down there for a look myself and the 5 percent land looks about seven feet higher than the land where the houses are to be built."

Back and forth it went until Whitton had her way. Campeau would be required to install storm sewers, asphalt gutters and catch basins for adequate drainage, at considerable additional cost. But, of course, the project went ahead.

In the city elections of November 1962, Whitton was re-elected, and the feud continued. Perhaps it reached its peak in 1963, when the developer appeared before the Board of Control to ask when he might expect building permits for a proposed new subdivision, Playfair Farm. Whitton immediately launched into a tirade, accusing him of wanting early approval so that he could "lure" unsuspecting buyers into prepaying for the homes. It is not clear why she considered preselling a sin, although records of the exchange indicate she was concerned that a buyer would not be able to back out of a deal. As in so many of their encounters, the emotions and the histrionics obscured the actual issue under debate. In this case, Campeau chose to beat a strategic retreat, presumably hoping that by the next meeting the mayor would have calmed down. The next day, her comments about preselling were reported in the newspaper.

One week later Campeau returned seeking an answer to his original question. This time, Whitton vacated her board seat to avoid another fight. Apparently even she realized that her opposition to everything Campeau did was getting out of hand. Campeau then rose, and, though he was there to ask about the building permits, referred instead to the newspaper account of Whitton's statement of a week earlier, which he tried to refute. The mayor, he stated, had had no business questioning his business practices.

At this, Whitton's short-lived composure collapsed. She leaped from her chair and threatened legal action against board members for illegal procedure, claiming they were circumventing her by allowing discussion not pertaining solely to Playfair Farm.

"This is concerning Playfair," Campeau responded.

"Where is that statement?" said Whitton, demanding to see the newspaper clipping that contained her allegedly damning statements about Campeau's behavior. "Where is that statement? Where is that statement? Where is that statement? Where is that statement? Where is that statement? Where is that statement? Where is that statement? Where is that statement? Where is that statement? Where is that statement?"

"Will someone *shut off* that gramophone" Campeau finally bellowed.

When calm was restored, he went on to say that he could prove that Campeau Construction had never enforced down payments on prepurchased homes when a buyer wanted to back out of a deal.

But Whitton was not to be sidetracked. Campeau would

have to present the newspaper clipping formally to the Board of Control if he wished to refute her comments.

"He has no more rights than anyone else," the mayor said.

"I insist on my privilege of democracy," Campeau responded.

"Come out on the hustings," Whitton challenged him.

When the argument finally ended, the board sided with Whitton, insisting that Campeau formally file a record of the offending comments. As for the original question of approving the subdivision, that had to wait for another day.

Whitton lost the 1964 election, but before she retired Campeau got at least some measure of personal revenge. Campeau and Tardif were trailing the mayor down a hallway as she headed, unescorted, for the exit after a black-tie dinner at the Chateau Laurier hotel. Whitton was dressed in her finest, a long formal gown, and somehow Campeau's foot landed on her dress, tearing it. Whitton stood embarrassed and speechless. Campeau apologized and the next day, through the press, said it was a terrible accident, offering the mayor money to buy a new dress.

"He stepped on her dress purposely," Tardif says unequivocally. "Bob was walking with me in the aisle and Whitton was ahead of us. And he picked up his speed a little, and she had a dress that had a thing that dragged on the floor, and he stepped on it."

Alban, who was in the vicinity, disagrees. He says it was a simple accident. Regardless of intent, the incident did nothing to improve Campeau-Whitton relations. "She was damned embarrassed," Tardif recalls. "She normally wasn't short on words, but that time she was. She didn't know what the hell to say. And me, because I was a Campeau protector, Jeez, I was embarrassed too."

Tardif soon became a Liberal member of Parliament and, after nine years in the House of Commons, would be appointed an immigration and citizenship judge. Whitton was temporarily gone from politics, but was not quite out of Bob Campeau's life for good.

7 / Ilse

"He was doing things that people didn't
understand."

— Andrew Perrier

BOB AND CLAUDA'S family life appeared to be blissfully tranquil in the early 1960s. In December of 1961 they celebrated their nineteenth wedding anniversary. Rachelle, now in her teens, was developing into a beautiful young woman, and the two boys, Jacques and Danny, were a delight to their parents. But Robert Campeau was leading a double life. Although Clauda remained in the dark for several years, her husband had fallen in love with another woman.

Robert Campeau and Ilse Luebbert met by accident. As Ilse would tell the story to her sister months later, she did not know the man was Bob Campeau, or that he was married, on that day in May 1961. She was simply cycling around the neighborhood in the area of the Queensway Terrace North subdivision, looking for work, scouting out offices, factories and other potential places of employment. At Allied Building Supply, she somehow stumbled into a management meeting. Those present must have found her a pleasant interruption. Ilse was a striking blonde twenty-one-year-old, recently arrived from Germany. In her charmingly accented English, she explained that she was looking for a job; a nice man with wavy hair gave her the name of someone in personnel whom she could contact the next day.

A few days later Ilse Luebbert was working at Allied Building Supply as a stenographer in the company's fuel oil

division. About a week after she started, the man who had been
so kind to her at the meeting phoned and asked her out for
dinner. It was not long before she was seeing Bob Campeau
regularly. Ilse's older sister Hilde, still living in Germany, soon
began receiving letters telling of the man she had met — Canadian, older. Ilse was no longer complaining about being
lonely.

This is the story Ilse told her sisters.

On the surface, Ilse Luebbert and Bob Campeau had
virtually nothing in common. At thirty-seven years old, Bob
was almost seventeen years her senior. He was Catholic and she
was Lutheran. Campeau knew nothing of war; Ilse had been
born into it. During the British bombing raids on Bremen, in
northern Germany, her mother and sister had carried baby Ilse
in a wicker basket as they sought shelter. One of her earliest
memories was of the family hiding out with several hundred
other people in a dank old iron mine, lit by torches and candles.
The mine was under a mountain near Minden, where the family
had moved in an effort to escape the air raids. In the dying days
of the Second World War, they hid in the mine while Minden
came under artillery fire from the advancing Allied forces.

Despite these unpleasant early experiences, Ilse was a
happy-go-lucky child who grew into a lively and attractive
woman. But she was apparently not satisfied with the jobs she
could find in Germany. So when her sister Annie — who was
seventeen years older and had lived in Canada since
1955 — asked her to come to Ottawa for three months in the
spring of 1961, she jumped at the chance. Annie needed
someone to look after her house in Queensway Terrace while
she and her family returned to Germany to visit their parents.
It was during this visit that Ilse began spending time with Bob
Campeau.

Word spread quickly throughout the company that Bob
was seeing another woman. It was not hard to notice a change
in him. The inner circle was still very close-knit — almost
family — and they all knew and loved Clauda. But Bob did
manage to keep the secret from his older brother Gilbert, now
one of the top men at Allied, the division Ilse had joined. It is

understandable that Gilbert did not find out: he was not at head office with the rest of the top executives, and it was unlikely that any employee at Allied Building Supply would dare suggest to his boss that his brother was having an affair. Gilbert's son René, who also worked in the oil division, was equally unaware of the situation. He actually got into a fight with another employee who repeated the rumor, which he took as a lie and interpreted as an insult.

But certainly Bob's behavior was indiscreet. He would regularly take Ilse out of her department to work for him as a translator. And although Gilbert did not realize what was going on, this frequent loss of one of his stenographers annoyed him and he complained to Bob about it.

Ilse eventually moved into a townhouse. Occasionally, Bob sent Jean-Marc Prud'Homme, now assistant general superintendent of Campeau Construction, to fix a screen or repair a countertop. And an employee who lived near Ilse saw Bob's white Lincoln parked there a little too often. He realized what was happening and got so worried that he considered quitting his job.

Many of the other senior people grew anxious as well. Bob either did not realize or did not care how deeply company morale was affected. Maybe he truly believed his involvement with Ilse was not widely known throughout the ranks of his senior executives.

Then there was the effect on Ilse. She was a beautiful woman, very young for such a relationship, and very vulnerable. Not surprisingly, she was resented by the Campeau old guard. "Everybody disliked her because she was a powerful employee, and they knew damn well where every story would go," recalls one former executive. "Things that Bob should not have known he found out. So everybody became very reluctant or displeased to have her around."

Bob and Clauda were still living in the bungalow on Applewood Crescent, four doors away from Alban and Laura, and at first it was as if all was well at home. Clauda did not notice any change, or simply refused to see it. Bob kept his secret well. At least from her.

At about the same time, Bob began thinking about his children's future. In the summer of 1961 he set up a trust fund for any of his offspring alive on August 29, 1965, at which time it would be divided equally among them. But each share would be held in trust for each child until he or she reached thirty-five. The fund ultimately held about 1.1 million shares of Campeau Construction, which, by the time the company went public in 1969, were valued at $10 each.

The first few months after she met Bob were very stressful for Ilse. After Annie returned from Germany, she grew worried. Ilse was so young and seemed genuinely afraid of the situation. Finally, about seven months after Ilse had started working at Allied, she flew back to Germany to talk to her older sister Hilde. The rumor circulating at Allied Building Supply was that she had left because she was suffering from leukemia.

Ilse told Hilde that she had not realized for some time that the man she had met, and who had helped her get a job, also owned the company and had a wife and three children. She was deeply troubled. After the two had talked it out, Hilde gave her baby sister this advice: "Don't see him again. Don't contact him. Stay here in Germany if you're scared you can't get away from it."

Then Bob arrived, having followed her across the ocean to this small town. In the next few days, the three held many long talks. They examined the situation endlessly and from every angle, discussed it over lunch and again over dinner at the various restaurants Bob took them to. Then they would start over again in the morning when Bob arrived from his hotel for breakfast. He just could not explain it, he said. Nothing like this had ever happened to him. He still loved Clauda, *and* he loved Ilse. "Your place is with your family," Hilde told him. "Ilse's young. She'll get over it."

Bob was torn by guilt, he told the women, and believed that he was destined for the fires of Hell.

When they weren't talking, Hilde put Campeau to work. "I gave him a pair of German wooden shoes and made him dig my vegetable garden," she recalls. "He came in his fancy clothes and shoes and everything and I said, 'Well, let's start to work

off some of your frustrations. Go in the garden and dig it up.'
And he did."

After a few days, the matter seemed to have been resolved.
Bob told Hilde that he was determined to remain apart from
Ilse, and he returned to Ottawa. Ilse flew back to Canada
several weeks later, also determined to start fresh. But she did
not return to work, and she did keep seeing Bob. A few months
later, Ilse fled to Germany again, and again Bob came after her
and they returned to Canada. They could not stay apart. And
all the while Bob kept up his normal family life with his
unsuspecting wife.

Early in 1963, Ilse realized that she was pregnant. When
Bob learned the news he bought a farm in Lachute, near
Montreal, where she could live after the baby was born. But he
was worried and often phoned Hilde in Germany. "I don't know
what to do," he told her. "She can't possibly stay there by
herself in the winter with a baby. Could you come over?"
Finally Hilde agreed.

Robert, Jr., was born in October 1963, and in November Ilse
moved to the farm Bob had bought for her. Those who knew the
couple say Campeau was pleased that the child was a boy. Hilde
arrived shortly after Christmas 1963 to live with Ilse and
worked days at a Dairy Queen several miles away.

Ilse's parents were now in Canada as well, living with Annie
in Ottawa, but they were not told that Ilse had a child.
Whenever Ilse visited them in Ottawa, she left Bobby, Jr., with
a friend. But eventually they learned about their grandson and,
when Hilde left the farm about a year later, they moved into a
separate log house on the property.

Meanwhile, Bob Campeau kept up appearances. He
continued to live with Clauda and their children, but would
often make the seventy-mile drive to Lachute to visit Ilse and
the baby. Since Campeau Construction was building in
Montreal at the time, Bob could be away from Clauda for
several days without having to explain his absence, and Clauda
still did not seem to suspect anything.

This was a particularly painful period for Alban and Laura.
They knew about Ilse but did not tell Clauda, obviously

wanting to spare her the pain. Inevitably, the relationship between the two couples deteriorated. Bob and Clauda and Alban and Laura still spent time together, but the closeness they had known before Bob met Ilse was gone.

Word that Ilse had a baby soon got around the office. And when they learned, many of the old guard were deeply offended; they were close to Bob, they were his friends, but this was too much. The tension at head office must have been almost palpable. Eventually it seemed as though everyone but Gilbert and his son René were in the know. But not one employee dared tell Bob's brother what was going on. Gilbert was a devout Roman Catholic who loved and respected both Clauda and his younger brother. When he finally did find out, the shock was violent.

Sometime after Bobby Jr.'s birth, Campeau called together his senior executives for a dinner meeting at the Motel de Ville in Vanier, a place where they often met. Most of the original Twelve were there: Alban, Jean Paradis, Ray Larocque, Marcel Lalande, Jean-Marc Prud'Homme, Eugène Lavigne, Clem Cadieux, Joe Johnston, Max Ballantyne, Gilbert — and Bob. They met in a private room. After dinner, Bob began talking, coolly and quietly, telling his long-time friends about his other life. He started with the basic information: he had two families. It was a strain on him, but he could handle it. He would not, however, tolerate any of his men trying to run the same kind of double life. Any who did would be fired. He told them that it was none of their business, and ordered that nobody bother either woman. He did not address Gilbert directly, but spoke to the group as a whole.

The room was tense. Many of the faces around the table were stunned. They were not shocked by the information — it was nothing new — but they were taken aback that he chose to tell them in this fashion. No one spoke. Then he praised Clauda.

"Clauda is a respectable woman — I have nothing to say against her — but so is Ilse," he said.

At this the tension finally exploded. Gilbert shot up from his chair, crimson, and pounded the dinner table. He was not sympathetic. Gilbert lunged for his younger brother, but was held back by a few of the others, who tried to calm him.

"It doesn't make any sense," Gilbert said.

"Does anyone have anything to say?" Bob asked once calm was restored. "Don't try to change my mind. This is my decision."

Everyone stared as Jean-Marc Prud'Homme rose somewhat hesitantly from his chair. It was not that he supported what Bob was doing with his life. But, he thought, what's done is done, and they all had to live with it. Gilbert, who was sitting beside Prud'Homme, kicked his foot under the table, trying to stop him.

"Let me talk, Gilbert," Prud'Homme said. Then he addressed the group. "Bob is not the first man to do this, and he won't be the last. In a man, sometimes, there is the animal instinct, and that's Bob."

Prud'Homme then turned to Gilbert and, alluding to their frequent squabbles, said, "You and I, we act like animals sometimes."

Gilbert said nothing further, and the meeting broke up, everybody knowing things would never again be the same. They filed out in silent amazement.

The news did not destroy Bob's relationship with Gilbert — they were brothers, after all — but Gilbert could not bring himself to accept it. The day after the dinner meeting at the motel, Gilbert met Prud'Homme.

"It doesn't make any sense," the elder Campeau said. "What will people think?"

"Gilbert, look around," Prud'Homme replied. "Look around."

Some time later, Bob let Prud'Homme know that his support had been welcome: "You see things the way they are, Jean-Marc."

Many of those who sat around the table that night at the Motel de Ville still speculate about why Campeau called the meeting and why he said what he did. One of them believes that Campeau threatened to fire anyone in a similar situation because he felt that he was the only one among them who could bear up under such strain. Another believes that the meeting was called solely for the purpose of informing Gilbert. "Gilbert was a very, very devout Roman Catholic," this former senior executive recalls. "He couldn't accept it, just couldn't accept it for one minute. He just got up and got red, as the Campeaus can get red, and just went for him." Family members who learned about the meeting believe he was telling his friends not to make the same mistake he had.

For almost three years, Bob traveled back and forth between his two families. He was away from Clauda and the three children for long periods. "As a boy growing up, I assumed my father was very busy," recalls Jacques, who was about twelve years old at the time. "He'd fly home, stay with us a few days, then leave." Yet he built them a lavish new house in the village of Dunrobin on the Ottawa River, just west of the capital. It was a ranch-style affair with high ceilings, somewhat like a chalet — his most beautiful home yet, befitting a man of his wealth and style. The new house kept Clauda busy, planning, moving, decorating.

Finally, Clauda sensed that something was amiss. And, inevitably, the gossip reached her. One day, she confronted Bob in the privacy of his office, away from the children. She asked whether he was seeing another woman. He denied it. It would be another several months before she learned the truth.

Although Bob loved Ilse, it was difficult to turn his back on twenty years of marriage and the woman who had been at his side since he was nineteen years old. Virtually everyone who knew him then says he was being wrenched apart. "He loved both these women very much and he did not know what to do, and he was torn very deeply, and it was a real source of concern and anguish," says Father Ovila Campeau.

The brothers were still very close, as they had been when Bob was a child. The priest visited often. Bob had been raised a strict Catholic, and the teachings of the Church had left their indelible mark: marriage is forever. One of Bob's close friends of that time suggests that if he could have, Bob would have continued to keep two families going: "He tried hard for many, many years, because I don't think he really wanted to hurt anyone."

Meanwhile, Ilse, a young mother tucked away on a farm with an infant son and no husband, must have wondered what had become of her life. One of their friends suggests that she was under a terrible strain, and likely was pressuring Bob to leave Clauda and marry her.

During this period, Bob told his friends that he did not want to hurt Clauda, and that when the right time came he would tell her. Just before Ilse gave birth to their second child, Giselle, Clauda and Bob took a short trip to a fishing camp in northern Quebec. A family member says it was probably here that Bob told her he was in love with Ilse and wanted a divorce.

Clauda was devastated. Up to now she had refused to believe the gossip. She had persuaded herself that she and Bob had a happy marriage. And, as she would later tell a Children's Aid Society investigator, who interviewed them during their divorce proceedings as a routine matter because minors were involved, "there were never marital difficulties." Bob, however, would tell the same investigator that, although there had been no marital problems and no arguments in front of the children, there had been a "gradual development" toward separation.

Bob left Clauda at the beginning of February 1966 to move in with Ilse and Bobby. Giselle was born that May. Bob later said that Ilse "fell in love with me. What could I do? We were married in the eyes of God." He continued to press Clauda for a divorce, but she refused. The restrictive Canadian divorce laws of those days ensured that, in the face of Clauda's refusal, Bob and Ilse would have to wait at least three years.

Clauda could not forget the teachings of the Church: couples did not divorce. She still loved the man she had been with since her teens. She had been at his side through the early struggles, hauling logs and lugging sacks of potatoes in Cornwall. They had shared the worry of Rachelle's long illness and the tragedy of not being able to bear more children. She had been with Bob when he and Tony built the first house on

Guy Street, as he became the biggest developer in Ottawa and as their children grew. How proud she had been of his success. She was not prepared to let go of all those years, not yet.

The breakup put an extra strain on Alban and Laura, who were left with the task of comforting her. The close bonds between the two families, who had lived side by side for fifteen years, had already been loosened. But at least they no longer had to shield Clauda from the truth.

Clauda remained at the Dunrobin house, caring for the two boys and living a somewhat lonely and isolated life. But Bob did not disappear from her life. He returned often to visit Jacques, who was thirteen years old in 1966, and Danny, who was seven. Rachelle, now nineteen, was studying in Switzerland.

Not long after the separation, the federal government expropriated Ilse's farm for the new Mirabel airport. She and Bob then moved to a house in Westmount, the headquarters of the English elite in Montreal. Since Campeau Construction remained based in Ottawa and was still doing most of its building in that area, he also maintained a suite at a hotel in the capital.

Although it might seem strange that Bob Campeau should move to Westmount, it was actually very much in character. Ever since his boyhood during the Great Depression, he had had a contradictory attitude toward the Establishment: he resented it and he wanted to be part of it. And no Anglo enclave was more symbolic of wealth and privilege in the Canada of the 1960s than the headquarters of the "white Rhodesians" of Westmount. As he later said, "With their attitudes of exclusiveness, they provoked the radical behavior we now see in the Parti Québécois."

Bob's decision to leave Clauda for his second family left a bitter taste in the mouths of his senior executives. In fact, it appeared to newer employees that the inner circle, largely Catholic, was drawing away from Bob. "Not that they didn't like him, but he was doing things that people didn't understand," recalls Andrew Perrier, a vice-president of leasing and development of properties in the late sixties. "Nobody really talked about it, but they all sort of scorned and they'd say, 'Oh shit, what's he doing?'"

After Bob's friend Joe O'Brien joined the company as a vice-president in 1969, he observed an increasing division between the old guard and the new. "There were two groups at Campeau Corp.," he says. "There were the officers of the company who had been with him for a number of years, who were all very much good friends with — and their wives were good friends with — Clauda. See, that meant they were sort of on Clauda's side. And I came along, and I was really the first one of the group of officers, when I joined him, who was on Ilse's side. And that ended up causing a bit of friction."

The separation was amicable. Clauda was never critical of Bob and, by coincidence, they often attended the same social functions. In 1967, they set aside their differences to throw a big wedding when Rachelle married Leonard Graham, an engineer from North Carolina whom she had met on a flight to Switzerland. Rachelle, who was just twenty and nine years younger than the groom, had grown into a beautiful young woman, a youthful version of her mother. Dark, slim and elegant, when she smiled in a certain way she bore more than a passing resemblance to Audrey Hepburn.

Father Ovila officiated at the marriage. The ceremony was followed by a lavish reception for hundreds of guests at Campeau's new Skyline Hotel in Ottawa. Sparing no expense, the president of Campeau Construction presided over the event, reveling in the role of smiling father of the bride. It was a formal affair, with the men in morning coats and the bride in a simple, elegant gown with ruffles at the neck and on the sleeves, and a veil of clouds of appliquéd tulle. There was a four-layer wedding cake. The after-dinner speeches included a toast to the bride by the federal public works minister George McIlraith, who had become a friend of the family. Bob brought in a group of violinists from Montreal to serenade the guests. For the wedding photographs, Bob and Clauda appeared together with Len Graham's parents. For this one night, it was as though Ilse had never existed.

Within a few months of the wedding, Bob and Clauda would

celebrate together their own twenty-fifth wedding anniversary, despite having been separated for two years. This strange event indicates just how torn Bob was. He continued to see Clauda often and, according to Clauda, even discussed the possibility of resuming a full married life.

For the most part, however, Clauda lived what friends and relatives say was an increasingly lonely life through the closing years of the 1960s. For a long time, she was unable to accept what had happened and remained reluctant to grant her husband a divorce. But by 1969, she had accepted that the breakup was irrevocable. She began divorce proceedings on August 29 of that year.

In her petition, Clauda wrote that "there has been a permanent breakdown of my marriage to the respondent by reason of the following circumstances: I have not deserted the respondent, and from on or about the beginning of the month of February 1966, I have lived and continue to live separate and apart from the respondent . . . The respondent spouse has been keeping company with another woman since prior to our separation in February of 1966, still continues so to do, and I believe it is his intention to remarry." The document stated that neither she nor Campeau had made any attempt at reconciliation.

Three days before Clauda signed the divorce papers, she and Bob reached a separation agreement that would provide her with $5,000 a month, with provision against inflation built in. As well, Clauda kept the house in Dunrobin. She also owned some 350,000 shares in the company, which were then worth about $3.5 million.

Colleen Coghlan of the Children's Aid Society, who interviewed Bob, Clauda, Jacques and Danny for the court, wrote of Bob Campeau: "Respondent cares very much about their two boys and wants to continue seeing them on a regular basis. He feels that he has a good relationship with the boys . . . Respondent states that petitioner (wife) is a good mother to the boys and feels that it is in their best interests that they remain with petitioner. He will be visiting them regularly and he wants to have them with him periodically."

The uncontested divorce was made final in the Supreme Court of Ontario on May 12, 1970, but some members of Bob's family never really accepted it. Bob's mother, Lucie, then in her seventies, asked herself what she had done wrong that could have influenced her son to leave his wife. "I blame Bob more than Ilse because he's older," she told one of her other children.

Some of Bob's brothers and sisters continued to consider Clauda their sister-in-law. And Clauda herself never really recovered. For a woman of her era and upbringing, divorce was something other people did. Recalls a friend: "She still loved Bob the day she died."

8 / Place de Ville

*"Construction is underway and we are not
stopping for anything."*
— Robert Campeau

WITH CHARLOTTE WHITTON apparently gone for good, 1965
promised to be a very good year for Campeau Construction.
With more than 6,000 houses under his belt, and new
subdivisions and apartment towers at various stages of
development and construction, Bob Campeau was firmly
entrenched as Ottawa's leading builder. His company now
boasted assets of about $20 million and annual sales and rental
income in the area of $12 million. Hundreds of homes were
under construction, but except for a few projects such as the
Britannia filtration plant and the Arts Building at Carleton
University, Campeau had so far built primarily only houses and
apartments. Now, for the first time, he was ready to claim
downtown Ottawa's skyline as his own, imposing his vision on
the very precincts of the Parliament Buildings. The name of
this vision would be Place de Ville.

Campeau was always looking for ways to make his mark, to
expand his horizons. Only recently, for example, he had jumped
into the dishwasher business.

The story began when he met F.W. Blanchard, a
seventy-seven-year-old Montreal inventor. Blanchard's brain-
child was a little water-propelled dishwasher that he was
manufacturing himself and trying to sell. It was the sort of
thing that might have intrigued Joseph Campeau, and it

certainly intrigued his son. Bob bought the patent and set out to conquer the kitchens of the world.

The Blanchard dishwasher needed no electricity. It operated on a system similar to a windmill, but using water instead of air. It involved a pivot and a tube that was punctured with holes at various angles and ran across the bottom of the machine. Water rushed into the tube, hitting the dirty dishes in a basket on the pivot and spinning the basket madly. A Blanchard — a three-foot tub constructed first of aluminum and later of fiberglass — could clean up after a family of four in a cycle that lasted all of four minutes. It cost about $18 to manufacture and sold for some $60.

Campeau Construction began arranging for patents in at least thirty-seven countries, but world-wide distribution apparently never materialized. However, the dishwashers did become popular in Canada, and a fair number were also sold in the United States. Canadian sales were considerably assisted by Campeau's captive market of new homeowners. "Every Campeau house had a dishwasher," says a former senior executive. "We got to the point where we probably sold 20,000 a year, mainly in Canada." Campeau continued to make and sell these dishwashers for many years.

But until Place de Ville, Bob Campeau remained primarily a residential builder. And although he was unquestionably one of the most successful businessmen in Ottawa, with wealth beyond what he had likely thought possible when he used to dream of opening a machine shop in Sudbury, he was still trying to impress — underneath his increasingly expensive suits, he was still the boy from Chelmsford.

Few knew this better than Andy Perrier, who at thirty-one years old had been put in charge of developing Campeau Construction's income properties. Perrier recalls an incident in 1962, just before the gala opening of Campeau's Champlain Towers on Rideau Terrace. The fourteen-storey, 243-unit apartment building was on the edge of the exclusive Rockcliffe Park district, and would be the most luxurious in Ottawa, attracting as residents many politicians, diplomats, judges and other leading figures. A German businessman, an acquaintance of Campeau's, was flying to Canada to attend the opening, and Campeau planned to meet him at Montreal's Dorval airport.

"How about coming to Montreal?" Campeau asked Perrier. "I'll drive on the way down and you drive back."

They headed out in Campeau's Lincoln. Campeau ate an ice cream cone and chatted amiably while he drove. When they arrived at Dorval, Perrier waited in the car as Campeau went inside to meet his friend. Some time later, Campeau emerged from the terminal building carrying his guest's luggage and signaled to Perrier to get out of the car.

"Here's the luggage," he said, handing the bags to Perrier and jumping into the back seat of the Lincoln with his German guest.

Campeau's manner had changed: Perrier's boss was far more serious, not joking around with *him* anymore. In fact, neither of the men talked to him at all. It became obvious that Campeau was trying to pretend Perrier was his chauffeur. The hell with this, Perrier thought, and joined in the conversation.

This was typical: one minute Bob was your best friend, the next you could be invisible.

It was this streak of ego and insensitivity that characterized Campeau's conquest of the heart of the capital. Even the name he chose for his development — Place de Ville — was assuming a lot. In France, the *place de ville* is the square in front of the city hall. It implies the focal point of a city. In fact, Ottawa's city hall was miles away.

The story of Place de Ville begins in April 1965, when the city offered for sale 65,000 square feet of land on a downtown city block. The block of land, bounded by Queen, Lyon, Albert and Kent streets, was in a rundown area just west of the downtown business district. It used to house the streetcar barns of the Ottawa Transportation Commission, but these had been abandoned when buses were introduced. The empty buildings were a century old and some were falling to pieces.

Campeau decided to bid, seeing in this property what others apparently did not: the chance to snap up a large parcel of what could be prime real estate and create his own downtown.

Development of the site, however, would be governed by an omnibus 1964 zoning bylaw that limited the height of any new buildings a buyer wanted to erect. But nothing had stopped him in the past, and Campeau saw no reason for a city bylaw to prevent him from reshaping the center core of Ottawa.

At this early stage, however, he held his cards close to the vest, promising only that there would be a major development on the site. In *Contemporary Cathedrals: Large Scale Developments in Canadian Cities*, author Robert Collier wrote that the municipality valued the property at $1 million, but that authorities, behind closed doors, agreed to settle for less: "Privately, the minimum acceptable bid was put at $850,000. They received only one bid before the deadline — an offer of $851,000 from Robert Campeau." The municipality set about studying the developer's offer.

In May, however, the city announced that Campeau's bid was too low, and so was not acceptable. A few aldermen also argued that the first bid had not met parking requirements for the district, but Campeau responded by saying he had agreed earlier, in a separate deal with the city's parking authority, to guarantee 300 public parking spots. There was nothing the embarrassed city officials could do. Bob Campeau had executed a perfect end run.

Though he had won on parking, there remained the question of price. Bob was adamant that he had bid fairly and that his price should stand. He complained in the media that municipal officials were conspiring to defeat him. From the tone of his public utterances, one would have thought Charlotte Whitton was back as mayor. He argued that he would improve the area, promising a development worth at least $10 million that would bring Ottawa some $200,000 annually in taxes. Then he set his own deadline — June 15 — and resubmitted his bid.

A group of local businessmen then entered the fray, offering $900,000 for the property. Even though Campeau's bid had originally been deemed too low and rejected, and this offer was higher, the city now did an about-face. It disqualified the new bidders because they had missed the original deadline. Since Campeau had met this date, they would sell it to him at his price. But, in what seems to have been a face-saving measure, the city demanded that he come through with his promised $10 million development, including those 300 parking spaces. He agreed.

With the land finally his, Campeau unveiled his plans for what he now began to call Place de Ville. Its two towers, just three blocks south of Parliament Hill, would give Ottawa a new focus, pulling it into the twentieth century with a sense of big-city downtown. The plans called for a twenty-two-storey, 300,000-square-foot office building and a twenty-six-storey hotel with 454 rooms, a development exceeding the density limits and the height restrictions of the existing bylaw. In particular, he wanted to build to 250 feet — 100 feet more than was allowed. One Ottawa alderman said that if the proposed rezoning went through, it would raise the property value of the Place de Ville site by $250,000.

The trouble was, Ottawa already had a focus: the Parliament Buildings. And the bylaw Campeau wanted to break was designed to protect their pre-eminent place in the nation's capital. These elegant buildings — with their distinctive copper roofs, turned green by time, dominated by the tall, slender Peace Tower — were steeped in history and drew thousands of tourists every year. Place de Ville would threaten the Peace Tower's dominance of the Ottawa skyline.

Ottawa had gone through years of study and debate to arrive at the official plan of which the 150-foot bylaw was a part and to develop policies that would protect Parliament Hill. In 1949, leading French planner Jacques Gréber developed a plan to improve the municipality, which included the city's much admired Green Belt, but kept the downtown height restriction where it had been since 1914 — 110 feet. In 1954, an official zoning plan was proposed. What followed was more than six years of study and two years of public hearings. Then, in 1963, two expert urban planners hired by the city recommended that the height limitation on downtown buildings be raised to 150 feet. Ottawa's rationale in adopting the 150-foot recommendation was that the Ottawa River preserved Parliament Hill on one side, so the city should protect it on the other. The recommendation became part of the official city plan finally approved in 1964, over which Bob Campeau and Charlotte Whitton fought openly. This plan guaranteed the Peace Tower, in the Centre Block of the Parliament Buildings, would remain the focal point of the city.

Under the official plan of 1964, then, no building was permitted to exceed 150 feet in a downtown area about one and a half miles wide and half a mile deep directly in front of Parliament Hill. Outside those limits, areas were governed only by a floor space index and a general principle that buildings should not exceed the height of the Peace Tower — 304 feet. Place de Ville was inside the restricted zone.

But what was an official plan compared to Bob Campeau's vision of the future? "Think of what it will do to the downtown area," he enthused. "It will make it live again." No matter that the height of his two new towers would almost equal that of the Peace Tower. Besides, he pointed out, he would not be the first to break the height restriction — the federal government, which was exempt from the bylaw, had done so twice, although not next door to Parliament Hill. He waged his campaign through the media and by lobbying elected officials.

The city gave Campeau an easy ride. The planning board, in a ninety-minute closed-door session in November 1965, agreed to his request to build to 250 feet — which would allow him to reach a height just above the center of the Peace Tower clock — and approved his density request. A few weeks later, city council duly passed the planning board recommendation.

Private citizen Charlotte Whitton had been watching these events from the sidelines, but she had not been idle. As soon as she found out what Campeau was up to, she urged the Ontario Municipal Board (OMB) to hold public hearings if the city approved the Place de Ville bylaw amendments. Then as now, all major zoning changes passed by Ontario city councils had to be approved by the OMB. But by the time Whitton learned that the initial bylaw amendments had gone to the provincial body, she was too late to meet the deadline for filing an objection. As a result, the first bylaw amendments were approved and, although it may seem astonishing now, without public protest.

It might have ended there if Campeau had not acquired another property and proposed a second twenty-two-storey office tower as part of the Place de Ville development. This required another amendment to the zoning bylaw and another approval by the OMB. And this time Charlotte Whitton did not miss the deadline for objections. Although she was the sole objector, her stature was such that the board decided on public hearings in April 1966.

But fate intervened. At the date on which she was to appear to make her case — she wanted to call qualified planning consultants to testify on the technical aspects of the project — she was in hospital and unable to attend. From her bed, she sent a telegram asking that the hearings be postponed "because of vital import on entire future concept of Ottawa as the capital of the granting or withholding of OMB approval on these items at this time." But the board was not prepared to wait, and again Campeau had his way. Whitton's frustration must have been colossal.

Bob Campeau got what he wanted with only the slimmest of opposition. The city councilors seem to have been more concerned about the money Place de Ville would bring in than about the overall planning of a nation's capital. Perhaps they believed that the development of the city had been dangerously stunted by what was unquestionably a restrictive bylaw. Although Charlotte Whitton may have been motivated in part by her dislike of Campeau, she seems to have been the only one who considered the larger implications of his vision.

Place de Ville eventually became the largest privately owned commercial development in the city, occupying an entire city block. The two office towers had a total of 550,000 square feet of commercial space (the federal government leased about 93 percent). The new Skyline Hotel had convention facilities for 3,000 people. The three buildings were linked by an underground shopping concourse. A five-level parking garage could accommodate 1,050 cars.

To help finance construction, Campeau sold the land he had bought for the development and leased it back for ninety-nine years. This way he had cash up front and was soon able to pay the lease out of income generated from renting the offices, stores and the hotel, which he continued to own. Skyline Hotels alone paid him $862,000 annually — four times what he was paying to lease back the Place de Ville site.

As Bob Campeau's schemes became more grandiose, his behavior at Campeau Construction became, if anything, even more high-handed. Perhaps it was partly the strain of his personal life — he was still shuttling between two families at this point — but Alban and Jean Paradis found themselves increasingly smoothing feathers that Bob had ruffled. Bob wanted a company run entirely his way. When he demanded something be done, there were to be no arguments. Even with Lionel long gone, Bob's shouts often echoed through the head office on Baseline Road.

Andrew Perrier recalls once, about a week before Christmas, bringing to Campeau's attention a particularly good photograph of one of their buildings in Ottawa.

"Bob, isn't this a nice shot?" Perrier said. "This would make a perfect Christmas card some day."

Campeau looked at the photograph and agreed.

"I want 5,000 Christmas cards done immediately, and send them out," he told Perrier.

"Christ, Bob, Christmas is only in a few days. There's no way I can get them printed, addressed and mailed," Perrier replied.

"Just do what I say," was Campeau's final word.

Perrier left Campeau's office, wondering what to do, and went next door to talk to Jean Paradis, Campeau's lieutenant. You could usually count on the gentlemanly vice-president for a sympathetic ear.

"This doesn't make any goddamn sense," Perrier muttered.

"Just let it ride a little and he'll forget about it," the older man advised him.

It would not have been the first time Paradis's patience outlasted one of Campeau's whims. But neither Paradis nor Perrier realized that the doors to the washroom linking the offices were open, allowing Campeau to hear their exchange. He shot up from his desk and bounded across the room.

"When I ask my top executives to do something, I want it done," he railed.

Timing prevailed, however, and the Christmas cards were never printed.

Campeau was often cavalier in his treatment of underlings and even of some executives. He would often drive his Lincoln to the office and leave the car at the door, sometimes in traffic, for someone else to park. If he was busy or if something was on his mind, he would ask an employee, be it Jean Paradis or another senior executive, to get him a sandwich or an ice cream cone.

One morning, he approached Perrier and asked him to get the Lincoln washed. Perrier turned the car over to the building superintendent, who returned a short while later to tell him that Campeau's car had a flat tire that would have to be repaired.

Returning shortly thereafter, Bob asked Perrier, "Where are my keys?"

"Well, Bob . . ." Perrier had given the keys to the superintendent, but was cut short before he could tell his boss about the flat.

"Never mind. Give me the goddamn keys. Oh, never mind."

And Campeau was off downstairs to the garage to find his car, despite Perrier's efforts to stop him. A few minutes later, having found out the truth for himself, he strode back. He needed a car right away, apparently to get to city hall.

"Give me your keys," he snapped. Perrier handed over the keys to his new Chevrolet. "I'll bring it right back."

Perrier had planned to go home for lunch. When Campeau did not turn up he thought, the hell with it, and took his boss's Lincoln. At the end of the day, he waited in vain for Campeau to show up. Finally he took the Lincoln home for the night.

Campeau returned the next day. He had been to Montreal,

where he had run Perrier's new Chev through a construction site; a piece of wood was still protruding from the punctured muffler. But Perrier wisely said nothing, going instead to see the company's chief financial officer, Clem Cadieux, who arranged to have it repaired.

Campeau's increasingly overbearing style was never more obvious than during the fight over Phase II of Place de Ville, which turned out to be much more of a battle than the initial development. The first phase had broken through a psychological and legal barrier. He had succeeded in amending Ottawa's official plan to suit his vision. Now he was growing bolder. In 1968, the year Phase I of the complex was completed, Campeau announced he now wanted to build a second phase on the entire block to the north, just 1,800 feet to the west of the Peace Tower. The plans included a 450-foot tower — thirty-nine storeys that would soar almost 150 feet above the Peace Tower, at three times the existing ceiling. He also wanted to *buy* the part of Queen Street that ran between the two developments and turn it into a pedestrian mall.

Buying a street was out of the question, even for Bob Campeau, but the city was prepared to talk about waiving the height restrictions yet again. After all, the greater the density of a commercial development, the greater the rental income. Some council members, however, were uneasy. Among them was Charlotte Whitton, who had been re-elected as an alderman in 1966. Why had he not disclosed the plans for Phase II from the start? Was he using the success of Phase I to bulldoze them into a favorable decision? The city's technical advisory committee and planning board recommended a maximum height of 325 feet. But Campeau was a powerful man, and ultimately the Board of Control agreed to the 450 feet he wanted, and city council approved it.

Enter the National Capital Commission (NCC), the federal agency that had been created to help develop, beautify and conserve the National Capital Region. The NCC is a unique agency: its jurisdiction extends no farther than the lands owned by the federal government, and so it has only limited power to protect its interests and pursue its mandate. The federal government owned about one-third of all the land in the

city and was the major tenant of privately owned buildings.
Yet when it came to city policy, even a policy that affected the
Parliament Buildings, the NCC could attempt to persuade, but
could not demand. It has no jurisdiction in zoning and can
control land development only by using its power of
expropriation. Furthermore, many city politicians resented
every attempt by the NCC to influence the course of Ottawa's
development. Did Ottawa control redevelopment of the city, or
did the federal government? they asked.

Although the NCC had kept quiet about Campeau's Phase I,
it could not ignore Phase II. It did not formally object, but
made its feelings known, appearing at another set of Ontario
Municipal Board hearings to advise the provincial body in
September 1968. Three citizens appeared to oppose the zoning
amendment, one of whom was Whitton. The others were R.A.J.
Phillips, who represented a group called Capital for Canadians,
and J. Zarzycki, a private citizen. They argued that the
rezoning not only set a bad precedent but amounted to urban
planning on a piecemeal basis.

The NCC warned that Campeau's new development would
obstruct the view of Parliament Hill. The city replied that it
wanted the additional tax revenues that would come with the
project. Campeau himself testified that he wanted to build a
comprehensive urban downtown scheme and that highrise
buildings were the trend of the twentieth century, supremely
acceptable to lenders and tenants.

This time, however, the OMB was not so easily convinced.
The city and the NCC had agreed to fund a study on just what
height restrictions should govern downtown Ottawa. So the
OMB decided to wait to hear the consultants' report and
refused to grant the bylaw exemption. In its decision, the OMB
said: "Although some side benefits would accrue to the public
sector, this particular development proposal is for the greater
economic advantage of the developer."

Campeau and the city officials were outraged by what they
saw as an unwarranted delay. "This is a serious blow to the
city's economy," Mayor Don Reid told the media. "In my
opinion, the NCC's contention that the Place de Ville tower will

spoil the view of Parliament Hill is utterly ridiculous."

Both the city and Campeau appealed to the Ontario government to overturn its own municipal board's decision, the city claiming that the bylaw was outdated. But the provincial government refused to interfere.

Campeau went further than the mayor. He vowed to ignore the OMB ruling and begin work on Phase II immediately: "We have an excavation permit, we already have shovels in the ground and I'm confident common sense will prevail in the end. We're going ahead." He added that he had been holding special workers in readiness at a cost to him of $100,000 a month and to the city of $70,000 in lost tax revenue. He saw no point in wasting time. Wrote Collier: "Whatever the outcome, he was going to build anyway, so he might as well get on with it."

Over the fall and early winter of 1968, Campeau forged ahead with the excavation of the site. Explosions rocked Ottawa's downtown several times a day as the Campeau men blasted away the bedrock. Forty trucks came and went, carting away the debris.

In February 1969, the consultants submitted a preliminary report summarizing their recommendations. Downtown development should resemble a saucer with the Parliament Buildings at the center, they argued. The further a new building was from the center of the saucer, the higher it could be built. Under this plan, Place de Ville II could reach a height of 342 feet.

Before the consultants' report was entirely ready, Campeau offered to compromise, asking for a bylaw amendment that would allow him to build to 375 feet instead of the original 450 the city had approved. The consultants agreed to study the proposal before making a fuller report.

But when the full report appeared, their original recommendation remained in place: no building should be allowed to rise more than 342 feet. The east end of the Place de Ville block, the side nearest Parliament Hill, would be limited to 300 feet. The report clearly supported the concept of protecting not only the beauty of Parliament Hill but also its symbolism.

"When a nation concentrates the major share of its national

government investment, decision-makers and international contacts within one city, that city takes on great symbolic significance. In almost every great national capital city the focal point of this symbolic role is a unique architectural element.

"In Canada, as in other major nations, the physical dominance or pre-eminence of this architectural element over the surrounding cityscape is equated by the citizens of the nation to whom it belongs with the pre-eminence of the nation itself. While this is a wholly psychological condition, it is viewed in very specific physical terms. Thus any other structure which is built to a height to exceed the Peace Tower is seen as degrading this national image.

"The consultants view this need for physical-psychological pre-eminence to be a valid national concern and thus a valid criterion for regulation in the Ottawa Central area ... Strict adherence to the height levels shown will ensure the conservation of the vistas of Parliament, the scale of Parliament Square and the pre-eminence of the Peace Tower."

Faced with this powerful argument, the Ottawa Board of Control decided in March to reject Campeau's 375-foot compromise and adopt the consultants' formula, which was approved by the Ontario Municipal Board on May 15, 1969. Ironically, it had taken an American firm, the main consultant on the project, to remind Canadians of the true importance of their Parliament Buildings.

Campeau knew when he was beaten, admitting that he had no choice but to live with the 342-foot limit, which would allow twenty-nine storeys. "There's no point delaying the project any further," he told reporters. "I'm willing to abide by the new formula provided it is adopted as the bible for building heights." But in a thinly veiled threat, he pointed out there were no such bylaws in nearby Hull.

The project Bob Campeau was allowed to build is attractive and has held up well. It consists of a twenty-nine-storey office tower, a 504-room Holiday Inn and a four-storey building in between that houses two theaters and some office space. The city allowed him to cut back on the number of public parking spots required, according to a formula based on building density. This was not unusual in Ottawa under what was known as the "cash-in-lieu of parking bylaw," which allows a developer to pay cash to the city to reduce the necessary number of parking spaces. In this case, the cash amounted to $1.5 million.

But the battle was not yet over. The National Capital Commission soon discovered a loophole in the new bylaw that meant Campeau could put a mechanical equipment penthouse on top of the twenty-nine-storey tower and so exceed the new height restriction. At issue was a twenty-eight-foot penthouse called for in Campeau's revised plans. "The consultants have confirmed that these were absolute height limits and that no penthouses or other parts of the building should exceed them," complained NCC chairman John Frost in a letter to the Ottawa Board of Control.

Campeau responded in typical form: "The bylaw has been approved, construction is underway and we are not stopping for anything." The city's solicitor, Don Hambling, added that the municipality had never planned to meet all the height limit recommendations, and that "what the NCC is really complaining about is a pimple of a machinery penthouse." The bylaw would stand. And a last-ditch appeal to the OMB fell on deaf ears.

All this fuss over an additional 28 feet may appear to have been somewhat petty, but it was not so small a matter to the NCC. Bob Campeau had already succeeded in radically altering Ottawa's downtown concept. Now he had found a way to build higher than the NCC had thought possible. If Campeau could add twenty-eight feet, someone else would find a way to add thirty, and so on.

Nevertheless, Charlotte Whitton must have taken some pleasure in the result. Campeau had been reined in, and Ottawa would have a workable downtown plan that preserved some of its essential character. She remained on council until she retired in 1972, and she died in January 1975.

Place de Ville Phase II would not be completed until 1972.

Beneath the office building and hotel was another shopping mall and an 850-car garage, both linked to the underground levels of Phase I. Campeau sold the land and buildings and leased them back at a favorable rent. And the federal government, which had opposed him so vehemently through the NCC, grabbed about 97 percent of the office space.

Campeau had lost a few battles, but he had clearly won the war. Still, he could not resist taking one last shot at his opponents. In February 1970, during a "topping off" ceremony to celebrate reaching the top level of Phase II, Campeau was asked about the twenty-eight-foot "pimple" by an *Ottawa Journal* reporter. The developer smiled and responded, "You'd better say 342 feet plus penthouse. Otherwise somebody will say I'm breaking the law."

Campeau had good reason to be pleased with himself. He had shown that he could not be stopped by governments and that he could tear up an official plan that had been many years in the making. He had wiped out the 150-foot height restriction and replaced it with one of 342 feet — more than double. Since the value of land increases with the permissible height of structures built upon it, he had profited greatly before the Phase II foundation was even poured. And a bigger building meant more rental revenue.

The bylaw exemptions applied only to Place de Ville, leaving the 150-foot limit in place in the downtown core. Within a few years, however, the limit was lifted in favor of a new plan that based height restrictions on preserving the view of Parliament Hill from six vantage points in the city. In March 1973, former prime minister John Diefenbaker, referring to the number of tall buildings in the downtown core and recalling his first visit to Ottawa, said in the House of Commons: "I saw the grandeur of Parliament Hill, the majestic location. Nowhere in the world is there the equal of it. I hope I do not speak out of turn when I say that I am concerned over the fact that more and more as high buildings are going up this magnificent structure is becoming a pygmy, or if I could invent a word, is being pygmatized. Let us do something now, before it is too late."

The face of downtown Ottawa is now largely the legacy of Robert Campeau. What was until the mid-1960s a town center of lowrise buildings, many of them built in the nineteenth century, is now a modern big-city downtown. Place de Ville is the dominant landmark in the western part of the downtown area. Queen Street, which cuts through the two phases, is Bob Campeau's street, and his name is prominent everywhere in his $100-million mini-city. Ten thousand people work in the office tower of Phase II alone.

The price Ottawa has paid for this highly successful development is most obvious as you drive east on Queen Street toward the center of downtown into the gloom of shadows thrown by Campeau's tall buildings. The oblong towers of Place de Ville spring up suddenly, and when you look up, instead of the spires of Parliament Hill, you see the tops of buildings. It is not until you turn the corner at Kent that you can see the familiar green-topped roofs. Place de Ville has blocked the view of the Parliament Buildings for a broad swath of downtown Ottawa.

As Robert Collier wrote, "To construct an isolated high-density commercial complex out of line with other developments and call it 'Place de Ville' reflects a kind of arrogance that flies in the face of proper control of a city in the public interest. Surely the basic lesson to be learned from this instance is that present municipal power may not be adequate, or may not be adequately exercised, when large-scale private development is introduced."

9 / The Reins of Power

"We sold our destiny and we got it back."
— Robert Campeau

IN APRIL 1969, as the final act of the Place de Ville melodrama was drawing to a close, Campeau took his company public. He needed money to fund the purchase of a large piece of land on Toronto's barren waterfront, where he wanted to build a luxury hotel as his first foray into that city's highly competitive market. He also needed money to service his considerable debt.

The company Campeau took public was a far cry from the cosy family partnership of the early 1950s. It included Campeau Construction, Allied Building Supply and Queensview Construction and Developments, now amalgamated under the banner of Campeau Corp. Ltd. It held more than $70 million in assets and was building about 500 homes a year. Total annual sales and rental income were netting more than $25 million and long-term debt was more than $41 million. Going public would reduce that debt level.

The twenty-one-acre Baseline Road complex now included a 20,000-square-foot office, an 87,000-square-foot components plant and a 50,000-square-foot warehouse. One Campeau division developed the raw land for commercial and residential use; another unit of forty-six people, including sixteen architects and engineers, designed and engineered the highrises and commercial complexes. The company maintained its own sales staff of six people and operated a home-improvement business for repairs and renovations. Allied Building Supply provided material to the construction operation. The components end of the business was diverse, producing ready-mix cement, trusses, insulated window units, stairs, cupboards, flooring and other items. It also sold across Canada and in Europe a patented truss plate for roof trusses. In short, Campeau Corp. was an elaborate, self-sustaining system, developing its land, designing its own projects, feeding its construction operation with supplies and components, and selling the finished houses.

There was no question that Campeau was the construction king of Ottawa. He was now building in the east and the south, to the far northeast in Gloucester Township and along the Rideau River, filing subdivision plans on hundreds of acres at an amazing pace. Place de Ville had already transformed the city's downtown. Since 1949, Campeau had built more than 10,000 housing and apartment units, about 2,000 of which were kept as income-producing properties, and a million square feet of commercial property. And it owned more than 3,000 acres of land for development.

The face of the capital had been altered irrevocably by this one man. Had someone thought to shade in on a map of Ottawa the Campeau projects either built or under construction in 1969, these would have formed a sweeping crescent enclosing the city and stopped only by the Ottawa River. This broad band was broken in spots, but it showed that over the last two decades Bob Campeau had left his mark on huge blocks of land, much of it formerly farmland. The city of Ottawa's expansion to the east, west and south since 1950 was largely Campeau's work. And scattered elsewhere on such a map would have been dots or lines marking Campeau apartment and office buildings and smaller housing projects. There would have been a big dot by the Deschênes Rapids where the Britannia filtration plant now stood, and two shaded squares near Parliament Hill to mark the site of Place de Ville. Ottawa was Bob Campeau's city.

Now he was looking for new fields to conquer.

In March of 1969, 1.6 million shares of Campeau Corp. were

offered to the public at a price of $10 a share. The offer was comprised of 1.2 million newly issued shares and 400,000 shares already held by Bob, Alban, senior executives and their spouses. This meant that the major shareholders before the company went public were diluting their ownership in two ways: each now owned fewer shares, and the shares they still owned were now part of a bigger total. There were slightly more than 5.1 million shares before going public and roughly 6.4 million shares after the public offer. In return, they were personally getting cash and collectively getting a company that had more money to work with — and presumably would be worth more to all of them in the long run. After subtracting the various costs of going public — primarily the costs of underwriting the share issue — Campeau Corp. had raised slightly more than $11 million. This was used to reduce bank loans associated with the waterfront land acquisition in Toronto.

After the share issue, Campeau's control dropped from about 31 percent of the company to 22.2 percent, but he remained by far the largest shareholder. Alban, the next largest shareholder, saw his stake fall from 12.5 percent to 9.5 percent. But 22 percent of the stock was controlled by Pat Kelly, a lawyer who joined the company in January 1967 as general counsel and executive vice-president. Although Kelly owned less than 1 percent himself, he was the trustee of the trust funds set up for Bob's and Alban's children, which accounted for 21.5 percent. The other major shareholders were Clauda, Alban's wife, Laura, and several of the original Twelve, primarily Jean Paradis. So despite the company's having gone public, an absolute majority of shares remained in the hands of very few, all of whom were answerable to Bob Campeau.

As a result of the public offer, Campeau Corp. was listed on the Toronto and Montreal stock exchanges. This was a major step for Campeau: he would no longer be able to operate in private, accountable only to a chosen few. Public companies are required by securities regulators to disclose much of their business dealings and are answerable to their shareholders. Although the public float of Campeau Corp. was modest, Campeau still had to answer in some respect to people other than the senior executives with whom he had been so close and over whom he had so much influence. Nevertheless, he still had the last word.

Given Bob Campeau's fiercely independent nature, it may seem odd that he would now be willing to allow his company to be swallowed by Paul Desmarais's Power Corp., but that is exactly what happened. Certainly Campeau Corp. was an attractive prospect, one of the largest fully integrated development concerns in the nation.

"Power Corp. came along and he was sold on the idea that if he made the deal with them he would no longer have any trouble getting mortgage financing," recalls Joe O'Brien, then a Campeau Corp. vice-president involved in mortgage financing. "That was part of the sales pitch — that if the two got together, Bob as the builder and the other guys as the financiers, so to speak, his money would be found for him. The rationale was that we would no longer have any trouble getting money for projects because at that time, I remember, interest rates had started going up on mortgage loans — apartment buildings were going to 10 percent, 11 percent, which was very high in those days — and making it almost economically unfeasible to build apartment buildings because of the rents you could achieve. We're talking mainly the Ottawa market at this time, and the whole idea was that Power Corp. would be able to be the facilitator for mortgage funding."

In other words, Campeau saw Desmarais as a source of cash. But the other big bait Desmarais had to offer was Canadian Interurban Properties, a jewel of a real estate company with almost $110 million in assets, including interests in twenty-two shopping centers and twenty commercial or residential buildings in twenty-six cities.

It would have been fascinating to watch Robert Campeau and Paul Desmarais as they hammered out their deal. Despite the superficial similarities in their backgrounds — both were self-made French Canadians from Sudbury — the differences between their styles and personalities were vast. Campeau was flamboyant and loud and loved nothing better than publicity. Desmarais was withdrawn and quiet and had always shunned the press. Campeau had started from a poor family and with little schooling; Desmarais was the son of a reasonably prosperous lawyer and had graduated from the University of Ottawa. "We grew up in the same city and it seemed that we could have an awful lot in common, so we made the marriage," Campeau said later. Even after the marriage went sour, they remained friends.

Although Desmarais had started a couple of years after Campeau, by 1969 he had become far more successful. He had started with a small, faltering bus company inherited from his parents in 1951 and had built a holding company with fingers in every pie. Power Corp. had interests in Imperial Life and Montreal Trust and other financial groups, as well as a real estate company, two oil and gas concerns, three manufacturing groups, Canada Steamship Lines and Consolidated-Bathurst, the mammoth pulp and paper firm. By the time Desmarais approached Campeau, Power's corporate web was massive, with assets of $270 million.

Campeau and Desmarais negotiated for months. When the deal was finally struck it amounted to what is known as a reverse takeover — Campeau took control of Canadian Interurban, and Power took majority control of Campeau Corp. Thus Campeau would acquire Power Corp.'s rich real estate assets and at the same time link up, in effect, with a big friendly bank — or so Bob Campeau believed.

Campeau obviously envisioned great things for his partnership with Power Corp. Says a former board member: "Bob knew Desmarais and they'd seen each other a number of times, and I think Bob at that time felt that if he could team up with Paul Desmarais, that between them they could really do a lot." Perhaps another factor in Campeau's decision was the prospect of taking over his old rival, Bill Teron, whose company, Teron Construction, had merged with Canadian Interurban in 1967.

But when Teron got wind of the Campeau deal, he decided it was time to move on. He had already learned that a link-up with Power was not the answer to a builder's dreams; Desmarais kept his purse strings tightly tied. By the time the

Campeau deal was in the works, Teron had begun to fight regularly with the Power executives, who usually did not want to back his projects. Teron believes that Desmarais expected Campeau to bring him into line.

"Desmarais had Canadian Interurban, he had Bill Teron, now he was going to buy Bob Campeau and Bob would reconcile the whole thing, he *thought*," says Teron. "I had indicated to Desmarais that Bob and I were two great guys, but we needed different cages. I mean, we were two tigers and needed separate cages because Bob had his way — and he was very successful at it — and he wasn't going to kowtow to me. I was very successful and I certainly wasn't going to bend to him. I left because they were going to do the Campeau deal."

The Campeau-Power deal was signed November 20, 1969, and completed the day after New Year's 1970, a little more than twenty years after Bob and Tony had built their first house on Guy Street. It was a complex agreement, a series of share exchanges that gave Paul Desmarais absolute control over Campeau Corp. at a cost of $37.6 million. After all the moves were executed, Power held 52.2 percent voting control of Campeau Corp., and Bob's personal voting power had fallen to just 7.4 percent.

Campeau also made a separate arrangement with Desmarais. He signed a management contract to serve as president and chief executive of Campeau Corp. for fifteen years. Desmarais, in turn, promised to sell only a limited amount of Campeau Corp. stock as long as the combined holdings of Bob, Clauda and the children's trust fund did not go below a minimum 2 million shares, or about 14.3 percent voting interest in the company. This personal deal was meant to protect both sides: Desmarais was not allowed to sell his control of the company; Campeau would be tied to a management contract to protect Power Corp.'s interest. Campeau promised that, if he decided to back out of the contract early and start up another company, he would not compete with Campeau Corp. in either Ontario or Quebec for a five-year period. (See appendix.)

"The deal was one that was typical of a Desmarais deal," says a former Campeau board member. "He did a reverse takeover. He took over Campeau and gave us some of his old assets to take it over, and in the end he still controlled Campeau, and I don't think Bob fully appreciated what that would mean. And Bob felt that he would probably get named to the Power board. That never happened."

What did happen was that Campeau Corp.'s assets and revenues more than doubled overnight. In 1969 the company was worth $111.2 million and had revenues of $36 million. In 1970, the assets were $272.2 million and the revenues $74.3 million. Most prominent among the new assets was a portfolio of highly profitable shopping centers from Quebec to British Columbia, including Eringate Mall and Golden Mile in Toronto, Wellington Square in London, Ontario, Place du Progrès in Gatineau and Place du Saguenay in Chicoutimi. Also in the package — and this must have been sweet indeed for a boy from Chelmsford — was the New Sudbury Shopping Centre. At one stroke, Campeau Corp. became strong in an area where it had been conspicuously weak.

In addition, Campeau acquired 700 acres of land on upper Mont St-Bruno near Montreal; 3,200 acres in Kanata, the satellite community near Ottawa that had been launched by Teron, and 68.8 percent of Blue Bonnets Raceway, with assets of more than $27 million, including two racetracks on the Island of Montreal on 146-acre and 214-acre parcels. Together, these acquisitions represented a windfall of prime development properties.

But it was not long before Campeau realized the negative ramifications of what he had done. He was no longer in control of his company and there was no easy access to the Desmarais millions to finance his dreams. In fact, according to Jean Paradis, who remained Campeau's right-hand man, Campeau Corp. was virtually cut off from Power Corp. funds. An independent company might have had better luck in seeking money from Power.

Campeau himself was to write in his 1972 annual report: "Although our relationship with Power Corp. has been pleasant and beneficial, the financing benefits ... have not materialized because the indirect relationship which has been created between ourselves and the financial institutions, which are also subsidiaries of Power Corp., make it inadvisable if not impossible for us to enter into financial arrangements with them."

And though Campeau had been given control over the real estate operations, he was still at the whim of Power's board of directors. True, he had been tied to a board of directors before the Power deal, but that board had been primarily made up of his close friends, over whom he had had great influence. Until the Power deal, he and his family had retained effective control. Furthermore, though Campeau got along well personally with Desmarais, he did not take well to Jean Parisien, the Desmarais lieutenant who now sat on Campeau Corp.'s board.

It is at this point in his story that the combination of personal and business pressures became too much for Bob Campeau. In the spring of 1970, Campeau's divorce from Clauda became final, but this does not seem to have made his life easier. Many of his friends were pushing for a reconciliation with Clauda, and although he was legally divorced, he was still married to Clauda in the eyes of his Church. Now, for the first time in his adult life, he did not control his business destiny. The company he had built from nothing was slipping from his grasp.

His friends saw the nervous breakdown approaching long before it happened.

Just a few months after giving up control of Campeau Corp., Bob gradually began to withdraw from corporate life, spending more and more time around the house in Westmount. In his absence, the company was run by a small group: Paradis, senior vice-president and secretary, chief financial officer Clem Cadieux, Marcel Lalande, the vice-president of housing, and Pat Kelly, the general counsel. Only Kelly was not a member of the original Twelve, and only Kelly seemed to like the idea of the link to Power Corp. The others, despite their differences with Campeau over his divorce from Clauda, were still devoted to him. But without his daily presence, they were becoming concerned about their future.

Bob still kept in touch by phone, but as the weeks became months he sank ever deeper into depression. "No question about the fact that it was a total breakdown," recalls a close associate of that time. "Bob aged ten years in one year. He looked like an old man. He looked like a ghost. The big thing at the time was whether he'd ever come back." Says O'Brien: "He just could no longer go on, and I'm sure Ilse was pressing too. She had a family and she wasn't married, and he loved her very much. And that pressure was what brought it all to a head. He just had to get away from it."

Those who saw him during this period found a starkly different man from the dynamic entrepreneur who had changed the face of Ottawa. "I'm dramatizing only a bit when I say he came close to being a vegetable," Jean Paradis said several years later.

Finally, Bob called his older brother Father Ovila for help, and the priest flew to Montreal. The two took long walks together and spoke of many things: the old days, the course their lives had taken, Bob's marital problems and Clauda. The priest was struck by his brother's anguish.

About a week after his arrival, Father Ovila persuaded Bob to come to Ottawa to see their mother, Lucie, who now lived in an apartment at Champlain Towers. When they got there, Lucie phoned Clauda. When she came to the apartment, Father Ovila, who was hoping for a reconciliation, asked her to take Bob back to Dunrobin. "He loved Clauda," Father Ovila says. "He loved her."

Clauda agreed, but, according to friends, she did so reluctantly.

Almost immediately after his return to Ottawa, in the summer of 1970, Robert Campeau moved in with Clauda, Jacques and Danny. One can imagine his conflicting emotions. He would be looked after; his mother, brothers and sisters, who still considered Clauda his wife, would be overjoyed at the prospect of a reconciliation. But he had left a woman he loved and their two small children. Ilse must have been devastated. For all practical purposes, Bob had returned to his first wife, although Clauda still had reservations. As Bob's absence lengthened, Ilse must have grown increasingly anxious.

Before Father Ovila left Ottawa, he suggested to his brother that he work once more with his hands, perhaps build a small garage at Dunrobin. "It will ease your troubles," said the priest. Bob took his brother's advice and, with the help of his chauffeur, began to build a four-car garage on the Dunrobin property.

One day that summer, Bidou Bisaillon dropped in at Dunrobin for a visit. Bob's sidekick from the days when he first met Clauda in Cornwall had kept in touch, but Bob and Clauda had seen him only occasionally over the years. Since the divorce, however, Bidou had visited Clauda several times. Bidou had heard that Bob was back, so he was not surprised to find Clauda's recently divorced husband hammering away on the new garage.

The two old friends greeted each other warmly. Bidou was shocked to see his old friend looking poorly and lacking his usual fire and self-confidence. Then Bob, staring at the ground, admitted to Bidou that he was ill.

"But I'm going to get better," he said.

After they had talked for a while, Bidou headed for the house to see Clauda. She was not the same Clauda he used to know, so lively and full of humor. Now she was nervous and strained.

"Bob is sick," Bidou said.

"Yes," said Clauda, "and he wants me to take care of him."

"Look, Clauda, let's cut the biscuits here," Bidou replied. "I would do anything to help him, and you should too. If he needs you, help him. He's done a lot for you. Be human and forget everything."

In the end, although Clauda was a proud woman, her compassion and love for Bob compelled her to accept him back into her life.

He still kept in touch with Ilse. Clauda told a close family friend: "She calls a lot, and Bob takes the phone into the bedroom and they speak for half an hour. Do they really think

I'm stupid and I don't know what's going on? This time if he leaves I won't take him back."

This friend describes Clauda as a strong woman who would not forget the Catholic Church's teachings on marriage: "It was the type of woman that she was, and it was the type of upbringing that she had. You're a Roman Catholic, so when you get married that's forever. If something happens that's unpleasant, you accept it, you try to cure it. But you don't throw everything away and move out. And that's one of the things that I'm sure influenced her a great deal. She was very religious at that time."

Bob sometimes spent evenings with friends at the suite he maintained at Place de Ville and often asked his old friend and political crony Paul Tardif to come to dinner in Dunrobin. Once, Father Ovila brought his sisters Beatrice and Gerarda from Hanmer to visit him.

Whatever her reservations, Clauda helped nurse her ex-husband back to health. And, as time passed, it must have seemed more and more likely that Bob would indeed stay with her.

Meanwhile, Ilse remained in Montreal. She was thirty years old and the mother of two children, and her life was in tatters. She became withdrawn and deeply troubled. "She looked very vulnerable in those days, and she didn't talk about it a lot, and we respected that," says her older sister Hilde.

Bob visited Montreal regularly for weekend treatments at the clinic of psychiatrist Dr. Alan Mann, whom he later named to the Campeau Corp. board of directors. Clauda accompanied him on these trips and they would stay together at the Château Maisonneuve.

In the fall of 1970, Bob was apparently feeling well enough to end his treatments. He suggested to his son-in-law Len Graham that they go down to Florida for a few months and build a house. So Bob flew with Rachelle, Len and their son, Len III, to Fort Lauderdale. Bob had purchased a house in the north end of the city along with two vacant lots across the street on the intercoastal canal. They would all live in the existing house while they built the new one on the empty properties.

Bob and Len worked sporadically, and the days slipped by. Len recalls: "We would get up and usually spend two or three hours [working] in the morning, and then he'd have lunch and a rest and a swim, and then we'd go back at it in the afternoon. At various times we did some work and not some work, but yet the thing was going along. Whether we had a subcontractor or not, it was always there for somebody to go over when they wanted to and pound some nails." Before long a beautiful vacation home was taking shape, with several bedrooms, a den, exposed laminated wood beams and an outdoor pool.

Clauda, who had remained in Dunbrobin looking after Jacques and Danny, flew to Fort Lauderdale in November for a visit of several weeks.

Bob also called his friend Joe O'Brien at his Campeau Corp. office.

"I'd like you to come down," Bob told him. "We'll relax and get this whole damn thing straightened out."

"How long are you talking about?" O'Brien asked.

"Well, it could be several months."

"Jesus, Bob, it'd be hard for me to do. You can appreciate that, with the kids and everything."

O'Brien had a wife and eight children, not to mention a full-time job at Campeau Corp. As it was, his wife had a problem with Campeau Corp.'s demands on his time. To abandon his family for several months was out of the question.

"Bob, I can't do it," O'Brien said. "But let me talk to Ann. Certainly I want to go down, and I'll spend some time down there with you."

About a week later, O'Brien flew to Fort Lauderdale. Clauda was already there.

"When I got down there he was spending a lot of time in his room — and it had to be dark," O'Brien recalls. "I remember that — having trouble sleeping and sleeping with an eyeshade on, that sort of thing, a mask. He was having regular days down there and he played a lot of chess with Len. He was down there to try and get organized to come back and straighten everything out."

It may have seemed as if Ilse was out of the picture, but Joe O'Brien knew otherwise. He maintains that there was never any genuine move toward reconciliation with Clauda at this time. During the two or three weeks he was in Florida, and while Clauda was still visiting, he and Bob fabricated a story to explain a whirlwind trip to New York. They said they had a business meeting to attend. In reality, they spent the weekend with Ilse and O'Brien's wife Ann, who flew in from Canada. The two couples went to a show and dinner, then Bob and O'Brien returned to Florida. O'Brien stayed a few more days before going back to Ottawa.

Clauda was not aware that Bob had seen Ilse again, and during this vacation in Florida she seems to have become convinced that she and her former husband would reconcile their differences. During one weekend when Campeau was away from Fort Lauderdale, Gilbert and his wife, Blanche, who were vacationing in Florida, dropped by for a visit. They found Clauda in good spirits, and she told them that she believed she and Bob would get back together. "I think things are getting better," she said.

The three had dinner and went for a boat ride, after which Clauda showed Gilbert and Blanche the house under construction. It was to be her home with Bob, she said. In early December, when Clauda returned to Dunrobin, she was not alone in believing that she and Bob were moving toward remarriage. Many family members seem to have had this impression: Clauda told some of them that he was staying with her, that he had told her his days with Ilse were over.

But shortly after Clauda's return, Bob made it clear to her that there was no possibility of reconciliation. Although she did not realize it, during their time in Florida Bob appears to have been agonizingly working his way toward a final decision between the two women in his life.

Father Ovila was privy to part of this internal debate. "He gave me a call from Florida and he was very tense," the priest remembers. "He was very, very tense and very torn. I was surprised. I felt things were going well between him and Clauda. And I know it was a real tragedy in his life then. He didn't give a damn for life at that time. He had to make a decision. And I forget what I told him, but not long after that phone call he decided he was going to marry Ilse. The worst thing in life is when you cannot make a decision. If you don't know what to do, it makes you sick."

During the few months in the sun, Bob Campeau had gradually built himself back up. And as his health improved, the fierce determination that has marked his life returned. Len Graham recalls that, as the house neared completion, his father-in-law started worrying again about the state of the company he had sold to Paul Desmarais and which he had all but abandoned. He did phone Campeau Corp.'s offices while he was in Florida, but he was not involved in the day-to-day running of the company.

Finally, in December of 1970, with the house almost complete, his health restored and his mind made up, Bob Campeau headed back to Ottawa to undo his marriage to Paul Desmarais and to marry Ilse. He wasted no time.

Robert Campeau and Ilse Luebbert were married before a justice of the peace just before Christmas 1970, almost ten years after they had met. Only Joe and Ann O'Brien, and one other employee whom O'Brien will not identify, attended. The O'Briens served as witnesses. Later there was a small reception at Place de Ville.

O'Brien, who had helped in the wedding arrangements, had drawn up a checklist of things to do that day. On his list was a call to Clauda. At the reception, he approached Bob. Clauda had to be told, he said. But Bob appeared reluctant.

"You know, Bob, there's no way that Clauda should find out that you're married through the papers or something," he said. "We've got to tell her. You can't go without her finding out. Look, Bob, I'll call her."

"That's a good idea," he replied.

So Joe O'Brien was left with the unpleasant task of breaking the news to an unsuspecting Clauda Campeau.

The call was brief.

"Bob and Ilse just got married," O'Brien told Clauda.
There was no reply.

The following day, Bob's sister Gerarda was at home in
Hanmer decorating her Christmas tree when Clauda phoned, in
tears. "Bob and Ilse got married," she said. And ever a lady
imbued with the etiquette of her era, she added, "Tell the
family not to send Christmas cards to Mrs. Robert Campeau
because he's married to Ilse. Tell the family to send cards to
Mrs. Clauda Campeau."

It is not known who told Bob's mother, Lucie, about his
marriage to Ilse, but the family matriarch would not have been
pleased. A few months later, her health began to fail, and she
expressed the desire to go to Hanmer to be with her oldest
daughter, Beatrice. So Lionel and Bob arranged to have her
moved from Ottawa to the small town near Sudbury where she
had met and married her husband. Bob paid for a team of
nurses to travel the distance from Sudbury to Hanmer by taxi
to provide twenty-four-hour care. Not long after, in August
1971, she died, at the age of seventy-seven.

A few days after his wedding, Bob showed up at the annual
Campeau Corp. Christmas party, at which some of the senior
executives first learned of his return. Early in the new year he
was back at the helm of Campeau Corp., but it was not easy to
regain the power he had relinquished for the better part of a
year. In his absence, control had centered in a group of
four — Jean Paradis, Marcel Lalande, Clem Cadieux and Pat
Kelly — who reported to Power Corp.'s Jean Parisien. It was an
uneasy alliance of the old guard and the new.

Pat Kelly had been the first real new blood among the
senior people in years when Campeau brought him in as general
counsel in 1967, a couple of years before O'Brien joined. Kelly,
who was the trustee of the children's trust estate, had known
little about the construction business, but he learned fast and
soon became one of Campeau's favorites. He was intelligent and
gregarious, a big man with a vulgar tongue. He had only one
lung, but this did not seem to slow him down. He was aggressive
and ambitious.

Campeau's withdrawal from the company saw Kelly

increasingly at odds with the old guard, for whom he apparently had little use. He referred to the Alfred Boys as "still having horseshit under their heels." Campeau Corp. was going to be a big company under the Power deal, and Bob's old group didn't have the refinement or the savvy to make the transition.

With Campeau out of the picture, Kelly saw his chance. "I think Kelly befriended Power, and I think he was hoping at one time that he could get rid of Bob," one former senior executive recalls. Adds Joe O'Brien: "Pat Kelly was spending a lot of time in the Montreal offices of Power Corp. because in Bob's absence someone had to be, and it was Pat. Pat was like I was. Pat was never wholeheartedly accepted. Yes, he was on the move to take control."

Campeau's return to his old office did not mean that he was automatically back in command. And if he had had any doubts about this, Joe O'Brien quickly set him straight. If Campeau was to try to win back control of the company, it would take time and determination. "There could be trouble, Bob," O'Brien told his friend. "I'm not so sure the senior people are all that loyal to you anymore."

O'Brien believed that Campeau faced a major task in winning back his own executives, who he felt were now firmly in the Power camp. Some senior people had even complained when the company paid for O'Brien's ticket to Florida to spend three weeks with Campeau. "There's no question in my mind that they had written Bob off," O'Brien says. "So Bob had a real battle on his hands in terms of deciding to try to buy the company back." O'Brien is perhaps overstating the case, but other former executives agree that most were skeptical that Bob could make a comeback.

Campeau decided first to assess the mood of his men and carefully lay the groundwork for a break from Power. He called a series of meetings in which he demonstrated that he had his finger on the company's pulse. He had returned under a cloud — mental health was still a taboo subject shrouded in mystery and misconceptions — and he had to prove that he was the same Bob Campeau. In reality, he was stronger than ever. And he wanted his company back, but he knew it would take time.

After several months, with most of his senior executives now firmly back in his camp, Bob was ready to reveal his plan. He assembled his vice-presidents — most of them old friends — and told them he was planning to see Desmarais and propose to buy back control of the company, retaining the real estate assets he had acquired in the initial deal less than two years earlier. But to do this, he needed their unqualified support. He was about to take one of the biggest gambles of his life. If Desmarais rejected the proposal, Bob was prepared to offer Desmarais the remaining interest in Campeau Corp. and start again from scratch with his senior managers. It would not be too difficult, if he had to, to get out of his five-year non-competition agreement with Desmarais. Each man at the meeting pledged his support. Pat Kelly presumably bit his lip, biding his time, but Campeau soon bought him out.

For all his faults, Bob Campeau is a remarkable man who can inspire great loyalty; a leader who regards his closest people as his most valued assets. Former employees recall that he often said he would spring right back if ever he went broke, provided he still had his men. And apparently his men returned the favor, willing to gamble their jobs and their security. Robert Campeau was definitely back.

It is not known what transpired between Bob Campeau and Paul Desmarais when Campeau went to the chief of Power Corp. with his buyback proposal. But Desmarais ended up agreeing to sell. However, he was in the midst of trying to gain the remaining stock of Consolidated-Bathurst and told Campeau that he wanted cash. And when Campeau set about trying to secure the money, he soon discovered that his traditional lending sources had dried up.

Joe O'Brien recalls that those traditional sources, presumably even the Bank of Nova Scotia, were not certain Campeau could do it: "I think they were probably still concerned about Bob. I think there was still that background there and, whether or not he could put the deal back on its feet, the company." So Campeau went to a lending source he had used only once before: the Vatican Bank.

In the late 1960s, Campeau Corp. had entered a joint venture with a French company to build Canadian-style timber frame housing on land just outside Paris. The project, sponsored by the Canadian government, which was trying to promote Canadian lumber in Europe, went so well that by September 1969 Campeau Corp. had developed a plan to build more of the same type of housing in other areas of France. Not wanting to use Canadian money to buy new land, Campeau began searching for a European lender. He was helped by Pat Gauthier of Canada's Department of Industry, Trade and Commerce, the Canadian government contact on the timber house project. Gauthier was well connected, and his connections included the Jesuits. Through them, Campeau arranged loans totaling about $15 million U.S. from the Instituto per le Opere di Religione, commonly known as the Vatican Bank.

Then, at the last minute, Campeau decided to phase out his French operations. But the loan was on favorable terms and, with Gauthier's help, Clem Cadieux persuaded the Vatican lenders to have it transferred to a Canadian project, the construction of the Journal Towers in Ottawa.

Now, with his traditional lenders not forthcoming and his company on the line, Campeau returned to the Vatican Bank. The bank was willing to talk, and he and Clem Cadieux flew to Rome twice as the negotiations progressed. "We dealt with Mennini and Marcinkus, basically," a former board member says, referring to Luigi Mennini, the bank's top layman, and Archbishop Paul Marcinkus, president of the Vatican Bank. "Clem and Bob had met Marcinkus, and we didn't need Gauthier anymore. I guess it hadn't occurred to us that there was that much money available."

Former employees say the money was lent to Campeau Corp. because it was a company composed primarily of practicing Roman Catholics. Bob had golfed with Marcinkus in the late 1950s when he was stationed in Ottawa as secretary to the apostolic delegation. This personal connection undoubtedly did not hurt him in his hour of need.

On March 21, 1972, Campeau announced that Power had agreed to let him buy back the company's shares for $28.5 million. The loan was then in its final stages. It came to 104 million Swiss francs (the Vatican often dealt through Swiss banks) or about $27 million, at 8.75 percent a year, due in 1977. The loan was secured by 3.4 million common shares of Blue Bonnets raceways and three large land parcels. Campeau Corp. did not publicly disclose the source, but, says a former board member, "it was probably fairly common knowledge within the company that that money came from Rome."

In the long run, the Vatican Bank loan turned out to be far more expensive than anyone could have foreseen. The Swiss currency was rapidly moving up in value against the Canadian dollar. By August 1973, the exchange rate would bring the value of the loan in Canadian funds to $34.4 million. It ended up costing Campeau an extra $16.8 million.

"When we had to pay it back, we had to pay practically double . . . but it was still a good deal," says Clem Cadieux, chief financial officer at the time. "In return, Campeau bought back its company from Power. Together with that were all the Canadian Interurban properties, Blue Bonnets and Bill Teron, and Kanata in Ottawa. That itself was worth a little fortune."

Campeau emerged from the Power Corp. deal with a strong base of shopping centers that, when the deal had gone into effect, had thrust him into a class far above that of residential builder. "The assets that he got out of Canadian Interurban are the basis of a big part of his success because they're all income properties," says Ira Gluskin, a Toronto securities analyst who followed Campeau Corp. stock after the company went public.

Campeau had learned a lesson. In a 1975 interview in *The Globe and Mail*, he said: "It was a very good exercise because it proved one thing to me — that we had to remain master of our own destiny. The way it ended up, the whole exercise was good for Campeau Corp. in the sense that we sold our destiny, we got it back and we made a very good deal in getting it back."

10 / The Liberal Landlord

*"The decision to proceed appears to have
rested on other than purely economic
considerations."*
— Senate committee report

OTTAWA IS A TOWN dominated by a single industry — government. And as in any such city, the industry fuels the local economy and supports supplier businesses. In Ottawa of the early 1970s, Robert Campeau not only built houses for government employees, he also housed a big chunk of the government itself. By early 1972, after the divorce from Power Corp., he was well on his way to becoming the Liberal government's favorite builder.

Campeau's connections with the Liberal Party actually dated to 1954, when he had hired Jean Paradis away from Central Mortgage and Housing's Ottawa branch. Paradis had been a Liberal appointee to CMHC. In the late 1960s, Campeau's friend Paul Tardif left municipal politics to sit in Parliament for the Liberals. Campeau also made a point of cultivating government ministers. When George McIlraith, the Liberal public works minister, gave the toast to the bride at Rachelle's wedding in 1967, he was doing a favor for an old friend. And in 1972, Liberal Senator Louis Giguère, Pierre Trudeau's first appointment to the Senate, was sitting on the Campeau Corp. board of directors. (Giguère would be charged with, and later acquitted of, accepting a bribe of $95,000 for using influence to win a lease extension for a duty-free shop at Dorval Airport in what became known as the sky-shops affair.)

After Pierre Trudeau's election in 1968, Campeau became

known throughout Ottawa as a prominent Liberal supporter
with easy access to the corridors of power. And throughout the
years that followed, he was criticized for the coziness of his
political connections. But these charges seldom bothered the
man who loved controversy. "I have supported friends in
politics," he once said, "but I have never leaned on them to get
anything special. If I believe in people, I will help them. If not, I
fight them."

He could not, however, escape entirely unscathed. The
story of how Robert Campeau became the government's largest
landlord can be pieced together from personal interviews,
government and corporate documents and published reports. It
forms the final chapter in the remarkable saga of his Ottawa
years.

The coming of Pierre Trudeau had signaled a new era for
French Canadians in Ottawa, and Bob Campeau was there
right from the beginning. The evening after Trudeau won the
Liberal leadership at a convention in Ottawa and became prime
minister — he was the third French Canadian to do so — Campeau threw a private party for prominent Liberals at his suite
in Place de Ville. "The whole bloody hotel was filled with
delegates celebrating," recalls former Trudeau minister Marc
Lalonde. "Campeau opened his penthouse or suite to all those
who were very active in the organization."

Trudeau, like Camillien Houde, was a man Campeau could
admire. He was sophisticated, cultured and well-educated. He
was a mover, a Napoleon-like conqueror, and it was thus that
Campeau saw himself. Trudeau's approach to politics was
much like Campeau's approach to business: both sought to
strike down the linguistic and cultural barriers standing in the
way of French Canadian achievement. Trudeau imposed his
vision of bilingualism on the civil service, giving French
Canadians a far larger role than they had had before. Campeau
had built a company run primarily by French Canadians
that had become one of the largest integrated developers
in the nation.

As different as the two men were, Campeau and Trudeau
became friends, and the prime minister often came to

Campeau's parties. But Lalonde says the two men "were not buddy-buddy." And a former Campeau Corp. board member and friend recalls, "I don't think he was as close to Trudeau as people say he was. Trudeau was not a friend of Bob Campeau's back in 1968." Still, Campeau was on good terms with many of the key players in the government. He played tennis with Jean Chrétien, who was at different times president of the Treasury Board and finance minister. He befriended Jean Marchand, one of Trudeau's closest confidants, who once said that Campeau "built half the city. He didn't do that without having good relations with many people in Ottawa." And then, of course, there was George McIlraith.

Having contacts on Parliament Hill made good sense for a local developer on the hustle. Says Lalonde: "Campeau was living in Ottawa and was a developer in Ottawa and was trying to lease office space or build office space for government, so he made a point of knowing every single minister around. He was the kind of guy to hobnob and, if you have met him, you know he's not shy. So he would make himself known to everybody. He would always come in for proposals that would go to Treasury Board and cabinet for renting space, like a lot of other developers in those days in Ottawa."

The first rumblings of criticism from Opposition MPs had come in 1969 during Campeau's government-backed venture building timber-frame houses in France. But Campeau Corp., with its many French-speaking employees, was the natural choice. The Liberals easily deflected the Opposition charges of favoritism.

Place de Ville had been Campeau's first major project to be leased primarily to the government. By the early 1970s, government leases were pouring in for office space in such buildings as Centennial Towers and Journal Towers.

Campeau's biggest and most controversial deal with the federal Liberals began to take shape in 1974, when he first approached the government — in the form of the National Capital Commission — with a proposal for a development in Hull, the French-speaking city across the river from Ottawa.

Back in 1969, the government had announced a plan to

relocate a quarter of the civil service to Hull by 1985, a move intended to help correct the disparity between Ottawa and Hull and create a truly national capital region. The NCC was to buy land in Hull and develop the projects, and the office buildings would be government-owned. The NCC even expropriated some of the necessary land.

The government's policy until 1963 had been to build its own office space, a task that fell primarily to the Department of Public Works. But the 1960s brought a spurt of growth in the civil service that created great demand for offices. And by 1963, the government was growing increasingly reluctant to provide the money to build its own buildings to meet this demand. So it cut the flow of construction dollars to the Public Works Department and began renting, a policy that greatly benefited developers like Campeau and projects such as Place de Ville. But in 1969 the Liberals under Trudeau tried to revert to the old policy of the government building government space. Among the first projects were plans for seven new buildings in Hull. The Trudeau government had bad news for developers that year: not only had the Liberals launched a concerted effort to halt the rapid growth of the civil service, but they were very concerned about the pace with which private developers were continuing to put up office space.

Douglas Fullerton, then the NCC chairman, recalled in a report a few years later: "At one Treasury Board meeting, I was instructed to go out and spread the news to the developers of the expected combined impact of the cessation of growth in the public service and the upsurge of new government building plans on future federal needs for rental space from the private sector. This was all done with the best of intentions and with the object of limiting losses for the speculators. I followed my instructions, crying woe in public statements; a study was prepared at the NCC reflecting the effect of slower federal employment on population and on the reduced need for homes and office space. The builders were slowed briefly, but they had a much greater trust in the inherent tendency of governments to grow rapidly than in my judgment or in federal preaching about economy. In the event, bulldozers kept scooping out new excavations for still more speculative office buildings to house still more public servants."

For a while, however, the primary construction occurring in Hull was being done by the government, which was soon at work on seven new buildings there.

Campeau waited for the right opportunity. This came late in 1973, when the NCC started eyeing the area near Standish Hall — one of the most popular entertainment spots in Hull when Campeau first started up in Ottawa — as the site for a government office building. With the Liberal plans to move large chunks of the civil service to Hull well underway, Campeau had a much grander vision for this site — something that he would build.

In January 1974, the NCC tried to buy the Standish Hall site for $1.5 million, but was turned down. Just two months later, Campeau signed a $100,000 option to buy the property for $2.25 million. About one month later, the NCC officials returned with another bid, for $2 million, only to learn of Campeau's option. So this bid, too, was turned down: Robert Campeau had been there before them.

Now that Campeau controlled some of the land the government wanted, he began talking with the NCC. In late April he sent Jean Paradis to see Edgar Gallant, who had recently become the NCC chairman, to discuss proposals for accelerating government development of the area around Standish Hall. Despite the government's standing policy of discouraging private development, Gallant was encouraging. He subsequently wrote to Paradis saying the NCC would be happy to discuss "ways of assuring a successful co-ordination of your development with other federal arrangements which may take place on one or another of the neighboring properties."

At this point, the government could still have assembled sufficient land for an office complex in the Standish Hall area. It could even have expropriated the piece Campeau had bought. Immediately to the east, the site of another building, known as Ottawa House, was still available, as was a nearby Hydro Quebec building. And the NCC had already acquired an old post office site in the early 1960s. In May, the NCC bid unsuccessfully for the Ottawa House site, offering $1.7 million. After that, the NCC made no further attempts to buy this or any other adjacent property.

Just eight days after the NCC's unsuccessful bid for Ottawa House, Campeau and Paradis met with Gallant and John MacDonald, the deputy minister of Public Works, to talk about a proposed office development. A day later, Campeau wrote to Gallant, advising the NCC chairman that he had already made a financial proposal to the Public Works Department and he wanted to build a hotel and commercial space alongside the office development.

Official government policy at this point was still for the NCC to buy the land needed for an office complex. But by December 1974, the NCC's planning management committee agreed that it might be wise to allow a private builder such as Campeau to develop the project instead. The government, they argued feebly, could still have some control, however small, because it would still own at least some of the land — namely, the old post office site.

In sum, Bob Campeau had played to his advantage the system to which he was so well connected. While continuing to talk soothingly to the NCC, he had used all his powers of persuasion on the federal Public Works Department. This double pressure had finally convinced the NCC to let Campeau build the project.

Although Campeau did not yet own Standish Hall, or any of the land required by the development, he now hired private planners to draw up a proposed lease-purchase deal that would allow the government to lease the project for a set period of time, and then buy it for a specified price. These planners met with NCC officials in the summer of 1974 and began negotiations.

It was not until February 1975 that Campeau closed the sale on Standish Hall and filed plans with Hull's planning department to build two office towers. That spring he negotiated a deal to buy the Ottawa House property for almost $2.3 million. When that deal closed in September, Campeau controlled much of the land needed for what would become Les Terrasses de la Chaudière, a complex that was to include three office towers, a hotel and commercial space.

The government now proceeded to negotiate the lease-purchase deal with Campeau. But before this could be done, the NCC's design committee had to approve Campeau's plans for the project.

Acting as Campeau's chief architect was Raymond Affleck, of Montreal, who was also a member of the NCC design committee that had to approve his plans. It is not clear just when Campeau hired Affleck, who has since died, but after Les Terrasses was built, the architect said of the design committee: "They knew me well and respected me a great deal. It may have eased acceptance by the NCC of that proposal. I have to say in all honesty I think that maybe it did affect acceptance of it. I raised the typical question of whether there was a conflict of interest. They were anxious that I remain on the design board ... It was an appropriate professional relationship with two clients who overlapped in their interests." Campeau's plans for Les Terrasses were approved in principle in July 1975.

But now the government seemed to get cold feet. The Treasury Board, the cabinet committee that must approve all spending, declined to approve the project until Gallant provided detailed information on how Campeau had assembled the land and how his negotiations with the NCC had progressed. Gallant gave the board a chronology but conveniently did not mention that the NCC had talked with Campeau in early 1974 or that, later that year, the NCC planning committee had agreed that a private developer could develop the sites. Satisfied with what the NCC revealed, the Treasury Board opened formal negotiations with Campeau. But it warned the NCC and the Department of Public Works never again to begin preliminary talks on lease-purchase deals unless the builder in question already controlled the land. A lease-purchase agreement with Campeau was duly completed and the project went ahead, with no tenders ever having been called. As part of this final deal, the government agreed to lease Campeau the 83,000 square feet of land it owned in the area for ninety-nine years at one dollar a year for the first thirty-five years. This additional property brought the total site area to about fourteen acres.

The way was now clear for Les Terrasses, later dubbed Place Campeau by Hull residents. The development would consist of 1.8 million square feet of office space (housing some 6,500 civil servants), 54,800 square feet of retail space, a 243-room luxury hotel with dining and convention facilities, and a four-level parking garage. Yet the story was not quite over.

The NCC had announced plans for a $3-million beautification program across the street from Campeau's hotel, along what was known as Brewery Creek. But after Campeau started building, the NCC decided on a two-year moratorium on this plan. Campeau promptly threatened to halt construction unless the beautification program proceeded, appealing directly to André Ouellet, then Liberal urban affairs minister and the minister responsible for the NCC, to intervene.

In his letter to new NCC chairman Pierre Juneau, Campeau let fly all his artillery: "I received a letter from the deputy minister and calls from the minister of public works and from the minister of state for urban affairs. They were all very anxious to have the hotel open its doors in July 1978. We have resumed construction in good faith believing that the problem would be solved ... I only want the NCC to abide by its agreement. I am taking the liberty of sending a copy of this letter to the minister of state for urban affairs." Faced with this barrage, the NCC backed down.

But as Les Terrasses neared completion, more and more questions were being raised about the original deal. When the Conservative Opposition got wind of the details in late 1976, its members were outraged and pressed the government for an investigation, saying it was paying too much.

The Senate Committee on National Finance decided to investigate lease-purchase agreements between developers and the public works department in general, part of a study of the department's office space programs. Campeau's was the most controversial, although he was not the only developer involved.

Of the four lease-purchase deals investigated, two were with Reichmann-owned Olympia & York Developments for office space in Ottawa and one was with Cadillac-Fairview for the Place du Centre project in Hull.

Then and subsequently, Campeau was put under particular scrutiny because of his known ties to the Liberals. In June 1978, Douglas Fullerton, who had preceded Edgar Gallant as chairman of the NCC, spoke in an interview with the *Ottawa Citizen* about Campeau's political connections and complained that the Les Terrasses deal had been approved despite opposition by senior government officials. After the article appeared, Senator Jean Marchand denounced Fullerton in the Senate. Public Works Minister Judd Buchanan, seeking further details, then asked Fullerton to a meeting. Fullerton emerged after twenty minutes, complaining again to reporters of Campeau's political connections. Added Fullerton: "All my life, I've been opposed to close ties between developers and politicians." On the day after the Fullerton-Buchanan meeting, Prime Minister Trudeau denied in the House of Commons that Campeau had benefited from his Liberal connections, saying Fullerton's charges showed either "his ignorance or his lack of memory in this particular matter."

On September 25, 1978, Campeau officially opened Les Terrasses, describing it as "a good deal for the federal government and a good deal for Campeau Corp." He denied that he had taken advantage of any inside information. Two days later, he sued Fullerton, the *Citizen*, its owner (Southam Press), and reporter Bert Hill for libel because of the original interview with Fullerton and other articles about Les Terrasses. Campeau sought damages of $100,000 from Fullerton, $700,000 from Southam Press and $60,000 from the reporter, saying in his statement of claim that the Fullerton interview and another article one day later "taken as a whole together with the headlines and colored photographs are defamatory.... The plaintiffs have been injured in their reputations and have been brought into public scandal, odium and contempt."

The suit was eventually settled out of court. No money was

paid, Fullerton says, but an apology appeared on the front page of the newspaper.

Only three days after Les Terrasses was officially opened, the Senate committee that had been investigating Campeau's and other lease-purchase deals released its report, which criticized the government for paying higher-than-normal rents at Les Terrasses and at the Cadillac-Fairview and Olympia & York developments. Indeed, the government did seem at the time to be getting a raw deal. At Les Terrasses, it was paying $13.67 or $14.67 a square foot, depending on interest rates, while the going market rate was $10.70. This amounted to $16.7 million in annual rent for thirty-five years and a purchase price of an additional $54 million when the lease expired. The committee criticized Ottawa for awarding the Hull contracts without calling for tenders.

"In entering into them the department . . . failed to observe precautions taken as a regular course in all other projects for the acquisition of space," the senators said. "Given the circumstances of that time — the intense demand for space by the federal government — the lack of capital funds to permit Crown construction and the legitimate desires to obtain firm costs in a highly inflationary environment and to control the architectural development of the National Capital Region — it is understandable that DPW [Department of Public Works] entered into the . . . lease-purchase agreements. However, DPW, with the approval of the Treasury Board, failed to observe precautions taken as a regular course in all other projects for the acquisition of space . . . . These agreements have committed DPW to pay rates for the space involved well beyond the prevailing private sector level."

The Senate committee concluded: "The decision to proceed appears to have rested on other than purely economic considerations . . . Even at the time of their signature, the economic benefits of these agreements were questionable. In light of the subsequent movement of rental rates in the National Capital Region, the agreements are clearly costly investments for the Crown."

The committee did not elaborate on the precise nature of those "other than purely economic considerations."

The day the report was released, Liberal Senator Douglas Everett, the committee chairman, told a news conference that it would probably not be possible to investigate further. His committee — or any other, for that matter — could not get access to the documents. But he assured the public that there was no evidence to suggest political pressure had worked in Campeau's favor.

The Senate committee report prompted Conservative calls for a Royal Commission into the Les Terrasses deal, but no commission was ever appointed.

All this publicity put Public Works Minister Judd Buchanan in the hot seat. Initially he argued that it would not have been ethical to expropriate the land and then go through a tendering process because Campeau already owned much of the property. This ignored the fact that it had taken Campeau about a year and a half to assemble the land after the government began planning its own development. But in 1979, Buchanan told a reporter that "in retrospect, my inclination would have been to expropriate and call for proposals . . . . This would have avoided any suggestion of favoritism." Referring to clauses in the deal that allowed Campeau to up the rent, within limits, if he was faced with higher interest on his capital, Buchanan added: "I would have fought like a stuck pig to negotiate it out of the lease . . . . In retrospect, that's a clause I would not have included."

Campeau told the same reporter that there was nothing whatsoever wrong with the deal: "I think I got a fair contract for the government and for myself." And in a 1987 magazine interview, he said he had built the complex at a cost far less than the government could have: "Les Terrasses is costing the government today about $14 or $15 a square foot, everything included. A project that they built in the Portage, on the other end of the bridge, is costing them $30 . . . . It's not Ottawa that made it for me. I made it for Ottawa."

In November 1978 (just after Les Terrasses opened), when

former NCC chairman Edgar Gallant was awarded a public service medal at a ceremony at Rideau Hall, Bob Campeau was one of the guests.

The Les Terrasses episode was not the last time Campeau's dealings with the federal government came under fire. In 1983, after completing renovations to his Centennial Towers and finishing Place Guy Favreau in Montreal, he leased all the office space to the government. Together with Place de Ville and Journal Towers, this made him by far the government's biggest landlord. Campeau Corp.'s total office and mixed-use space amounted to more than 6 million square feet, some 97 percent of it occupied. Fully 70 percent of the net rental area was leased to the Government of Canada. And Auditor-General Kenneth Dye took notice.

In Dye's 1984 annual report, he outlined how the Public Works Department withheld information from cabinet and wasted taxpayers' money in its dealings with Robert Campeau. Dye said that in 1983, Public Works withheld information in connection with three downtown office sites — Centennial Towers, Place de Ville's Tower C and the two Journal Tower buildings — leased from Campeau for about $400 million. According to Dye's analysis, the terms of the deals cost taxpayers more than $50 million in excess of what they should have. Among his findings: the department rang up $42.7 million in additional costs over the term of a ten-year lease at Place de Ville; lost the chance to acquire Centennial Towers through lease-purchase for just $15 million more than the cost of the lease payments; rented space in Journal South for $72 a metre *more* than it charged government departments, meaning a difference of $8 million over the first five years of the lease; and entered into leases valued at a total $135 million for Journal North and South without public tender, saying no alternative space was available when it had 18,000 square metres of Crown-owned space in Hull that had been vacant since mid-1978.

Dye found that "in arranging these long-term leases, the department did not disclose essential information to the ministers of the Treasury Board, entered into direct negotiations with the landlord without public tender, failed to negotiate in a timely manner and acted beyond its authority by not obtaining the necessary approvals from Treasury Board."

At a later hearing, Arthur Wilson, assistant deputy minister of operations for Public Works, revealed a Treasury Board official had authorized leasing Place de Ville's Tower C, the headquarters of the Transport Department, which Dye said cost $43 million more than Campeau had originally been asking. Furthermore, the department's records showed the Treasury Board had approved the higher rate without written authorization. The leasing deal had been made by phone.

Wilson concluded that Campeau "appears to have a great deal of clout" and that little could be done in negotiating lease renewals with him because there were few options when huge departments took up entire buildings. Just before the Liberals lost the 1984 election, the government retroactively passed a Treasury Board resolution ratifying the Place de Ville Tower C lease signed in 1982.

And 1984 brought a further revelation. In December 1983, the government had rented, but was not yet using, twelve floors in the sixteen-storey Centennial Towers. This had already cost more than $2 million. The space was to be used as headquarters for the new Canadian Security Intelligence Service, or CSIS, but the legislation to create the new spy agency had been bogged down in Parliament. Although Deputy Public Works Minister John MacKay explained that the government had to rent the building when it did because the rental would have increased had it postponed the December 1 possession date, Auditor-General Dye ridiculed his comments. The Solicitor-General's Department did not even know when the government began negotiating whether Centennial Towers would meet the security requirements for a spy agency, he said.

And in January 1985, it was revealed in a memo that in 1981, senior officials in Public Works had blocked an attempt by juniors in the department to "make Treasury Board aware of the total picture of our negotiations with Campeau about the Journal Tower leases . . . . We were directed by headquarters to delete from the submission any reference to negotiations for the Journal South and North and to proceed with negotiations. The Treasury Board submission was amended as requested and resubmitted."

These revelations and allegations tell a story of monumental government inefficiency, and graphically show Campeau's shrewdness as a businessman. There is no question that Campeau Corp. made millions from its dealings with the Liberals, and that sheer bungling on the part of the government wasted taxpayers' dollars in certain deals.

(The tables turned somewhat in the spring of 1989 when the Liberals, now as the Opposition, attacked the Conservatives for renewing a lease at Place de Ville. The Transport Department had planned to move 3,000 employees from the building and move into new offices. But the Tories cited restraint and decided instead to renew the lease and apparently pump millions of dollars into helping Campeau renovate and remove asbestos from the office tower. The Liberals claimed the government decided on the lease because Campeau, a traditional Liberal supporter, publicly backed the Conservatives, and their free trade agreement with the United States, in the 1988 election.)

There is one footnote to this story. Campeau had been a staunch Liberal supporter, yet his company had throughout the years donated to both the Liberal and Conservative parties, as all smart businesses do. Between 1974, when disclosure of sizable political donations became mandatory, and 1987, Campeau Corp. contributed a total of $139,127.88 to the Liberals and $93,087.16 to the Conservatives. Bob Campeau may have been the Liberals' landlord, but he was equally willing to play the same role for their political opposition.

A formal portrait of Bob and Clauda Campeau in 1944, soon after their marriage.

Clauda in 1956. (Courtest of Gerarda Ste. Marie)

Bob at Lake Dechenes, the site of his cottage, in 1955. (Courtesy of Gerarda Ste. Marie)

A get-together at Bob's sister Gerarda's house. Left to right: Gerarda's husband Sylvio Ste. Marie, Gilbert Campeau, Lionel Campeau's wife Rolande, Lionel, Gilbert's wife Blanche, Bob and Clauda. (Courtesy of Gerarda Ste. Marie)

Jean Paradis (in bathing suit), Bob's key lieutenant in the 1950s, relaxes with Jean-Marc Prud'Homme. (Courtesy of Jean-Marc Prud'Homme)

Bob (back to camera) instructs his assistant superintendent, Jean-Marc Prud'Homme, on his golf swing at Lake Muskoka in 1958. (Courtesy of Jean-Marc Prud'Homme)

47 Guy Street, the first house Bob and Tony Campeau built. (Ottawa Citizen)

Father Ovila Campeau stands in front of Bob and Clauda's first big house, the bungalow on Applewood Crescent. (Courtesy of Gerarda Ste. Marie)

*A friend and a foe — Ottawa councillor Paul Tardif,
Bob's main ally on city council, and Mayor Charlotte
Whitton, who did everything in her power to thwart
Bob's projects. (City of Ottawa Archives, Ottawa
Journal Collection, CA #3956 and CA #3952)*

The first phase of Place de Ville nears completion in 1967. The Skyline Hotel is in the foreground. (Canapress Photo Service)

Bob autographing a steel beam for Place de Ville Phase II, March 3, 1970. (City of Ottawa Archives, Ottawa Journal Collection, CA #3963)

Although separated for more than a year, Bob and Clauda got together to celebrate the marriage of their only daughter Rachelle to Len Graham in 1967.

Lucie Campeau and her four sons in 1967: (left to right), Father Ovila, Gilbert, Bob and Lionel. (Courtesy of Lionel Campeau)

Bob joins his former partner, Alban Cadieux (far left), in the winner's circle for the Prix d'Ete at Blue Bonnets racetrack in 1977. (Campeau sports his latest toupee).

Bob Campeau, sans toupee (City of Ottawa Archives, Ottawa Journal Collection, *CA #3966)*

Bob and his second wife Ilse in 1980. (City of Ottawa Archives, Ottawa Journal *Collection,* CA #3967)

Lieut.-Col. Kenneth White (left), chairman of Royal Trustco, and Richard Thomson, chairman of the Toronto Dominion Bank, who bought up Royal Trustco shares during Campeau's unsuccessful attempt to take over White's company. (Photo by Peter Redman, Financial Post)

Albert Reichmann and Bob Campeau at a topping off ceremony for Scotia Plaza, February 1988. (Photo by Peter Redman, Financial Post*)*

Scotia Plaza, the second-tallest office tower in Toronto (Photo by Lenscape)

Allied Stores chairman Thomas Macioce around the time of Campeau's takeover bid.

Shopping centre magnate Edward DeBartolo, the white knight who tried to ride to Allied's rescue. (Photo by Brian Condron, Financial Post)

Campeau takeover strategists, merger lawyer Allen Finkelson (left) and merchant banker Bruce Wasserstein. (Photo by Peter Redman, Financial Post)

Edward Finkelstein, chairman of Macy's, entered the bidding for Federated Department Stores at the eleventh hour just when Campeau thought he had won. (AP/Wide World Photos)

The victorious Bob Campeau with John Burden, recently appointed chairman of the Federated-Allied empire, at a news conference just after Campeau Corp.'s June 1988 annual meeting.

Bob and Ilse's youngest son, Jan Paul, shows his trick bike riding skills at Campeau-owned Oshawa centre. (Photo by Carl Ferenez, Oshawa Times)

Bob and Clauda's adopted son, Danny, before his American Racing Series race at the 1988 Molson Indy in Toronto. His car was badly damaged during the race. (Photo by Mike Barrett)

Bob and some members of his extended family at a dinner where he received B'nai Brith Canada's award of merit in March 1986. Standing left to right: Danny, Hilde Luebbert (Ilse's older sister), Ilse, Bob, Robert Archambault (Rachelle's second husband). Seated left to right: Susan Ball (Danny's wife, now divorced), Rachelle, and Giselle (Bob and Ilse's daughter). (Courtesy of B'nai Brith Canada)

(*Photo by Peter Redman*, Financial Post)

PART III

The Outsider

11 / The Changing of the Guard

"The Toronto establishment didn't think he belonged in Toronto."

— Joe O'Brien

ALTHOUGH DURING the 1970s Robert Campeau continued to build in Ottawa, his attention increasingly shifted elsewhere. He had emerged stronger from his personal crisis; he had sorted out his marital troubles and had escaped from Paul Desmarais's embrace. He was back in control of his company and there were new worlds to conquer. By the end of the decade, Campeau Corp. would no longer be primarily an Ottawa development concern. The first new frontier was Toronto, and Campeau's first move in Canada's largest English-speaking city was the Harbour Castle Hotel and condominiums.

Toronto's waterfront had been a seamy stretch of dingy docks and warehouses when Bob Campeau first turned his sights there in 1968. For $10 million, he acquired some sixteen acres with 2,000 feet of waterfront. This was the deal he would finance a year later by taking his company public. Campeau would do for Toronto's undeveloped harbor area what he had done for Ottawa's downtown with Place de Ville: create something where there had been nothing. Here he would build a $300-million lakefront development, including a luxury hotel, two upscale apartment towers, a convention center, office towers and shops.

The only trouble with this vision was that the land was cut off from the city by the railway tracks and the Gardiner Expressway, a barrier no Toronto developer had yet successfully crossed. His detractors predicted failure. "It was a maverick thing to do at that time because he was literally on the other side of the tracks," recalls Bill Teron, Campeau's competitor from Ottawa, who would also soon be building in Toronto. "He had the audacity to do what no one else would do. He was pioneering, risking."

Toronto did not know much about Robert Campeau at the time. It was not familiar with his supreme self-confidence. He was a housebuilder from Ottawa, and that was all. And besides, he was French, and this was the heart of English Canada. "I remember being told by everyone that the Toronto establishment didn't think he belonged in Toronto and certainly didn't think he'd get it off the ground," says Joe O'Brien. "A couple of other guys had tried and failed, and who was this pipsqueak who thinks he's going to come in and show us how to do it?"

Construction on the first apartment tower was scheduled to begin in May 1969, but Campeau was forced to delay building until sufficiently favorable long-term financing could be obtained. When work on the hotel and the first thirty-six-storey apartment building finally began in 1972, it was headed by Len Graham, Rachelle's husband, who had been brought into the Campeau organization as vice-president of heavy construction in 1969. Graham finished off some projects in Ottawa and then headed to Toronto to work exclusively on the waterfront development. If it succeeded, it would firmly establish Bob Campeau in the lucrative but highly competitive Toronto market.

This project was going to be his showpiece, and Campeau was meticulous in its construction. He demanded that nothing go wrong and frequently traveled from Ottawa to personally inspect the work in progress. Graham recalls a time when he and Campeau were inspecting some wood paneling work in the hotel, done by a contractor with whom they were not familiar: "Bob looked at the wood, and the grains were not matched and the staining wasn't uniform. And he said, 'This isn't the quality we want, and if it delays us, it delays us.' So I met with the company and I said, 'It's not up to the standards that we expected. Take it out.'"

When the hotel was 90 percent complete, Campeau suddenly decided that there were not enough sports facilities for the guests. He demanded that ten rooms be ripped out and converted into additional health club space.

And later, when the second condominium tower at the lakefront was under construction, Campeau became so concerned about the quality of the work that he sent Eugène Lavigne to Toronto to take charge. Lavigne arrived with authorization to take whatever steps were necessary to improve the quality of the waterfront development. "Bob would visit a project like that once in a while, and he was able to detect the faults in walls, doors, whatever, and to him that was totally unacceptable and he'd raise the roof," Lavigne says. "To him, the quality-control had gone down to its lowest level. They had gone up to the twentieth floor, so I brought them back to the second floor to start over again, floor by floor, wall by wall, by door, everything."

In late 1974, after the first 538-unit apartment tower had been completed, Campeau decided to convert it into a condominium. The rents were high, and only about half the apartments were leased. Many of the tenants, who had been offered five-year leases, were livid. "We went through hell with that," recalls a former Campeau executive. "We rented over 200 units and then told those 200 tenants that we were going condo, and some of them wanted to kill us." Campeau was expected to gain more than $10 million in profits by the conversion.

Toronto greeted Robert Campeau with a mixture of derision and fascination. The city had not seen his like before. Just before the Harbour Castle Hotel opened in April 1975, journalist Hartley Steward wrote a profile of the developer for the *Toronto Star*. He described Campeau as "a handsome little fellow in a rough-and-tumble way, with his collar loose and his dark, wavy hair unorganized." Campeau put on something of a performance for the reporter, showing him the development from his seven-seater plane, then flying him to Ottawa for a visit to Campeau Corp. headquarters at the Baseline Road complex. There he ushered Steward into a plush room with wood paneling — a complete model of one of the rooms in the hotel.

"This has got to be the very best hotel room in the world," Campeau said. "By Jeez, I've seen a lot of hotel rooms in my day, but this has got to be the very best."

He then showed the reporter another model room, this one without paneling.

Then Steward was granted a glimpse of Bob Campeau's decision-making process. Campeau had just learned the difference in cost between the two rooms; now he mulled over the figures.

"Twenty cents a room," he said. "That's all. Twenty cents more on the room rate will pay for the difference. That'll do it. We go with the paneled room. We'll cut the cost elsewhere. I want to talk to Len. He's got the figures. Where's Len? Let's meet in my office."

Campeau's son-in-law arrived and, as the reporter looked on, began detailing the cost of the more expensive room. "It's a lot more for that room. It all adds up."

"Twenty cents more a room," Campeau replied. "We'll go with this one. Besides, Len, you haven't bought any of that stuff yet. Now's the time for some tough negotiation. Get those prices down. Hell, if I were buying that cabinet, I'd get it for $75, maybe $65."

The official opening of the Harbour Castle Hotel took three days. Hundreds of guests drank Robert Campeau's wine, stuffed themselves with his hors d'oeuvres and laughed behind his back. Members of Toronto's elite toured the hotel and attended a private party in the Royal Suite, snickering at the overly ornate furnishings. Chronicling the event in *Toronto Life* magazine, Barbara Amiel wrote: "Ephraim Diamond and wife (Cadillac-Fairview), tanned and buoyant, were standing alone in one corner while deliberately dowdy matrons and their blinking husbands swept by, talking about Hunt Club doings. Old Toronto had come to see the hotel and was amused by it all. The Roman-style baths in the royal suite, all marble and gilded columns, the pride of Robert Campeau, were a special source of twitters. 'We must have one installed, there's no question,' trilled one guest, obviously known in her set for her quick humor, 'but maybe we'd better put it in the basement.' "

The guests then filed outside for an opening ceremony that began with Campeau reviewing the Royal Regiment Guard of Honour at the front of the hotel. Barbara Amiel saw it this way: "Moving briskly toward the saluting stand, his moire tuxedo shimmering subtly, just a hint of frilled shirt showing ... Campeau stepped in front of the crowds. Solemnly he acknowledged the presentation of arms by the commander and, with a little skip that put him in step with him, he began the inspection. Slowly he slid his feet in an imitation of all those inspections he had seen performed by countless members of the House of Windsor. It was a dream come true: the tough little French-Canadian kid from Sudbury, public school dropout, doing it just like Her Majesty. A dream of free enterprise."

Then the group went inside the hotel, where Campeau served dinner to 350 people. He sat up front at a head table with Cedric Ritchie of the Bank of Nova Scotia and J.C. Barrow of Simpsons-Sears. Every woman in the place received six Bavarian long-stemmed crystal wine glasses. After the meal, Robert Campeau gave a rambling speech, ranging from his adventures with Charlotte Whitton to his opinion of governments in general — that they interfered too much in the economy.

The hotel, which had opened with such fanfare, turned out to be a big drain on the corporation. Campeau had built two hotels before — the Holiday Inn and the Skyline at Place de Ville — yet this was the first he would both own and operate. He opened it in a period when the supply of hotel rooms in Toronto far outweighed the demand, and the following year he struck a deal with Hilton International to operate and manage the hotel and the adjoining convention center, soon to be completed. Even then, the hotel continued to lose money, and he finally sold it in the fall of 1981 to a Hong Kong investor for $81 million.

"The hotel was something Bob had wanted to do for years, but it was an absolute disaster," says a former senior executive.

"That place lost as much as $7 million a year for at least three years."

In the final analysis, however, Campeau's lakefront development was a success. Although he lost money on the hotel venture, the two condominium towers joined Toronto's most fashionable residential addresses. And the first phase of the distinctive and beautiful Waterpark Place, a $75-million, twenty-six-storey tower of rose-colored granite and glass later built across the street from the condos, was rented quickly and profitably. But, perhaps even more importantly, the development vindicated the vision of Bob Campeau. He was the first to realize the potential of the waterfront and actively develop it. When it was built, the project sat alone at the foot of Toronto's Bay Street. Now the district boasts a glitzy shopping area and an antique market, and is lined with some of the most expensive condominiums in the city.

Even while conquering the Toronto waterfront, Campeau found time to dabble in a scheme reminiscent of his fling with the Blanchard dishwasher. This time it was cardboard housing, and although the idea sounds far-fetched, it almost worked.

At first Campeau Corp. wasn't involved; this was a personal investment by a man who had money to burn. Campeau sank $50,000 into a venture that would develop, manufacture and market prefabricated fiberglass-reinforced cardboard houses. The company, Panokraft Corp., would sell these inexpensive dwellings primarily in underdeveloped countries with warm climates. The entire development process took about three years, and initial surveys were taken in Africa, which they considered a major potential market.

"Bob is that kind of a guy," says a former manager familiar with the project. "He would see something and have a vision that this is it — I've gotta sell this to the world — and take it and go with it. And some of us had trouble with some of those things."

A plant was set up in Montreal, where experimental houses using the panels were built. Supporting beams were made from pieces of the reinforced cardboard that were scored, or indented, and then folded. Unfolded panels were used for the roof and walls, to which paint or a stucco-like finish could then be applied.

But there were problems. The boards were actually quite strong, but fiberglass-reinforced polyester is susceptible to fire and rain. Some progress was made on slowing the rate at which the reinforced carboard burned, but the main problem was water. Workers on the project could not properly seal the ends of the boards. The resulting water seepage led to swelling and loss of strength. John Stark, a former Campeau Corp. employee who worked on the project and whose job at the time was studying new materials on the market, believes that the water problem could have been overcome, but only at a prohibitive cost.

Before long, Campeau seems to have got cold feet. In April 1973 he sold his interest to Campeau Corp. for the price he had paid, and the company assumed bank loan guarantees of $500,000. It also advanced Panokraft $70,000 at the end of that year. There is no record that the Campeau Corp. board was bothered by this costly buyout. A year later it bought the remaining 50 percent interest in Panokraft at half price and decided to write off its research and development expenses. The bite on the company's profits amounted to almost $500,000, or 8 cents a share, in 1973, and more than $270,000, or 4 cents a share, in 1974. Campeau Corp. spent a lot of money, at shareholders' expense, trying to perfect this cardboard housing.

Campeau remained very much in charge of his company during the 1970s, but his management team was changing and, with it, his business focus. The changes were gradual, but by the end of the decade Campeau Corp. had evolved into a major force on the North American scene. And the key management players, who had almost all been French Canadian and learned the business on the spot, were gradually superseded by a group of Anglo professionals.

The first important new arrival was Ronald McCartney, who had been vice-president and general manager of Canadian Interurban and had joined the Campeau organization at the time of the merger. He stayed on after Campeau bought the company back and soon emerged as senior vice-president of development. He later succeeded Jean Paradis as Campeau Corp. president.

Joe O'Brien, who had by now become a member of the old guard, was the first to leave. In December 1972, he was offered the chance to form a new mortgage insurance company in Toronto. Still bitter over the divisions in the company during Campeau's breakdown and withdrawal, and never really accepted by the French inner circle, O'Brien decided to take the job. He asked Campeau to lunch and told his friend he was quitting.

"Why in the hell are you leaving?" Campeau asked.

"It's a chance to start a company from scratch," O'Brien replied.

"Well, if you want to do that, go start it up and come back in a year."

O'Brien never returned to the Campeau team. He is now affiliated with Canada Mortgage and Housing in Toronto as director of the NHA Mortgage-backed Securities Centre. He did not often see Campeau after he left the company but says, "I still love the guy."

The next to leave was Alban, the first of the Alfred Boys, who had been at Campeau's side for more than twenty years. He had developed a passion for horses and, in 1973, at the age of fifty-two, wanted more leisure time. So he opted for a deal under which he would run the Blue Bonnets racetrack in Montreal under a ten-year lease, although Campeau Corp. would continue to own it. Alban operated the track independently and made a success of Blue Bonnets, which by 1980 boasted the highest attendance of any track in Canada. He had finally emerged from Bob's shadow.

The next important step in the changing of the guard came in 1974, when Campeau hired David King from shopping center developer Cambridge Leaseholds. King was one of Canada's most knowledgeable people in shopping center development and would become a key strategist of the company's transition away from Ottawa and residential building. A sign of this shift was King's prompt move to a Toronto office.

By the time King arrived on the scene, Campeau's business was being forced to change by circumstances beyond his control. The overall residential market was fast eroding. As his market for single-family homes declined, Campeau began to focus more on luxury condominiums, office towers and industrial parks and to enter new markets such as western Canada and the United States.

In 1974, Campeau Corp.'s housing revenues fell to $19.6 million from $28 million in 1973, and by 1975 Robert Campeau was complaining about the effects of spiraling mortgage rates and high inflation on his housing and lumber divisions. (He now owned a lumber company in northern Quebec and a building supply operation in Ottawa.) So it was no surprise when he threw his support behind Pierre Trudeau's anti-inflation program in 1975. During 1975 and 1976, as inflation in Canada dipped to below 7 percent from levels of more than 11 percent, the housing market rebounded and Campeau's sales rallied, bouncing back to almost $66 million in 1976. But the levels could not be sustained, and in 1977 Campeau decided to consolidate some head office operations and launch a cost-cutting program, slashing his housing division by cutting staff, decreasing inventory levels and restricting the numbers of new houses to be built. That year, three architects, three draftsmen and sixty construction workers were laid off.

At the same time, Campeau began to cut back on his manufacturing operations, partly because of high production and transportation costs and partly because the demand for his products was slackening as the housing market declined and as other companies began supplying more and more of their own material.

In 1978, Campeau adopted a policy of building new homes only after they had been presold from models. He slashed housing inventories from 1,700 in 1977 to 1,160 a year later, while housing sales fell to 880 units from 1,100. Most of the units in each case were in highrise condominiums.

Not surprisingly, the next of the original Alfred Boys to go was Marcel Lalande, who was in charge of housing. He had been with the company almost twenty-five years. After a fight with

Bob, he resigned in June 1977 and joined real estate developer Costain in Ottawa.

In 1978, Bob's lieutenant, Jean Paradis, who had been close to him for many years and had served as president of the company from 1972 to 1974 and then as deputy chairman, suffered a heart attack and was forced into semi-retirement.

In December 1978, just after Paradis's heart attack, Don Carroll was brought in as executive vice-president of finance. At the accounting firm of Peat Marwick, he had handled the Campeau Corp. account for the past several years. He quickly joined Ron McCartney, now president, and David King, now executive vice-president for commercial development. With Campeau, they formed a four-man management team that orchestrated the company's accelerating departure from residential development.

By 1980, an interesting new management structure was in place at Campeau Corp. Not only had the old guard been largely replaced but the company's focus had shifted from Ottawa to Toronto, where King and Carroll were working. Soon McCartney was transferred there as well. Yet Campeau remained a phantom to the Toronto financial community, living in Ottawa.

Financial analysts liked the combination of King and Carroll; what they saw was an able and seasoned developer coupled with a proven financial manager, a strong team moving the company away from its traditions. Says Toronto securities analyst Ira Gluskin, "As long as they were there, this was a company to be looked at."

This new team was taking Campeau Corp. in a number of novel directions. Besides the development of office towers and the refurbishing of the Canadian Interurban shopping centers, the company was entering new markets. The one that grabbed Campeau's attention was the rapid expansion, begun in 1972, into the prime U.S. market.

Years later, Campeau said he had moved into the United States because Canada was overbuilt, with too many schools, too much office space and enough houses. Private enterprise, he said, worked beautifully in America. And his solution for

Canada was "fiscal responsibility and selective immigration to get the population growing again. And maybe the girls should start having babies again."

Bob Campeau does everything on a grand scale, and his move into the United States was no exception. His first acquisition was in northern California, where he scooped up 637,000 square feet in ten commercial and industrial buildings, plus ninety acres of commercial-industrial land already zoned for development. Soon he had large holdings in northern and southern California and had made inroads in Florida and Texas. By 1980 he had offices operating in all three states and owned thousands of acres of developable land, as well as income properties ranging from condos to office buildings. He had done some new building: highrise condos in Houston, Texas, and Jupiter, Florida, and office buildings in North San José and Lake Forest, California, and in Palm Beach Gardens, Florida. As the eighties got underway, he was poised to build on many fronts.

You could build big in the United States without someone like Charlotte Whitton breathing down your neck. There would be no Place-de-Ville-style fights here. So he built a forty-two-storey office tower in San Francisco and another in Houston. And there were plans for an eighty-storey tower, also in Houston.

Robert Campeau was making up for lost time. Other major Canadian developers had been in the United States for years. By 1981, about 60 percent of Daon Development Corp.'s total assets were held in the United States, followed by Cadillac-Fairview and Costain at 45 percent, Carma developers at 35 percent and then Campeau Corp. at about 25 percent. As David King said a few years later: "We were three to six years behind competitors in entering markets in western Canada, California, Texas and Florida, but these markets are growing so aggressively that it didn't matter when we came to town." At least, it didn't matter until the recession of 1981.

It is interesting to note that, even with David King and his successful background in developing shopping centers, Campeau did little in this area in the 1970s. He emerged from the

Power Corp. buyback with an impressive portfolio of shopping center properties — a ready-made business — yet did not take it much further in the years that immediately followed. Securities analysts still wonder why, with shopping center development such a lucrative business and housing revenues on the decline, Campeau did not do more.

"In 1976, let's say Trizec had six, Cadillac-Fairview had eight and Bramalea had four," says Ira Gluskin. "Now, twelve years later, those other guys have shopping centers all over the place. Campeau doesn't have that many more. Where was he? He missed the whole boom. Why? Because I don't think he understood the business, paid attention; he had no interest."

Bob Campeau always paid attention to who owned his company, though. And throughout the 1970s he kept a firm grip on its ownership. He had learned his lesson from the Desmarais deal. In 1972, in order to secure interim financing from the Bank of Nova Scotia that would allow construction to start on the Harbour Castle Hotel project, Campeau asked his senior executives to grant him the right to vote their shares. It was a bizarre bank financing agreement, and at least some of these people were not told why Campeau had to have control.

"I know that Bob was quite concerned after we'd become public and we had collectively a fair number of shares, and I guess he didn't want any of us to start flooding the market with those shares," says one of the former executives. "If all of us collectively decided to unload our stock in the marketplace, it could have a tremendous impact on the price of the shares."

About one year later, the company created a new class of 1 million shares, all of which were sold to Campeau for $200,000 to bring his personal voting control up to about 66 percent. Since this eliminated the need for his agreement with his executives, the voting rights Campeau had acquired reverted to them.

In 1977, when his housing travails began and Campeau Corp. stock was trading at levels far below the original issue price of $10, Campeau decided that the company should buy back shares from the public. They were dirt cheap in August 1977, trading at between $3.70 and $4.40, and it was a good opportunity to take stock out of the public's hands. He offered initially to take up the stock at $5.50 a share, but an independent appraisal, which was required by securities regulators in Ontario, put the net asset value at at least $22.63 a share, and one securities analyst called the offer an "insult." So Campeau boosted the price to $7. But some analysts still advised their clients not to sell. Stockholders were given the choice of taking the cash for their Class A shares or converting them to another class of stock. The buyback scheme succeeded — shareholders approved the plan — and Campeau Corp., though it did not go completely private, took a lot of stock out of the hands of the public.

The share buyback scheme may have been good for Campeau Corp., but it was not good for minority shareholders. William Pershaw, for example, had bought 100 shares for $1,000 when Campeau Corp. went public in 1969. His son had been working on the site of the Skyline Hotel at Place de Ville and told him about the stock offer. A life insurance policy for $1,000 had just come due and this seemed like a good place to invest the money. An inexperienced investor, Pershaw did not seek a stockbroker's advice. He later told a reporter, "I figured if the wife gets a fur coat there's nothing in the pot." So Pershaw gave Bob Campeau $1,000 to help him pay off the debt on the Harbour Castle land. Eight years later, having been paid dividends of less than 1 percent a year, Pershaw got back just $700. So he had lost $300 and whatever interest he could have made had he put the money in the bank.

After the buyback, Campeau Corp. was delisted on the Toronto and Montreal stock exchanges. The company was 90 percent owned by Bob Campeau and his senior executives. Within four years, the stock was trading over the counter at $16.50.

Although Campeau's business focus was increasingly moving

out of Ottawa, he continued to live there throughout the 1970s. One reason may have been that it allowed him to stay close to Jacques and Danny.

Clauda, though, may have found him too close for comfort. Early in the decade, in what seems on the surface a rather callous act, Bob had built a $600,000 home in Dunrobin, just about a mile to the east of where his ex-wife still lived in their old house. This new mansion, which he called Stoneayre because of its fieldstone walls, sat on a hill overlooking the river. It was a large home well set back from the road, with an indoor pool — the lounge chairs had built-in stereo headphones — and maid's quarters upstairs. Its wine cellar was well stocked with imported champagne.

Clauda and Bob would sometimes pass each other on the unpaved road near their homes, or she would run across him at social gatherings. There was no tension, friends say, and Clauda, though bitter, was proud of Bob and his accomplishments.

The breakup had been hard on the children. Danny, still a teenager, moved into the new house with his father and Ilse, who in October 1973 had given birth to a third child, Jan Paul. Jacques, who was studying business administration at Algonquin College, stayed with his mother, still angry with his father for what he had done. Jacques said several years later: "The distance between father and I started growing when he realized I preferred living with my mom. I loved my mother. I knew the kinds of things he was doing. But he convinced Danny to go live with him." Nonetheless, at his mother's urging he joined Campeau Corp. in 1974 and eventually became president Ron McCartney's assistant.

The trappings of money were now extravagantly evident in Bob Campeau's lifestyle. He and Ilse entertained lavishly — Pierre Trudeau was a guest at their Stoneayre parties — and took exotic vacations. They often went skiing and occasionally visited spas in Europe. One of the vacation spots they frequented was a large hunting and fishing retreat on about thirty square miles of virgin wilderness some twenty minutes by floatplane from Roberval, Quebec (several hundred miles from Quebec City). The land was owned by Gagnon Frères, a lumber company Campeau had purchased in 1969. On it he had put several chalet-style buildings, including a large central dining room and several cabins. Here he hunted moose, bears, wolves, pheasants and partridges, although he does not like to be seen as someone who slaughters animals: "I only kill one moose a year. Did you know the meat is low in cholesterol? We do love moose meat."

Ilse's sister Hilde recalls one occasion when the hunter became the hunted. "He was once jogging down from the camp where we were sleeping to the camp where we were eating, where the staff prepares the meals. It was one mile apart, and we used to take that mile in a truck because we were told by the guide that there were lots of bears around. If fishing parties were there, there was garbage created, and that's what bears love. But he wouldn't listen, and he jogged down the lane. And he was about halfway down to the next cabin and encountered this big black bear. Fortunately, the black bear must have just had a good fill at the dump, so he decided to dump Mr. Campeau and not eat him. We were all sitting at the breakfast table when the door flew open with a big explosion and Mr. Campeau scrambled in, and he was foaming from the mouth, telling us his experience — where he suddenly confronted, a few feet away from him, this big black bear who gave a few grunts and got up on his hind paws. He took a close look at him and then decided he was not the right meal."

In the late 1970s, Campeau bought from Paul Desmarais a chalet atop Mont Gabriel, in the Laurentians. It was near a ski resort but was secluded and featured a private ski run under one of the balconies. He, Ilse and the children spent many a winter weekend there. Campeau often sat in the comfortable living room, reading one of the historical biographies on which he doted.

Such vacation spots offered an opportunity for Campeau, ever conscious of his health and appearance, to indulge his passion for exercise. He still swam, jogged, played golf and tennis and did strenuous calisthenics. Even today, he swims about a mile and a half five times a week when at home. Recalls

Hilde: "He used to do push-ups and everything when I lived with him and Ilse. I was still in a deep sleep and I was woken up because the whole house was shaking. He's a fanatic when it comes to exercises and health." According to his old friend Joe O'Brien, "He wanted always to be in great shape. We were jogging all the time, and he was very proud of looking and being a good skiier and being a good golfer and being in good physical shape and looking young."

But no fitness regimen could combat wrinkles or thinning hair, the inescapable signs of aging. Bob was particularly concerned about his hair loss and, in the late seventies, bought his first toupee. Jean-Marc Prud'Homme remembers this hairpiece as being less than flattering. One day, he walked into a meeting with a few other men, not having seen Bob for several days. He did a double-take when he entered the room.

"Hey, what happened to you?" everyone kidded Bob.

"Well, what do you think of it?" Bob asked.

"It's not the best."

Soon Campeau bought a toupee that suited him better, but life was not without its embarrassing moments.

Campeau used to take his vice-presidents and their spouses for weekend retreats at a Lake Placid resort. At one such retreat, David King (then president of the company) and his wife, Bev, were having breakfast at Campeau's table with a few others. Doing her best to make small talk, Bev asked, "Did you see the guy out there at the pool this morning with a bathing cap on?"

There was silence until Campeau broke it.

"That was me, Bev," he said.

The silence resumed until she broke it, apparently unaware of her gaffe.

"Why were you wearing it?"

Campeau's answer, if any, has been lost.

Campeau later sported a wig with curls, but eventually opted for hair transplants. Then there were facelifts, part of his campaign to look as young as his fitness regime was stringent. Employees of the company in the late 1970s and early 1980s recall Campeau being away from the office for long periods and returning with some evidence of a hair transplant. Says one former executive: "He doesn't make this common knowledge around the office. He doesn't come back and say, 'Blah, blah, blah,' but he goes away on holidays, to Europe on a number of occasions, and I gather he has them done there. It's quite evident when you have a hair transplant done, these little plugs on your head."

Campeau also became involved with homeopathy, an alternative system of medicine in which the patient takes infinitesimal doses of a substance that would in larger doses produce the symptoms of the disease treated. Some family members believe that Campeau sees such remedies as rejuvenation tonics and goes to European spas for the same reason. One of them says he has always been concerned with death, and that the deaths of those around him have affected him deeply: "He just can't come to grips with death, I think. He can't understand why he can't buy his way out of having to die."

The late 1970s were a period of upheaval in Campeau's family life. Despite the divorce from Clauda, he remained the head of the extended family. When his brother-in-law Matte, Beatrice's husband, was struck by lung cancer, Bob arranged to fly him and Beatrice to Germany so he could be treated. Matte died in 1977, and Bob soon gave Beatrice the first installment of a $25,000 gift that would be spread over five years.

At the same time, Len Graham and Rachelle were having marital problems, which precipitated Len's departure from the company in 1976. He and Rachelle separated two years later and were eventually divorced. Rachelle eventually married Robert Archambault.

And Clauda was coming out of her shell. In 1973 she began seeing David Smith, an extroverted Ottawa restaurateur who had earned the nickname "Caterer to the Stars" because he hobnobbed with the likes of Liberace and Shirley MacLaine. Smith owned Nate's Deli and the adjoining steakhouse, The Place Next Door, on Rideau Street. Divorced and eight years Clauda's junior, he met her at a party he was catering, thrown by one of Clauda's friends. Clauda mentioned that she was

having guests to lunch the next day, so Dave wrapped up two
cakes for her to take home. They did not get together for
another year, when Clauda happened to be in the restaurant
with some friends.

Dave recognized Clauda, ambled over and, as is his nature,
soon got the group laughing. Clauda invited him back to the
Dunrobin house, and a week later he asked her out for dinner.
Soon they grew close.

As Dave remembers it, they always had fun together.
Clauda was full of surprises. He recalls getting lost on a back
road on the way home to Ottawa from a friend's cottage on the
Quebec side of the river. His friend had given him directions,
but he had not been paying attention and did not know which
way to go when they came to a fork in the road. He had no idea
where he was, it was the middle of the night, and he was
peeved.

"I think this is a fuck-up," Clauda said.

Dave laughed harder than he had in a long time. He had
never heard this proper lady swear before.

On one occasion, Dave took Clauda to Manotick Marina to
buy a boat. They spotted a twenty-foot runabout, a day cruiser
with an inboard motor and a price tag of about $13,000.

"Do you like it?" Clauda asked.

"Yeah, for what we need, it's a great boat."

Clauda was about to write a cheque, but Dave stopped
her.

"What are you doing?" he asked.

"I'm buying the boat."

"Wait a minute. You just don't do things like that."

Dave grabbed her hand as the salesman shot him a dirty
look, and he took her outside.

"Clauda, you can't pay $13,000," he said. "That's what he's
asking. Let's see what we can get it for."

"If it was $12,000, he would say $12,000," she replied.

"There's no harm in trying. Come on." Dave led her back
inside.

"Listen, the boat's great," he said to the salesman. "But it's
only worth $9,500."

"You're crazy," the salesman said. "It cost me more than $9,500."

"Fine, that's all I want to pay. Come on, Clauda, let's go."

Clauda wanted the boat, but relented and followed him out. As they were climbing into the car, the salesman ran out after them and invited them back inside to talk. They eventually bought the boat for $10,300.

Clauda liked this game. Some time later, Dave arrived at the Dunrobin house and an excited Clauda ran to show him two expensive dresses she had bought that day.

"Did I get myself a deal," she exclaimed. "I told the salesman I would pay full price on the one and half price on the other. So he let me have it for that."

Clearly, whatever her feelings about Bob, Clauda was ready to move on with her life. Perhaps she would even have married Dave. But fate intervened. In the mid-seventies, Clauda had been diagnosed with breast cancer, and one of her breasts was removed. But the cancer spread, and in the late seventies she was having a rough time with chemotherapy treatments. Dave was there to provide strong moral support; his charm and happy-go-lucky ways brought joy to Clauda's life as she battled the disease. He brought Liberace to her home in Dunrobin and introduced her to Ginger Rogers and Luciano Pavarotti. Liberace and Pavarotti, Dave recalls, adored Clauda.

In 1979, Clauda and Dave decided to take a month-long vacation in Europe — Paris, the French and Italian Riviera, Venice and the Greek islands. Shortly after their return to Ottawa, she was admitted to hospital. Dave visited a couple of times a day. At one point she seemed to improve and actually went home, but the reprieve was brief. During Clauda's final days, Dave sat in her hospital room and they talked about the possibility of buying a home together, closer to the city. But Dave is sure that Clauda knew it would never come to pass.

One day, Gilbert's daughter Nicole came to visit her aunt in hospital and spied the flowers Bob had sent.

"Oh, *ma tante*, he's so mean, sending you flowers after what he did to you," Nicole said.

"Don't talk like that, Nicole," Clauda said. "He's a good

man, a sensitive man, and he's always been good when I've been sick or needed anything."

Dave Smith was holding Clauda when she died that April.

Jacques was deeply affected by his mother's death, the anger he felt toward his father rekindled. Soon after Clauda died, he quit the company.

Clauda's death coincided with the end of an era at Campeau Corp. With Jacques's departure, Danny was the only member of Bob's immediate family still at the company, and the old inner circle was all but gone. Gilbert had been diagnosed with cancer a couple of years earlier and had gone on disability. Jean-Marc Prud'Homme retired. Eugène Lavigne, already suffering from kidney troubles, had a heart attack in March 1980 and never returned to work. Ray Larocque, the last of the Alfred Boys, retired not long after. Only Clem Cadieux, now senior vice-president of special projects, remained from the inner circle of the 1950s. It was a whole new company that prepared to meet the 1980s.

12 / Taking On the Old Boys

*"I'll stop you, Campeau, and my friends are
going to be on my side."*
— Kenneth White

BOB CAMPEAU COULD not have known in the spring of 1980, as
he was shopping for a suitable company to take over, that he
was preparing for a battle the likes of which he had never
fought before. He could not possibly have anticipated the
ferocity with which Toronto's business elite would come to the
aid of one of their own to fight off an upstart outsider.

Admittedly, the multimillion-dollar fight for Royal Trustco was not Campeau's first clash with the Toronto establishment, but it would be by far the most bruising. In the fall of
1973 he had attempted his first hostile takeover, in this case a
company called Markborough Properties, a medium-sized
developer whose major project was the 3,200-acre Meadowvale
in Mississauga, just outside Toronto. The company also held
180 acres in Whitby, to the east of Toronto, and 860 acres in
Markham, to the northeast. A takeover would give Campeau a
ready-made presence in Toronto, substantially boosting his
exposure in that market. Except for the harbor lands and a few
Canadian Interurban properties acquired from Power Corp.,
Campeau had no holdings in Toronto in 1973.

On October 16, 1973, Markborough shares were trading on
the Toronto and Montreal exchanges at about $10 each when
Campeau launched a $64-million takeover bid with financing
from the Bank of Nova Scotia. He offered $16 each for all 4
million shares, a fair but not overly generous bid. One day later,

he agreed to buy 356,000 shares at $16 each, or about $5.7 million, from three corporate shareholders, and thereby handily secured almost 10 percent of the stock in one fell swoop.

Markborough's board of directors immediately urged stockholders to reject the Campeau bid because the offer did not reflect the true value of the shares. "We believe that 1973 will mark the crossing of the threshold to years of substantial profits and cash flows," the company wrote in a letter to its shareholders. "In the years prior to 1973 much of the company's resources and energies were spent developing its principal asset, Meadowvale, and the company is just now beginning to reap the benefits of this work."

There is no question that Campeau would have been getting his money's worth. Markborough's assets were estimated that year at about $104 million, and revenues at about $35 million. In a directors' circular to stockholders, the company said it had conducted a study that indicated its pretax asset value was about $27 a share and after-tax value was $17 a share. Taking over Markborough would thus be a lot cheaper than buying the equivalent amount of land and other assets on the open market.

Hudson's Bay Co. obviously agreed with Markborough's self-assessment. On Saturday, November 17, it entered the fray with a bid of $17.50 a share, or about $70 million. Hours later Campeau moved to $18.50 a share, or about $74 million.

The several institutions and companies that owned the majority of Markborough stock liked Campeau's offer and agreed to sell. The shares tendered to the bid or owned by Campeau Corp. comprised 57.9 percent of the stock. Campeau that Friday night held a party in the Skyline Hotel in Place de Ville to celebrate his apparent conquest.

But at 3:30 P.M. the following Monday, Hudson's Bay came back with a $19-a-share offer worth roughly $76 million. Campeau maintained that the shares that already had been tendered to his bid could not be withdrawn. For all practical purposes, he owned Markborough.

But there was a dispute between Campeau and tendering

stockholders over whether they were allowed to withdraw their shares. Immediately after Hudson's Bay raised its bid, people started demanding their shares back. The matter was set to go to the Supreme Court of Ontario when Campeau decided to back down and withdraw his bid. He said later he decided to bow out because of the uncertainties of litigation and the effect of a court fight on Markborough's small shareholders who had tendered. And a higher bid, he said, could not have been justified.

Campeau covered his expenses and even made a small profit by selling Hudson's Bay the shares he had already purchased. But he would not forget this defeat. "On Friday we had the company and we celebrated, and then on the Monday we didn't have it anymore," recalls a former executive. "The Markborough deal was in his hands, and I don't think Bob has ever forgiven Bay Street boys for that."

He could not blame Bay Street for his next rebuff, this time an attempt to acquire Bushnell Communications, the owner of Ottawa television station CJOH and two cable television operators. One year after the Markborough setback he arranged to buy almost 1 million shares of Bushnell — about 52 percent of the stock — at $10.50 each from Western Broadcasting Corp., which had been ordered by the Canadian Radio-Television Commission to sell its shares. Campeau said he saw Bushnell purely as an investment, although neither the broadcast nor the real estate industries could figure out why exactly he wanted it. The *Financial Post* wrote that in an interview, Jean Paradis had appeared concerned that the takeover not be misconstrued as "an ego trip for Robert Campeau."

There was no hostile management this time, and no rival bidder. There was just the CRTC, the federal regulator that had to approve all changes in ownership in the broadcast industry. The CRTC rejected the takeover. In its ruling, the commission said it was not satisfied that Campeau had "considered adequately and made provision for the obligations and responsibilities inherent in the operation of Bushnell's various broadcasting undertakings." The agency also ruled that

Campeau failed to satisfy concerns that his real estate interests could interfere with the "responsibilities of broadcasters to provide balanced opportunity for the expression of differing views on matters of public concern" such as housing and land policy.

Campeau's next move, in 1979, was against a U.S. company, and the $25-million bid was made through Campeau Corp.'s 60-percent owned affiliate Johncamp Realty Inc. The target was Prudent Real Estate Trust of New York, which owned ten apartment complexes, three shopping centers and two small office buildings in ten states and in Ontario. Prudent fought the bid, but Campeau succeeded and won a majority of the stock.

It was a relatively small acquisition, and one that was outside Canada, where Campeau had twice been rebuffed. But Bob Campeau is not one to be easily discouraged or to lower his expectations. His next target was far bigger than even Markborough and back on home turf. In 1980, Royal Trustco was Canada's largest trust company and thus one of the country's most powerful financial institutions. It fit Campeau's specifications; he had been looking for a major acquisition, possibly real estate, possibly a financial institution, in an attempt to diversify. And, obviously, Campeau enjoyed the thrill of the hunt.

Campeau set his sights on Royal Trustco almost by accident. In July 1980 he held a series of meetings with George Mann, the president of Unicorp Financial Corp., to discuss buying into some real estate investment trusts Unicorp had formed in the United States. During the meeting Mann pointed out to Campeau that Unicorp also owned about 5 percent of Royal Trustco.

This 5 percent became the cornerstone of Campeau's takeover bid. He made a deal with Unicorp that committed the company to selling him its shares if he was successful. He in turn was committed to paying Unicorp the equivalent of his final per-share offer to Royal Trustco shareholders. In this way Campeau tied up 5 percent of Royal Trustco's stock before there was any indication of his intentions.

In the event Campeau's bid failed, his deal with Unicorp provided him with some insurance. For two months following an unsuccessful bid, Unicorp could not sell any of its shares without Campeau's approval and was required to pay him half the profits if it did. Furthermore, if within the same two-month period an offer was made to Royal Trustco's shareholders for at least $20 a share — the shares were currently trading in the $14 - $16 range — Unicorp could be required to sell its shares. This meant that if a rival bidder appeared and knocked Campeau out, he would still make money, as would Unicorp.

Campeau was essentially proposing a leveraged buyout, acquiring a company with borrowed money and enabling his much smaller Campeau Corp. to take over a far larger concern. In the majority of such takeovers, the target company's assets are used as security for the loans, which are repaid out of its cash flow or in part by selling off some of its assets. To finance the takeover bid, Campeau had arranged a seven-year loan from the Bank of Nova Scotia at one percentage point over prime; the security would be the Royal Trustco shares that were tendered. Campeau planned to service the debt partly with the dividends on the Royal Trustco shares.

Royal Trustco Ltd. was very English Canadian and very rich. Opened in 1899, it had become one of the pillars of the Anglo Montreal financial community. After the Parti Québécois came to power in 1976, it joined the corporate exodus to Toronto, where it maintained its executive offices. By 1980, it owned almost $7.5 billion in assets, compared to Campeau Corp.'s less than $1 billion, administered some $19 billion in estates, trusts and agency accounts and held more than $7 billion in deposits. In addition, it was the country's largest residential real estate broker. At its helm was Lieutenant-Colonel Kenneth White, sixty-six years old and every bit as English and Establishment as the trust firm he controlled.

Campeau had been introduced to White about fourteen years before by his friend Joe O'Brien, who then worked at Royal Trustco in Ottawa. O'Brien figured it would be a good idea if his boss Ken White, then president of the trust company, met the successful developer: it could lead to some type of business interaction. So he arranged a lunch at the Beaver Club in the Queen Elizabeth Hotel in Montreal. White and Campeau had little in common, though, and the meeting had been a failure.

O'Brien believes the problem was White, not Campeau: "I thought Bob handled himself very well at the lunch because he did a lot of reading and he was well-spoken. He had a lot of ideas, but I left the lunch feeling that Ken wasn't impressed. I think it was just — and this was the thing that Bob was bucking through these years — that he was not Establishment. And that was the thing that really made it tough for him everywhere. He really didn't care. That's one of the traits of Bob's personality. He was not going to try and ingratiate himself. Here was a French Canadian guy, no formal education, who Ken didn't think belonged."

This time Kenneth White would not so easily dismiss Bob Campeau. In late August 1980, after cutting his deal with George Mann and Unicorp, Campeau phoned White and tried to arrange a meeting. He did not disclose what he wanted to discuss.

"I want to see you before the twenty-seventh," Campeau said. "It's important."

"I'm going to be in Montreal on the Friday," White replied. "I can see you then."

"I'd like to see you before," said Campeau.

"Well, call me back," was White's response.

For the next several days, Campeau tried unsuccessfully to reach White again, then decided to show up on his doorstep. But first he phoned William Mulholland, the president and chief executive officer of the Bank of Montreal. It was about 10:30 at night and Mulholland was at his home in Montreal. Campeau and Mulholland had a meeting scheduled for the next day.

"I want to postpone tomorrow's meeting until the afternoon," Campeau told the bank president.

"Fine, I haven't got my schedule, but we'll work it out," Mulholland replied. "Come by whenever you want."

"I want to talk to you about the takeover." Campeau simply dropped this into the conversation.

"Yes?"

"It's Royal Trustco."

"Stop!" Mulholland interrupted. "We have a conflict of interest. You probably know we're Royal Trustco's bankers and we're also shareholders. You should not divulge your plans to me unless you care to in the light of our relationship with Royal Trustco."

"Would you feel you had to call White right away and relate to him what I'm saying?" Campeau said.

"No," Mulholland countered.

"Well, I want to tell you what we are doing," Campeau continued. "We're going to announce a takeover bid in the morning and we hope to secure White's cooperation."

He told Mulholland that Campeau Corp. wanted to buy the Bank of Montreal's shares. At the time, it was believed the bank held some 10 percent of Royal Trustco and was its largest shareholder.

"Do you think that I should go and see White or should I call him? Campeau asked.

"In my opinion, if you're serious about wanting to secure his cooperation, I certainly would not break the news just over the phone to him," Mulholland responded. "I'd try to see him and at least do him the courtesy of discussing it with him face-to-face."

The following morning, Wednesday, August 27, Campeau flew to Sherbrooke, Quebec, and called White at his summer home near Bromont in the Eastern Townships. He told the Royal Trustco chairman he was coming over, and White agreed to meet. Not that he could have stopped him.

Campeau's taxi driver waited outside the gate as the two men sat on the lawn, making small talk over coffee for about twenty minutes. Then Campeau told White he was preparing to launch a $413-million takeover bid that afternoon.

"We don't plan to change management," Campeau told Royal Trustco's stunned CEO. "We don't want to get involved in the fiduciary part of the company or in the mortgage part.

But we *do* want to have two or three members on the board and we want to be involved in the development of the real estate arm. Commercial real estate."

White was obviously concentrating on something else as he responded. "We haven't been able to pierce the commercial real estate market very well," he said, "but on retail we're very successful."

"That's the contribution we think we can make," Campeau went on. "You're administering pension funds, you want to get into real estate, and this would be a good opportunity. We've decided this is a good fit. And as far as I'm concerned, you will remain chief executive of the corporation. I've known you for a long time and I understand you're sixty-three. I think you're a young sixty-three. I think you're managing this company well. You can retire whenever you want to. I'm sure when the time to retire comes, you yourself would want to step down. That would be up to you."

(In fact, White was sixty-six.)

"You know, you may not be getting the company that you think you'll be getting." White was growing angry. "There are an awful lot of things in this company that you may not be aware of, and just looking at it may be cosmetic, and you're getting yourself involved in something that you really don't think you are getting involved in."

"Do you feel that the price is a good price?" Campeau asked.

"Yes, it's a good price, but it's a lot of money for those shares," White replied.

Campeau then told White that Unicorp had already agreed to sell its 5 percent and that he had agreed to pay either in Campeau Corp. shares or in cash the same amount as the final offering price under his bid. By this point White had had enough.

"I don't see why you don't go and take over something else," he told Campeau. "Really, this is my company."

"It may be your company, but we're making an offer to the shareholders," Campeau responded firmly. "I don't see where this is going to disrupt your role in the corporation whatsoever."

"I'm telling you right now," White spluttered, "I won't work for you and if this bid is successful, I'm going to quit. And I really don't like you, Campeau, and I don't like Paul Desmarais and I don't like Conrad Black and I don't like Edgar Bronfman. I don't like all these guys making bids for public corporations, and I wish to hell you would stay where you are and don't bother us. This is really going to complicate the Bank Act, and it's really not helping the French Canadian and English Canadian situation."

"What do you mean by that?" Campeau asked, becoming angry himself. "Our money is money, isn't it? I don't see the point in that at all."

"Look, I'm telling you now that you should pull this bid."

"I came down here to tell you that we *are* going to make a bid, and the bid is going to be announced by noon," Campeau insisted. "I wish I could have told you a week ago. But we are certainly going to go ahead with it."

"Well, it will not be successful," White shot back. He was plotting strategy as he spoke.

"You may want to go and get a white knight," Campeau responded. "But I've known you for a long time, and you may not get a white knight. Of course, if a white knight bids more money, we would have to examine that, but I think we have concluded here that the price is fair, and I feel there is no reason why we couldn't get along very well."

(A white knight is a company that is invited by the target of a hostile takeover to come to its rescue with a friendly bid to buy the shares of the target company.)

"There isn't going to be any white knight!" snapped White. "I'm going to stop it. I'm going to call my friends and I'm going to lock up 51 percent of this stock before you can turn around. You may think, or you may tell me, money talks. And really, in the end, shareholders are going to make up their minds. But I'm telling you that I have got ways to persuade these friends of mine to go along with me, and they *will*. I think this conversation is pretty well over."

With that, White grabbed Campeau's arm, escorted him to the gate and threw him off the property.

"You should pull the bid," White repeated. "Pull that damn bid!"

"I'm sorry, Ken. We are not going to pull the bid. The bid is going to go ahead."

White headed back toward the house and, turning suddenly, he shouted, "I'm getting on the phone now, I'm getting my team together and we're going to stop you. It's *my* company. I'll stop you, Campeau, and my friends are going to be on my side."

That afternoon, Campeau announced in a press release his $413-million takeover bid, consisting of $21 a share for common stock and $29.93 each for preferred shares, conditional on his obtaining 51 percent. The offer was set to expire September 19, leaving three weeks for shareholders to tender their stock. Executive vice-president Don Carroll would be the chief architect on the Campeau team.

Campeau said in his offering document that he planned no major changes to the company or its management. He said he would conduct a review of operations that would focus on ways Campeau Corp. could help in Royal Trustco's real estate business. But, as Royal Trustco would soon point out to its shareholders, Campeau had not obtained the approval from U.S. regulatory authorities necessary to acquire Royal Trustco's American subsidiaries. Therefore a successful Campeau bid under those circumstances could force him to divest the trust company's sizable U.S. banking operations, seven Florida banks, which accounted for 4 percent of its total assets under administration.

Shortly after the takeover announcement, Campeau arrived at Mulholland's office at Bank of Montreal headquarters in Montreal.

"It didn't go very well," Campeau said.

"I gathered that," Mulholland said. "He just left here."

"Was he unhappy?"

"He was very unhappy."

"I guess he's going to fight us."

"He's going to fight you tooth and nail."

Campeau later told securities regulators that he expected a fight but had not taken seriously White's threat: "The threat Mr. White made to me, that he was going to stop the bid — I couldn't believe that. I couldn't get that through my head. I had never seen that and I did suspect, however, that he was going to get to work and get a white knight."

The Mulholland-Campeau meeting that day lasted two hours, a rambling conversation that included about thirty minutes devoted to moose hunting. Mulholland made it clear that the Bank of Montreal was not prepared to sell its shares. Campeau had already arranged financing with the Bank of Nova Scotia, but he told Mulholland, presumably in an attempt to secure his support, that he could arrange for the Bank of Montreal to join in and finance half the deal if he wished. Mulholland replied that it was the bank's policy not to finance hostile takeovers involving major clients.

Mulholland realized that Campeau believed that a French-English contest was involved here — something to the effect that an English cabal would try to defeat him. The bank president told him that was not the case.

"I recall pointing out to him a lot of people, who would have no objection otherwise to what he was doing, would have very serious reservations about the desirability of any person or company obtaining unilateral sole control of an institution like Royal Trustco, including me," Mulholland told the 1981 Ontario Securities Commission hearings into the Royal Trustco affair. "And a lot of people, who he might find unsympathetic to his bid, would probably feel more comfortable if that was not one of the conditions he was insisting on, absolute control of the Royal Trustco as part of his plan . . . I was trying to explain to him that there were a lot of people, in perfectly good faith, who had very serious reservations about that aspect. And it didn't mean that they were part of some club that is sometimes referred to as the Westmount Gang, or that they did not like French Canadians or something like that."

Campeau disagrees. "Kenneth White just doesn't like French people. If my name had been MacDonald, it would have been a completely different story. What happened was that the remnants of the Westmount business establishment, who are now in Toronto and are feeling pretty sore about French people, organized to keep me out."

He later said: "It was the first French Canadian attack on a major financial institution controlled by Anglo-Saxons. There were two fights. One was because an English Montreal guy didn't want to see a French Canadian own it, and then there was a battle between owners and managers."

White maintains that his defense was in no way connected with French-English divisions and that Campeau blew it out of proportion by interpreting it thus. Says White: "We had a business the ownership of which should not be in the hands of somebody who is doing exactly what he's doing today, dismantling businesses for the purposes of the real estate or whatever. He told me how he was going to take over the company. It had had nothing to do with being French Canadian. It was a raid on the company."

There may be merit to the argument that a financial institution should not be controlled by one person, but there was a very personal element to White's response to Campeau's bid. Says Joe O'Brien: "Here was Ken with this big establishment institution, the largest trust company in the country, and to think of Bob Campeau owning it just drove Ken out of his mind."

Whatever the accuracy of Campeau's assertions, the events of August 27, 1980, set in motion a battle that pitted him against some of English Canada's most powerful companies and banks. The debate would continue for years over whether it was a fight between English and French, Establishment and outsider, or a fight to keep majority control of a financial institution out of the hands of one large stockholder. Whatever the case, it was a terrific fight.

After Campeau put the ball in play, White called a Royal Trustco special board meeting for 2 P.M. on the following Tuesday. Royal Trustco needed someone to organize the defense and act as strategist. That man turned out to be Austin Taylor, the 325-pound chairman of investment dealer McLeod Young Weir, an able man from a Vancouver mining family who had trained in New York with investment firm Morgan Stanley. Taylor once said that his father gave him little advice in life except to "never sell your Royal Trust shares." As soon as the takeover rumors reached his Montreal office, Taylor, whose company was Royal Trustco's investment broker, had called John Scholes, Royal Trustco's chief operating officer.

Taylor flew from Montreal to Toronto later the day the takeover was announced and met with Scholes and other Royal Trustco executives that night. White was still in Quebec. They discussed the Campeau bid and any legislation that might apply, but it was not a major strategy session. Thursday and Friday the meetings continued, this time with Ken White in attendance. At these sessions they discussed various defences, such as a friendly merger with another company or launching a counterbid for Royal Trustco stock. Taylor believed they did not have enough time to line up a proper candidate with which to merge. By Friday afternoon, nothing had been decided, so the key players — White, Scholes and Taylor — arranged to meet again on Saturday. Presumably they wanted to have a strategy in place before the markets reopened on Tuesday, after the Labor Day long weekend.

As strategy was being plotted in private, the war was already heating up in the media. White called a news conference on the Thursday and declared: "I will not work for Robert Campeau." One day later, Campeau responded with a news conference in the Bank of Nova Scotia building in downtown Toronto. He told reporters he had been planning this for months and was trying to diversify. He dismissed concerns over a single company owning a financial institution the size of Royal Trustco and said he did not feel combines officials should become involved. "We do not want to have any mix-up between the two industries," he said. "In our decision, we placed particular importance on the large residential real estate arm. It has one of the largest residential real estate operations in North America. What we are interested in doing is moving Royal Trust further into the commercial field, a little faster than it now appears to be going. We feel we can make a real input to help them get into commercial real estate and the management of property.

"In the end," he added, "it will not be the color of my eyes or of Ken White's that will make up shareholders' minds. It's how good the offer is."

Royal Trustco soon took out full-page advertisements in newspapers across Canada appealing to anyone with a mortgage or invested savings and contributors to pension funds. The ads declared: "The attempt to take over Royal Trust concerns over one million Canadians and twenty-six billion dollars of their savings and investments." Bob Campeau responded with his own ads. Said Toronto securities analyst Ira Gluskin at the time: "Ken White elevated it almost immediately into a holy war, pitting the sacred trust of widows and orphans against a development mogul." An interesting approach, considering the development mogul in this case was David and Royal Trust the Goliath.

White and Scholes had been busy on two fronts since Campeau's Wednesday announcement. They did not yet have a defense strategy, but they had been busy canvasing support among major shareholders. Some, such as Stelco, called up White as soon as they heard what Campeau was doing and pledged not to tender. In other cases, White or Scholes made the first move. For instance, Scholes met with Thomas Galt, chairman of Sun Life Assurance. Not only did Sun Life own a lot of Royal Trustco stock, four Sun Life directors also served on the Royal Trustco board. (The day after White met with his board, he knew Sun Life was prepared to buy up to $10 million in Royal Trustco stock. Before the battle was over, Sun Life purchased 685,961 shares, or 3.51 percent, and owned in total more than 930,000 shares, or almost 5 percent.)

White personally went to work on Russell Harrison, chairman and chief executive officer of the Canadian Imperial

Bank of Commerce. He phoned Harrison at home, indicating that he would appreciate any help. (Although the Commerce did nothing at first, by the September 19 deadline it had purchased 516,000 common shares for about $10 million.) White also took advantage of his position as chairman of the board of Commercial Union Assurance Co. He contacted Commercial's investment manager, Robin Denman, who promised not to tender his shares. (Over the long weekend, Denman decided he would help while increasing his holdings to 1 percent.)

On a second front, on August 28 and 29, Royal Trustco purchased 352,110 of its common shares and 33,600 preferreds for its pension fund through McLeod Young Weir for more than $8 million. It then decided to sell those shares to Sun Life.

In sum, Royal Trustco was trying to keep whatever stock it could out of Campeau's hands. The battle was warming up.

Meanwhile, the Bank of Montreal was moving to Royal Trustco's defense, although there is no evidence it did so at White's request. Mulholland quickly ascertained that the bank owned only 8 percent of Royal Trustco shares and ordered his men to buy the total up to the 10 percent ceiling the Bank Act permitted a bank to hold of a trust company. (By September 3, the Bank of Montreal would purchase the equivalent of 519,043 common shares for more than $10 million to hold the maximum 10 percent.)

On Saturday, August 30, Austin Taylor of McLeod Young Weir met again in a strategy session with White, Scholes and other Royal Trustco executives and proposed what became known as Plan A. This would involve forming a syndicate of major institutions, companies and pension plans to make an unconditional rival bid also at $21.

Taylor's list of those to approach was a virtual who's who of the Canadian business world. Included were fourteen life insurance companies, among them Sun Life, Crown Life, Canada Life, Manulife, Dominion Life, North American Life and London Life; twenty-seven companies or their corporate pension funds, including Canadian National and Canadian Pacific, steelmakers Stelco and Dofasco, Bell Telephone, Gulf

Oil, Mobil Oil, Chevron, Imperial Oil, Shell Oil, Molson, Air Canada, MacMillan-Bloedel, Noranda Mines and Hiram Walker; three banks, the Toronto Dominion, the Royal and the Canadian Imperial Bank of Commerce; and individuals such as media czar Ken Thomson, Vancouver financier Sam Belzberg and the Eaton's department store family. Also on the list were the pension funds of all ten provincial governments.

Plan A never came to fruition. Some of Taylor's targets did eventually decide to buy Royal Trustco stock, though not as part of Taylor's proposed syndicate. Yet in the course of contacting those on the Plan A list, Taylor helped spur the formation of a much less formal, but no less formidable, alliance, which later became known as "the friends." In this way he was complementing the informal strategy Ken White and his colleagues were pursuing in lining up support.

One of the first people Taylor contacted was Richard Thomson, chairman of the Toronto Dominion Bank. Thomson was a banker's son with an MBA from Harvard who had joined the TD in 1957 and was now a very powerful man. Thomson, whose black curly hair topped a frame over six feet tall, was at forty-seven the youngest of the chiefs of Canada's five major chartered banks, and his bank was the smallest. He was also the most aggressive of the five bankers. Taylor called him at home on Sunday, August 31, and they met at Thomson's house at about eight that evening, along with Timothy Hale, the bank's equity portfolio manager, and Alan Hockin, its executive vice-president of investments. Taylor sold his scheme with fervor, but the bank executives were cool. He also told them Royal Trustco believed at this point that some 6 million of its 19.6 million shares would not be tendered to Campeau's bid.

Before Taylor left, he agreed to meet the Toronto Dominion executives at his office the following morning, at which time they would give him their decision about Plan A. With Taylor gone, Thomson and his men discussed buying Royal Trustco shares and the possibility of going up to the maximum 10 percent. At this point the Toronto Dominion Bank owned no shares of Royal Trustco, though on Friday Thomson had discussed buying Royal Trustco shares with a select group of his top executives. He later told the Ontario Securities Commission that the meeting was held to find out what the bank's investment division thought about Royal Trustco and that the recommendation was to buy.

Thomson now phoned Don Love of Oxford Development Co. to gauge his reaction. "We felt that if we were going to make an enemy of Campeau, we had better make damn sure we were not making ourselves an enemy of the [development] industry," Thomson later testified. "Because we are bankers to many developers, and if the developers, a large one — and there are only a handful — if they decided that they are each going to take over a trust company, we had better know before we start muddying the waters."

Richard Thomson's involvement in the Royal Trustco defense particularly sparked Campeau's wrath. Campeau said later of the TD chairman: "When he was the architect of the friends in 1980, I'd never met him. But Dick Thomson is a Wasp of the old kind, old family. He told me one time when we were talking at the Bank of Nova Scotia, 'You have no business here, you shouldn't be in Toronto.' Sure, he said that. Thomson thinks he controls Toronto, and to some degree he controlled a fair amount of it at that point. But he controls a hell of a lot less of it today."

When Thomson called Don Love, there were already strong ties between Oxford and the Toronto Dominion Bank. The bank had recently financed a move by Love to take Oxford private and currently owned 40 percent of the company's equity. On the phone, Love told Thomson that he did not approve of the Campeau bid. Thomson then tentatively agreed to finance a purchase of Royal Trustco shares by Oxford.

The Sunday meeting at Thomson's house broke up at about 11 P.M. The TD executives agreed to meet with their lawyer and then with Austin Taylor the next day, Labor Day. Thomson then phoned Toronto Dominion president J.A. Boyle to inform him of the decision: "Look, this thing is developing. Let's meet at McLeod's office on Monday morning," he told Boyle.

The club was starting to form.

The next morning, Alan Hockin arrived at McLeod Young Weir's offices to tell Austin Taylor that the Toronto Dominion was not interested in Plan A. When Thomson and the others arrived, they discussed Campeau's offer and applicable legislation. The talk turned to how aggressive the Bank of Nova Scotia had been in financing Campeau's bid and the possibility of it going higher. Thomson related his phone call to Don Love of Oxford: both the Toronto Dominion Bank and Oxford were prepared to buy up to 10 percent of Royal Trustco stock. Presumably White learned this news after the meeting broke up.

Later that day, McLeod Young Weir decided it did not want to handle two such large orders, and Love was told to place an order with someone else.

That night, the Toronto Dominion's Hockin gave Austin Taylor his order for up to 10 percent of Royal Trustco stock. The bulk of it was filled the next day, September 2. (By September 8, the Toronto Dominion had bought 1.6 million common shares, some at more than Campeau's bidding price, and 239,990 preferreds, for about $40 million. On September 3, Oxford purchased more than 1.7 million shares, also for some $40 million.)

The Royal Trustco directors met on Tuesday in the forty-fourth-floor boardroom of the Toronto Dominion Bank Tower in downtown Toronto. Chairman Ken White outlined the sequence of events beginning with the morning of Campeau's visit. He told them Campeau had asked for his support on the basis that White could "name his own price." He then described the steps he and his colleagues had taken to organize a defense in case the board agreed it wanted to fight the takeover. Chief operating officer John Scholes told the meeting that various shareholders were making market purchases and that Austin Taylor was taking action that could lead to a counterbid. But the full details of Plan A were not disclosed. White told the board that he had assembled an in-house team while McLeod Young Weir evaluated the Campeau offer. And he informed them of the promises he had received from various major shareholders who were appalled at the Campeau bid and would not tender. Just before 3 P.M., White told the directors that Royal Trustco stock was trading at $21.50, 50 cents more than Campeau's bid price.

The directors voted to oppose the bid and to do all they could to stop Campeau. Before the meeting broke up, White informed them that 1.9 million Royal Trustco shares had been traded — 86 percent of them through McLeod Young Weir and Dominion Securities, the trust company's financial advisers. Although White did not identify the Royal Trustco shareholders already entering the market, he presumably knew they were mostly his "friends."

Even while the Royal Trustco board was meeting, White's, Scholes' and Taylor's groundwork of the previous week was beginning to pay off as more of their friends began to enter the market and buy up available shares. This pattern would continue right up to the September 19 deadline.

A strategy was now falling into place virtually of its own accord. Austin Taylor would continue to try to sell his Plan A, but to no avail. The "friends approach" had been set in motion, and now it gathered steam as White, Scholes and other Royal Trustco executives worked their contacts and friends at other companies, using Taylor as backup. If someone expressed interest, Taylor would follow up and a share order usually resulted. Campeau and his vice-president of finance, Don Carroll, waited, aware of the trading but not of the players.

On September 2 and 3, National Trust Co. bought 100,000 shares, or 0.51 percent. On September 3, Commercial Union Assurance bought 110,000 shares for about $2.25 million. (To finance its investment, it sold its shares of Bank of Nova Scotia, which was financing Campeau's takeover bid.) On September 7, Alf Powis of Noranda Mines, whom White had contacted, agreed to buy. Within four days his company owned the equivalent of 500,000 shares, or 2.6 percent, at a cost of $10 million. Simultaneously, Canadian Pacific purchased 81,200 common shares, about 0.42 percent, and by the deadline had bought 51,000 more.

Royal Trustco did not limit its campaign to Canadian firms. The Midlantic National Bank in New Jersey ordered

100,000 shares and Deutsche Bank in West Germany, which already held 150,000 shares, purchased 350,000, both through McLeod Young Weir. Hong Kong & Shanghai Banking Corp. bought 546,200 shares or 2.8 percent.

It took until September 8 for Royal Trustco to respond formally to its shareholders. On that day White sent out a letter advising that McLeod Young Weir had studied the takeover offer and found it to be inadequate. He did not disclose the extent of Royal Trustco's defensive actions. "Regardless of the terms, the issue of single ownership is a significant one in the opinion of the directors," White wrote. "The philosophy that no one individual should be in a position to control a large financial institution serving the public has been recognized in the Bank Act. No one person can own more than 10 percent of a Canadian chartered bank and your directors believe that the same principle applies to the ownership of a financial institution of the nature and size of Royal Trust." An accompanying document added: "The directors and officers of Royal Trustco have been advised by a large number of persons acting independently that they intend to purchase shares of Royal Trustco in the market during the offer period."

Campeau, his lawyers and his investment firm, Green-shields, had heard rumors that forces friendly to Royal Trustco were buying up its stock, but there was nothing they could do but watch and wait. It was obvious, with the incredibly heavy trading in Royal Trustco shares, that something was happening, although Campeau and Carroll could not pin down exactly what. When he was asked at the Ontario Securities Commission if he had known for certain that Royal Trustco's friends had in fact bought up stock, Campeau replied that he knew only what he had read in the newspapers. "I have no hard facts to prove who, but it was referred to in the press," Campeau said. "We got all kinds of telephone calls. Some were very much against us and some were very much sympathizing with us . . . . We discussed this with our lawyers very often."

During the first two weeks, Mulholland of the Bank of Montreal had remained on the sidelines. Despite having tied up

10 percent of Royal Trustco's stock, he did not appear to be one of the active "friends." Now he decided to play the role of peacemaker, although his motives are not clear. Perhaps because of the amount of business between Campeau Corp. and the Bank of Montreal, he did not wish to offend Campeau.

So he broached with Campeau the possibility of his taking a lesser stake in Royal Trustco. When they met to discuss this over breakfast, Campeau told Mulholland that he had consulted with his lawyer and his banker, chairman Cedric Ritchie of the Bank of Nova Scotia, and that he was more interested in the financial aspects of the trust company than in voting aspects. He wanted a large stake but he was not adamant that he be allowed to vote all of the shares he would buy, although he appeared still to want at least majority voting power because, he told Mulholland, he feared Royal Trustco could double-cross him.

"I don't think you really need to worry about that," Mulholland said. "With the kind of board the Royal Trustco has, they are not people who knowingly acquiesce in that sort of thing, and neither would some of the shareholders, like us."

Mulholland proposed what he called his peace plan. Would Campeau settle for 50 or 60 percent ownership and agree to vote only 25 percent?

"I really don't know if you could do that," Campeau replied. "It seems to me that in the press, and the statement Mr. White has made, that it is obvious he wants to fight us and wants to stop this bid. And I don't see how this would work. How would you go about enforcing a contract like that in any case?"

"We don't need a contract," Mulholland responded. "We'd have a press conference. There would be you and your management and the management of Royal Trust, and it would be in bold letters in the press that the bid is now acceptable, providing you only voted 25 percent of the stock and providing you only had — whatever you want on the board."

Campeau would think about it.

At a subsequent meeting with the Bank of Montreal CEO, Campeau agreed, and on September 10 Mulholland took the

idea up with Ken White. Mulholland added that the Campeau
bid apparently had support among senior federal officials — Campeau was a Liberal supporter — and said something
to the effect that Royal Trustco could win the battle but lose
the war. When White asked what that meant, Mulholland
suggested that federal authorities could become more severe in
regulating the trust company. Mulholland proposed that
Campeau be allowed to acquire 25 percent and nominate three
directors. White predicted that more than half the stock would
not be tendered to Campeau, and although he did not like the
compromise, he said he would discuss it with his executive
committee. The committee also rejected the proposal.

As the expiration date of the Campeau bid drew nearer,
several of the major shareholders in the group of friends began
to get cold feet. Primary among them was the Toronto
Dominion's Richard Thomson, who began to worry about the
possibility of being stuck as minority shareholder in a
Campeau-controlled Royal Trustco. On September 16, Austin
Taylor relayed Thomson's concerns to White, warning him
that the bank could decide, after all, to tender to Campeau. The
next day, White met with Thomson and assured him that 59 or
60 percent of the shares would not be tendered to the Campeau
bid. He disclosed some of those who had bought shares — the
Bank of Montreal, Sun Life, Noranda and Oxford. He also
disclosed that Royal Trustco's management was thinking
about increasing the dividends on Royal Trustco stock. White
gave similar assurances of a failed Campeau bid to Alf Powis of
Noranda and Thomas Galt of Sun Life the same day. As a
result, the friends held firm.

What they had done that day in desperation would come
back to haunt them. White and Scholes could by now be
reasonably assured that about 60 percent of the Royal Trustco
shares were locked up in friendly hands. Though they disclosed
this to Thomson, Powis and Galt, they did not disseminate the
information to all their shareholders. This was "tipping,"
providing the Toronto Dominion executives with material
facts that had not been generally disclosed. All other

shareholders were entitled to the same information when trying to decide whether or not to tender.

White clearly knew what he was talking about. By the September 19 deadline, only about 30 percent of the Royal Trustco shares had been tendered to Campeau's bid. Campeau was stunned. He could not understand why, in a 100 percent cash bid, he was not successful. "I have never seen another example where somebody made a 100 percent bid in cash for all the stock and it was not successful . . . . It has happened, there have been some fights, in fights when there has been 51 percent of the stock or something like that, but not when it was 100 percent. But when the cash bid was made for 100 percent of the company, there is only one way to stop that, and that is a white knight and that is fair ball. And then there is maybe counterbidding. So we were very baffled by the fact that the shares had not been deposited . . . and there was no white knight. So of course we concluded there was a group buying shares out there."

On the deadline day, Campeau and his executives held a series of meetings to decide whether to bow out or up the ante. Campeau decided that he would not buckle, extending the offer to October 2 and increasing his bid to $435 million — $23 a common share and $32.78 per preferred. Said Don Carroll: "It's very discouraging, just like starting all over again."

"It was a matter of testing," Campeau later explained. "If the price was excellent at $21, it had to be considerably better at $23. A lot of us felt that probably this bid was not going to be successful because of the trading that had taken place under the other period. But we decided to make the bid, and it was certainly the upper limit that we wanted to pay for that stock . . . we wanted to know if this group that the press was referring to was going to stand the heat of another two dollars . . . . We wanted to know if the other people who had bought shares on the open market would decide to make a profit and sell."

Campeau called Mulholland of the Bank of Montreal and pressed him to sell his shares "to avoid embarrassment" because the Ontario Securities Commission was investigating

what was taking place in the market. Mulholland did not
tender.

Would the informal alliance continue to hold? Even though
70 percent had not been tendered by the first deadline, White
and company clearly were not sure. So McLeod Young Weir
went back into action. The day after Campeau's new bid was
announced, it approached Paul Reichmann, vice-president of
Olympia & York, to see if he was interested in acquiring Royal
Trustco stock. Reichmann said he probably would be
interested in 50 percent. White rejected this idea — he was not
prepared to give up control — and there the matter stood for
several days. He must have been doing a lot of phoning to shore
up his support. He called Thomson of the Toronto Dominion,
wanting to know if he had tendered. When told the bank had
not, White added, "I hope you won't at $23." At a board
meeting on September 22, White told Royal Trustco directors
that the company would continue with the same strategy and it
appeared that at least 60 percent of the stock would not be
tendered. Still, he was worried.

Two days later, Reichmann got in touch with McLeod
Young Weir and indicated he would be interested in 20 percent.
He would buy up to 10 percent right away if he could be assured
that Royal Trustco would welcome a 20 percent stockholder
and promise that Olympia & York would be invited onto the
board and executive committee. Royal Trustco agreed and
Olympia & York immediately began buying. In the next five
days, it purchased 1.78 million shares, or 9.1 percent.

The final nail in Campeau's coffin was driven by Caisse de
dépôt et placement, the Quebec government's pension fund. At
the last minute it pulled out about a million shares it had
tendered to the first bid, leaving Campeau with just 25 percent
of the stock.

The eventual defeat came as no surprise to the Campeau
team. Yet the night before the bid was withdrawn, a
determined Don Carroll was still in his Toronto office trying to
find a way to win, though he knew he could not. Campeau
phoned from Ottawa and Carroll tried to soothe a bruised
ego.

White's "friends" had locked up 55 percent of Royal Trustco at a cost of about $164 million; fully 75 percent had not been tendered. During the tender period, more than 10 million common shares were traded, meaning almost 63 percent of the stock changed hands. Late on October 2, Campeau withdrew his bid. He did end up buying the shares held by Unicorp. He later sold his shares to the Reichmanns, making them the largest shareholders in Royal Trustco. Even though this left him with a profit for his trouble, it was a stunning defeat for Robert Campeau. He would, however, receive some small vindication.

Campeau had complained to the Ontario Securities Commission, which could not overlook the matter. In 1981, commission hearings called as witnesses some of the top corporate executives in Canada. In its final ruling, the commission said of the executives who formed the friends: "Each was motivated to cause the corporations they managed to purchase Trustco shares and not to tender them because of commercial, financial or personal interest in the outcome of the Campeau bid . . . Since all of these purchasers are investors and not speculators, the only real justification for entering the market at the new market highs must have been to support and assure a continuing business relationship, to foster a new one or to help a friend fend off the advances of an undesirable bidder."

The commission found that White and Scholes had acted improperly. They were able to determine, reasonably accurately, the percentage of outstanding shares held that would not be tendered but had not provided this information to all shareholders. The key piece of evidence against them was their disclosure to the Toronto Dominion Bank officers of the percentage of shares that was locked up. The commission ordered White's trading rights suspended for sixty days and Scholes's for thirty days.

One aspect of this story must have raised questions in the minds of many ordinary shareholders of the companies involved in the Royal Trustco defense. Some of the Royal Trustco stock had been purchased at higher than Campeau's bid price. This is not unusual in the early stages of a takeover fight, because the buyer may plan to sell when the bid is later pushed up. It was also reasonable for the friends to assume that if the Campeau bid failed, the value of their Royal Trustco stock would soon fall, perhaps to as low as its prebid level of about $16. In fact, the share price fell $1.25 immediately after the bid expired. Yet by holding on to their stock, the companies knowingly risked losing millions of dollars. It is a wonder that their own shareholders did not make more noise about this.

Richard Thomson's Toronto Dominion Bank suffered the effects almost immediately. Under U.S. law, the Toronto Dominion, with a subsidiary in California, could not own more than 5 percent of a bank in another state. Apparently ignorant of the law, it now held almost 10 percent of Royal Trustco, which owned banks in Florida. The Toronto Dominion was forced by the U.S. Federal Reserve Board in November to divest half its interest in Royal Trustco at a loss of $650,000. Don Love's Oxford, however, sold its shares at a profit in March 1981.

Campeau emerged from the affair with his integrity intact. But he complained that the Royal Trustco executives got only "a slap on the wrist" and was soured on doing business in Canada. "Royal Trust was a disappointing, downgrading experience for me," he later said.

13 / Scotia Plaza

"We either settle this or I tear the building down around your neck."
— Robert Campeau

CAMPEAU CORP. HAD grown so large by 1980 that, like many a vast company, it was having trouble keeping track of what was happening on its many fronts. Complicating matters was the fact that Campeau and head office remained in Ottawa while most of the key executives were now in Toronto. The system of governing the development of shopping centers was also somewhat strange: one group conceived a development, another planned it and a third carried it out, each with a vice-president who exercised individual executive discretion. Vice-president Don Carroll said later of the company: "It was getting historical information far too late. As a result, budget projections were largely based on wishful thinking." So David King and Carroll developed a monthly reporting system under which the company could keep tabs on every department's finances and activities and oversee how the numerous projects were moving along. The new system allowed the company to make quick decisions on where to funnel money and what assets to sell.

At about the time of the Royal Trustco bid, David King hired John van Haastrecht to run Campeau Corp.'s shopping center division. Van Haastrecht had built shopping centers in western Canada, Manitoba and Ontario for Columbia Commonwealth Ltd. and had been running a small development company of his own for about eighteen months when King

197

approached him. But even though van Haastrecht knew and liked King, he had heard gossip in the industry about Campeau Corp. and about what Bob was like to work with, and his first reaction was to say no. King persevered, promising him a free hand with shopping center development. Van Haastrecht finally agreed, but only on two conditions: he would not operate out of Ottawa head office, where Campeau was, and he would have no Campeau offspring working directly for him.

The first thing van Haastrecht did on arriving was consolidate the three separate groups of the shopping center operation. He set up the shopping center division as a separate business unit and set about to build new malls and renovate many of the tired properties in the Campeau portfolio. Work began in 1981 on the new Pinecrest shopping center in Ottawa and Intercity in Thunder Bay, Ontario.

When van Haastrecht arrived, the new management team was firmly in place — Campeau as chairman, Ron McCartney as president and David King and Don Carroll as executive vice-presidents — and the company was running smoothly. It was a good thing, because business conditions were changing and a recession was looming.

By this time Campeau Corp.'s traditional business had all but disappeared. In 1981, the housing inventory amounted to just seventy-one units. Sixty-three of these were in highrise condominiums and just eight were single-family detached homes. Campeau was also rapidly divesting pieces of the operations associated with residential building. He sold one of the four parts of the building products division, discontinued another and reduced production at the remaining two. He was negotiating the sale of the lumber division when prices plummeted and hopes of completing any divestiture faded; he temporarily suspended the division's operations and continued to hunt for a buyer.

In June 1981, Campeau decided to relist Campeau Corp. on the stock exchange. The recession had hit, money was tight, interest rates were rising and the company would thus be in a position to issue shares if it needed more financing. Said Campeau: "Some of our people felt that since we had problems in privatizing completely, we should remain public. By doing this, we were not losing anything and we were keeping our options open should we want to go to the equity market later."

In the United States, Campeau's options had suddenly become very limited. He had approached land acquisition in the United States like a small boy in a candy shop, so with the recession he was forced to pull back. The retrenchment took the form of a major housecleaning that began in late March 1982. One-third of Campeau Corp.'s assets of more than $1.5 billion were in the southwestern United States, where he was having trouble obtaining financing and finding tenants. That year he laid off half his staff in Texas and delayed indefinitely plans for the eighty-storey building in Houston and two projects in Dallas. Other plans in California and Washington State were postponed, though work under construction was not suspended. The trend continued for a number of years, and Campeau was still dumping U.S. holdings in the late 1980s.

The key orchestrators of this painful withdrawal were Ron McCartney, Dave King and Don Carroll. Bob was not as interested in strategic retreats as he was in daring advances and glorious victories. And by early 1982 it appeared to Toronto's investment community that Campeau was taking a backseat approach to the day-to-day running of the company. Where was this "one-man show" they had heard so much about in the past? Indeed, Campeau seemed to have learned to relax more and enjoy the fruits of his success. He was spending time with Ilse and the children, skiing more, taking longer vacations. He said then: "At one time our company was a one-man show. The whole load was on my shoulders. But now we have strong management, and I don't need to be involved daily." This was not the Bob Campeau of the previous three decades. However, he would not be content in this looser role for long, and by late 1982 he became more active again, realizing his hand was needed in the reshaping of Campeau Corp.

By early 1983, the transformation of Campeau Corp. that had begun in the mid-1970s was complete. On January 14, 1983, thirty-three years after he had built his first home, Bob

Campeau announced that he was pulling out of housing and residential land development. His board of directors approved a strategic plan to focus entirely on developing and managing office buildings and mixed-use properties, shopping centers and business parks. In 1983, commercial properties already accounted for more than 80 percent of operating profits as Campeau set about to dump all residential assets, which were valued at some $850 million, over a three-to-four-year period. Included were residential real estate holdings and lumber property. One year earlier, Cadillac-Fairview had dumped its residential holdings. It was no longer the lucrative business it had once been. Several months later, Campeau said he had decided to pull his company out of the residential business because it had lost its "entrepreneurial flair." Then, in a final indication of how changed the company was, head office was moved from Ottawa to 320 Bay Street in Toronto, where McCartney, King and Carroll were already operating.

In early 1983, Ron McCartney resigned as president of the company, and Dave King was named his successor. Former executives say McCartney took the blame for the troubles caused by having purchased too much land, primarily in the United States. He was later named president of the company's Florida operations.

Although the company was retrenching in the United States, it was still developing in Canada, completing the Place Guy Favreau complex in Montreal and a renovation of the Centennial Towers office building in Ottawa. Business park properties were developed in the Ottawa area. In the United States, Campeau completed preparation of the site for a stunning $170-million (U.S.) building at 333 Bush Street in San Francisco's financial district. The polished granite building would rise forty-two storeys. It also developed several business park properties in the Santa Clara area and would soon begin construction on another office building in south San Francisco.

As part of his shopping center responsibilities, John van Haastrecht, who by 1983 was senior vice-president of development, oversaw the multimillion-dollar renovations of Eaton Square in London, Ontario, the Oshawa Shopping

Centre, the New Sudbury Shopping Centre and the Place de Ville plaza.

The plaza at Place de Ville required new flooring. Marble slabs had been put down on the plaza floor when Campeau built Place de Ville, and the underlying rubber membrane, which stops seepage, had by now deteriorated, and water was leaking into the parking lot below. Repairing the membrane meant the daunting task of raising the huge marble slabs from the floors. After replacing the membrane, van Haastrecht chose to put down interlocking stone in place of the marble. The stone was cheaper and future repairs would be easier. But he had not reckoned on the reaction of Bob Campeau.

Van Haastrecht was in his Toronto office one Friday afternoon in 1983 when the head of Campeau Corp.'s National Capital Region division, responsible for the Ottawa projects, phoned.

"I've got Bob Campeau in the office, and he says there's a problem."

"What is it?" asked van Haastrecht.

"You'd better talk to Bob."

Campeau came on the line. "You're putting interlocking stone into Place de Ville."

"Yeah, I guess we are," van Haastrecht agreed.

"I don't like interlocking stone," Campeau said.

"What the hell do you want me to do, stop the job?" van Haastrecht asked.

"Yes."

"Fine, it's stopped."

There the matter stood for about one week, when David King phoned van Haastrecht to discuss the situation. Something had to be done to appease Campeau and prove the boss had been right in halting the project. So van Haastrecht suggested they spend more money for landscaping, but leave the interlocking stone. So the project went ahead with an additional $100,000 in its budget for landscaping.

Despite Dave King's promise that van Haastrecht would never have a Campeau child in his direct employ, Danny, now twenty-five, was placed in the shopping center division in 1983.

Before this he had worked in other Campeau operations, including a stint as assistant to McCartney when he was president. Van Haastrecht's response was to get Danny out of his office, so he sent him as maintenance manager to the Oshawa Shopping Centre. Within no time, Danny had completed a list of complaints about the center's staff, wanting a few people fired. So van Haastrecht took him out of Oshawa and placed him in the construction division, advising him to calm down and learn how to deal with other people.

Van Haastrecht's real problems continued to be with the boss himself, who had by now moved to Toronto. One day in 1983, Campeau invited van Haastrecht, now senior vice-president of development, to a private lunch in the new boardroom at the Bay Street office. During lunch, van Haastrecht listened with growing annoyance as Campeau told him how he ran his company and all that he had accomplished. Finally, van Haastrecht could take this talk no longer.

"What the hell do you think I've been doing?" he told Campeau.

Campeau said nothing for several seconds before responding. "I wanted to talk to you about that," he said. "You took the Pinecrest project over budget."

Campeau was referring to the 200,000-square-foot Pinecrest shopping center in Ottawa, which had opened a year earlier. Van Haastrecht thought he had done a superb job in a period of tight money. It had cost $16.3 million to build, and he had put a $17-million mortgage on it, spreading the risk and giving up 50 percent of the equity to Confederation Life. The result was a quick $700,000 profit for Campeau Corp., which retained half ownership with a relatively small investment.

"What are you talking about, I took it over budget?"

"David King told me all about it," Campeau replied.

The rest of the conversation is not recorded, but clearly the lunch was not a success.

Later, King called van Haastrecht to find out how he had got on with Campeau.

Van Haastrecht told him about the Pinecrest discussion.

"Oh yeah," said King. "Well, you know your deal where you

did the financing and you gave 50 percent to Confederation Life? Bob wouldn't do that deal. So I had to make it look like he was bailing you out of something. So I said you had to do it because you'd gone over budget, that if we didn't do it, it would be bad for the company."

Van Haastrecht's problems with the Campeaus came to a head in the fall of 1984. During the $6-million redevelopment of the Sudbury shopping center that had begun in 1983, Danny offended Fred Perlman, the head of Dalmy's, one of Campeau Corp.'s biggest tenants. This was the last straw, and van Haastrecht relieved him of his duties.

"I just can't afford to have you out there as an ambassador," he told Campeau's son.

Danny continued to have an office in van Haastrecht's division, but van Haastrecht left him there with nothing to do. He never heard directly from Campeau on the action he had taken, but it is safe to assume that Bob was not pleased.

About a week later, van Haastrecht asked Campeau to attend the opening of the redevelopment of the Sudbury shopping center because of his ties to the region. Campeau obliged, but at some point during the day remarked that he was disappointed in the shopping center division because it basically had no talent. On hearing of this, van Haastrecht decided to take a one-week vacation to think about his future. Immediately on his return he had lunch with David King.

"I'll give you two choices," van Haastrecht told King. "I'm gonna walk out the door right now or I'll clean everything up and turn it over to whoever you want as my successor and stay for the end of the year."

Van Haastrecht left in December, leaving a more efficient shopping center operation and several refurbished properties.

The early 1980s were a difficult time for Bob Campeau the family man. His older brother Gilbert's cancer grew worse and Bob did what he could. He sent his jet to fly Gilbert and Blanche to Houston for treatment, and then back to Canada, paying for the expenses. Gilbert died in 1983, leaving his wife and five children. Bob later phoned his sister Gerarda, who by then had moved to Ottawa and was close to Blanche, wanting to know if Gilbert's wife was financially secure. "Because if she's not, I'll look after her," he said.

Bob was always generous with his family, though he drew the line when his eldest son, Jacques, when he was thirty years old in 1983, demanded his share of the children's trust estate. (According to the terms of the trust, he could not get at his shares until he turned thirty-five.) Since Clauda's death, Jacques had rarely spoken to his father. Now he sued Campeau in an attempt to obtain his portion of the stock. By now, the trust estate held about 25 percent of Campeau Corp.'s common shares and Jacques's portion was valued at about $20 million. In Jacques's suit, he also named Danny, now twenty-five, and Bobby, Jr., now nineteen, who both opposed his application. (Giselle, who was born in 1966 after the trust's "special date," was not eligible for a share in this trust fund.) Rachelle had turned thirty-five in January 1982, and had already received her shares. In the end the judgment denied Jacques's claim and upheld the original terms of the trust that "upon reaching thirty-five he will be entitled to payment forthwith of his shares." Jacques had to be content with the income from the trust estate for another five years.

Along with the retrenchment in the United States, in 1984 Campeau was pushing ahead with the biggest Canadian office building he had ever built, and his biggest project to date. This was the giant Scotia Plaza development in downtown Toronto, the $400-million sixty-eight-storey home for the Bank of Nova Scotia at the corner of King and Bay streets, one of the most expensive and prestigious intersections in Canada. Scotia Plaza, a slender, attractive building of Red Napoleon granite, would be the second-tallest office tower in Toronto, a monument both to Bob Campeau and to the bank that had supported him since he was just a small housebuilder.

Standing in Campeau's way, however, was Toronto's official plan. But anyone at city hall who had bothered to check his history would have quickly learned that Campeau would not flinch at such a minor obstacle. The man who had built Place de Ville knew his way around city hall and the ways around city bylaws. The official plan's density requirements allowed a developer in the downtown core to build office space equal to eight times the lot size plus housing equal to four times the lot size. Campeau wanted to double the density and build an office complex that would be sixteen times the lot dimensions.

His way around the problem was to swap density rights with planned buildings at the waterfront. Campeau already owned rights to build twin forty-storey buildings across the street from the harbor condominiums — the Waterpark Place development. He took his residential density rights at King and Bay streets — four times the lot size, or some 532,000 square feet — and transferred them to the waterfront. Then he transferred his 592,000 square feet of office space rights at Waterpark Place to Scotia Plaza. This meant Waterpark Place would be reduced to seventeen- and twenty-six-storey buildings, but he would be able to build much higher on the much more valuable Scotia Plaza land. He then received additional density "credits" for Scotia Plaza by promising to preserve some historical sites nearby and agreeing to provide land for 200 nonprofit homes while also putting daycare centers in both Scotia Plaza and Waterpark Place. It was an incredible piece of manipulation, yielding him a development worth at least $30 million more than before the swap.

Why did the city agree to go along with Campeau and gut what little remained of its official plan? The argument seems to have been that the reduction in Waterpark Place would hold down density on the lakefront. Yet just a short while earlier, the city had amended its official plan to allow construction of a five-building World Trade Centre close to the Waterpark site. And after Campeau got his density swap, other developers began demanding similar treatment. The city had clearly made a mockery of its own rules.

In the old days in Ottawa, having got this far, Campeau would have encountered no further difficulty. But now Richard Thomson, the Toronto Dominion Bank chairman who had played a role in the successful defeat of Campeau's 1980 attempt to take over Royal Trustco, moved onto the field to fight the French Canadian builder and the Bank of Nova Scotia, one of his main competitors. At the same intersection as Scotia Plaza, the Toronto Dominion and Cadillac-Fairview were already building a fourth tower to the Toronto Dominion Centre.

In the spring of 1984, after Campeau had assembled the land for his project, Thomson launched an all-out campaign to stop him, declaring that Scotia Plaza violated Toronto's official plan. The Toronto Dominion took out full-page newspaper advertisements and complained to the media that Campeau would reap almost $50 million in benefits because of the increased density and that the project would strain the already overburdened transit system in the area. Said Thomson to the media: "They can put the building somewhere else."

Thomson then proceeded on the political front. The Toronto Dominion appeared before the city's land use committee and objected to the Scotia Plaza project. Meanwhile, Thomson began personally lobbying city council members.

City council's final debate on Scotia Plaza was scheduled for a special meeting June 28, 1984. The Toronto Dominion wanted to speak, but the city's policy was that neither citizens nor companies could appear before a full council meeting, and it turned down the bank's request. About 600 people packed the council chamber that night, hundreds of them Toronto Dominion employees who had been promised free dinners by the bank if they stayed to the end of the meeting.

It was a heated debate. Mayor Art Eggleton, who had accused the Toronto Dominion Bank of not disclosing its interests, was, in turn, accused by NDP Alderman Richard Gilbert of not disclosing his interests. The alderman pointed out that Campeau Corp. had donated $3,000 to the mayor's election campaign. As expected, all New Democratic Party council members — who found themselves in the strange position of siding with a major bank — were opposed to the

Campeau project. Said Alderman Joanne Campbell: "I cannot sell my soul for 50 daycare spaces." In the end, the seven NDP aldermen, cheered on by the bank workers, were the only members of council to vote against the project. Campeau's plan was now through council.

Campeau's Scotia Plaza troubles were not over. Downtown Action, a citizens' group that was expecting the city hall defeat, was planning to challenge the project at the Ontario Municipal Board (OMB). Behind the scenes, Campeau had been negotiating to head them off. He had first proposed giving $2 million to the city for nonprofit housing, but its planning commissioner advised Mayor Eggleton against such a move. Said the commissioner, "Any city that starts to sell zoning is doomed to failure."

So Campeau Corp., primarily through a new vice-president, Walter Jensen, entered into secret negotiations with NDP aldermen Jack Layton, David Reville and Dale Martin, who were allied with Downtown Action. The NDP had itself considered taking Campeau to the OMB, but then backed down, worried it might be forced to pay up to $50,000 to pay Campeau's legal bills if it lost the challenge. So these aldermen decided instead to take up Downtown Action's fight in secret talks with the developer, while the citizens' group proceeded with its objection to the OMB. But the NDP aldermen ultimately accepted Campeau's offer of $2 million in land or materials to a co-operative housing group for nonprofit housing; in return, Downtown Action's objection to the OMB was withdrawn. All parties to the deal agreed to remain silent in an effort to prevent anyone from scoring political points. Eggleton, who had turned down Campeau's first offer, later disclosed that he talked four times with Campeau Corp. and the NDP and was aware of their negotiations.

In late 1984, when the deal became public knowledge, a storm of controversy erupted. Even the Canadian Institute for Public Real Estate Companies, a developers' lobby group, spoke out against the deal, saying it could lead to third-party pressure on developers to enter agreements outside proper channels. Campeau president David King defended his company's actions in a letter to the mayor: "It was determined that it would be advisable to make an investment in public housing if that would result in removal of the objections." Indeed, $2 million was a small price compared with the money that could have been lost to a delay in construction while they were before the Ontario Municipal Board.

As it turned out, there was a delay anyway. The Toronto Dominion's Richard Thomson played his trump card: one of the buildings on the Scotia Plaza site housed a Toronto Dominion branch with a lease that ran until 1996. Thomson now demanded $36 million from Campeau if he was to move. Campeau offered $500,000 and there the matter stood for almost a full year, with neither side willing to budge. Meanwhile, wrecking crews tore down eight other buildings around the holdout. It got to the point where the Toronto Dominion was the sole tenant in an otherwise deserted building.

Finally Campeau met face-to-face with Thomson in the office of Cedric Ritchie, chairman of the Bank of Nova Scotia. Campeau recalls that he told the Toronto Dominion Bank chairman, "We either settle this or I tear down the building around your neck. I'll leave you there." Thomson's reply is not recorded, but it was probably not polite. The meeting failed to break the stalemate.

At this point, Campeau's lawyer wanted to take the case into the courts, but the Bank of Nova Scotia chairman refused. Negotiations continued. At last, in April 1985, Thomson met with Ritchie and David King and reduced his demand to $24 million, which would be split between Campeau Corp. and the Bank of Nova Scotia. Campeau was already behind schedule on construction and reluctantly agreed. But he still fumes over Thomson and probably always will. "He's a gouger," Campeau says of the TD chairman. "He makes a lot of money for his bank, but he's a gouger. Against Robert Campeau, he's just a son of a bitch."

As Robert Campeau had grown older, his tastes had grown richer, his cars fancier, his homes more lavish. In the middle of the Scotia Plaza fight, in 1984, he moved into by far the most grandiose home of all, and in so doing left Ottawa behind for good. His new address was on Toronto's exclusive Bridle Path, a $5-million home occupying about 25,000 square feet if you include the pool and finished basement. He and Ilse designed the house and borrowed Gilbert's son René from the company to build it. Construction, which began in 1981, was a lengthy process; things had to be just right, and Bob, as usual, had a tendency to change his mind at the last minute. At one point after the hole for the pool had already been dug, he ordered it moved to the other side of the house.

The mansion sits on a four-acre site and is a beautiful stone-walled imitation French chateau. The grounds and interior are lavish enough to overwhelm the already stunning neighboring homes. The house is surrounded by rose gardens and meticulously landscaped lawns. Inside, several tons of marble — apparently one of Campeau's favorite materials — grace the fireplace, the bathrooms and other areas.

Bob and Ilse's bedroom alone is the size of a small house, an estimated 1,200 to 1,800 square feet. Each of them has a big bathroom. Campeau's is equipped with a shower with three heads. Ilse's sports an old-fashioned tub with gold-plated faucets and feet and a large circular stained-glass window. The house contains more than ten bathrooms in all. The main bedroom area has an alcove, large cedar closet and changing areas. A specially crafted circular wood staircase from a hall off the bedroom runs down to the deck of the Olympic-size pool, affording Campeau easy access. In addition to the master bedroom, there are five other bedrooms — two are for guests — plus a small two-bedroom apartment over the three-car garage.

The pool system is considered one of the best in the country, with an ozone system that requires no chlorine and yet cleanses the water to the point that it is drinkable.

Compared to the grandeur of the rest of the house, the kitchen is almost cosy, with lower ceilings, cabinets on three walls and a special marble countertop for making pastries. The dining area is about 25 or 30 feet wide by 40 feet long. The family and living rooms have large French doors opening onto a patio.

Campeau's library is paneled with special burled wood from a company in Montreal, and every doorknob and hinge throughout the house is made of specially finished imported brass.

Of this mansion the *New York Times Magazine* said: "The house reflects the way its owner sees himself: the outsider as self-made man. The architecture of the mansard structure, which he and Ilse, his second wife, designed together, is based on Norman style — an architecture self-consciously signaling a French Canadian's conquests over the Anglo financial establishment in Toronto."

To mark his arrival in Toronto, Bob Campeau threw what he considered the ultimate in housewarmings in September 1984. Among the guests were the just-retired prime minister Pierre Trudeau, businessman Conrad Black, Toronto Archbishop Emmett Cardinal Carter, Ontario Premier William Davis and Italian Ambassador Paulo Fulci. The assembled multitude dined on top of the indoor swimming pool, on an aluminum-and-plywood structure that takes two men about six hours to install and converts the pool into a dance floor or banquet area.

After dinner, in a special marquee on the lawn, the guests listened to singer Paul Anka's tribute to the boy from Chelmsford, a bastardized version of Frank Sinatra's "My Way" written specially for this party. Conrad Black, author of a fine biography of Maurice Duplessis, could certainly have done better.

> *It's clear, we're here to cheer,*
> *A great career, and very loudly.*
> *A man, none better than,*
> *Who had a plan, fulfilled it proudly.*
> *With Ilse his wife, Bob Campeau's life,*
> *Did reach each goal and in a whiz way.*
> *I toast with you, this newsboy who,*
> *Sure did it his way.*

This boy found work was joy,
Through self-employ, like Jackie Horner.
Each day, he'd rush away
To earn his pay on the prize street corner.
He earned his gold through papers sold,
And Campeau sold the old show-biz way.
You all can see, he's a lot like me,
But he did it his way.
For what is a man, what has he got?
If not real friends then not a lot.
And Bob has some, as you can see.

— Anka looked around at the crowd at this point to show that Bob Campeau indeed had friends —

But most of all, his family,
Jacques, Jan-Paul, Giselle, Bobby, Daniel, Rachelle,
He did it his way.
His fame, and his acclaim,
Are like his name, on introduction.
The mob have praise of Bob,
And of the job he does in construction.
Does Campeau thank Dominion Bank?
That's asking if the pope is kosher
Now Toronto has a tremendous plaza
Known as Scotia.
Hotels and centers, towers and tracks,
Give him a project — he attacks.
All Canada loves Bob Campeau,
This Taj Mahal he calls chateau.
Is he extrordinaire? Bet your derrière,
But he did it his way.

Stoneayre, the Dunrobin mansion he had shared with Ilse, now stood empty. In 1985 he sold it to Rachelle. Father and daughter were on vacation together in Europe when the sale was supposed to close, so the deal was wrapped up about a month later than scheduled. Campeau's attorney's sent Rachelle a bill for $40,000, interest on the late closing.

Outwardly, Bob Campeau's life was comfortable. His company had weathered the recession, he was one of the five biggest developers in Canada and he had every material thing a man could ask for. Nonetheless, in late 1985 he suffered another bout of depression. Perhaps it was business pressure, or perhaps just the pressure of being Bob Campeau. "Everybody gets depressed," Campeau remarked a couple of years later. "To what degree I was depressed I don't know. They say Churchill had depressions in his life quite a few times."

It got bad enough that he ended up in hospital, where Father Ovila came to see him. During one visit, Bob asked his older brother about the possibility of a Roman Catholic marriage to Ilse. Now that his first wife was dead, Campeau was considered a widower in the eyes of the Church and a marriage would be sanctioned.

Father Ovila recalls that Bob had first raised the subject about a month after Clauda's death six years earlier. He wondered what would have to be done, what type of ceremony they could have, whether the banns would be published and whether Ilse's children would be baptized in the Catholic Church. Bob put much emphasis on the question of the children, and the priest wondered whether his younger brother had yet broached the subject of a Church wedding with Ilse. Father Ovila had heard nothing more of it until now.

Bob told Father Ovila he wanted to marry Ilse while he was in hospital. "I can do something for you if you're willing," the priest responded. Soon afterward, the priest received Cardinal Carter's permission to marry Bob and Ilse in hospital, and everything was arranged for a ceremony one night. But Ilse suggested that perhaps they should wait until her husband's health improved. Bob agreed.

A few months later, in early 1986, Father Ovila happened to be in Toronto the day of the ceremony — he was looking for a car Bob had said he would pay for — and was at the Bridle Path home that evening with a couple of his brother's friends when Bob said he was going to be married by Cardinal Carter in a private ceremony. "He wanted to be faithful to his Church," his brother says. That same day, Bob and Ilse were married by Cardinal Carter at the cardinal's home, the Episcopal Palace.

PART IV

I'll Take Manhattan

14 / Manhattan Express

*"It was the vision that the complement of
retail and real estate was the way to
go — the vision was in Allied."*
— Allen Finkelson

IT WAS, BOB CAMPEAU would later recall, the devastating Royal Trustco defeat that pushed him to New York. He had failed in three takeover attempts in Canada; perhaps he would find his big success in the U.S., where they played the game differently and far more frequently and where his one modest hostile takeover success had taken place. He had spent the six years since the Royal Trustco fiasco getting his company in shape, retrenching in the U.S., completing the shift away from housebuilding and getting major Canadian projects such as Scotia Plaza and Waterpark Place under way. By 1986, Campeau Corp. was a mature company with assets of $1.5 billion Canadian and revenue of more than $200 million. Campeau was in a position to acquire an attractive American business, and he began searching for the right target in a range that extended from real estate developers to financial institutions.

The United States was definitely a country where megadeals were made. In 1985, General Electric had spent almost $6 billion* to acquire RCA, Philip Morris had spent $5.6 billion on General Foods, and buyout specialist Kohlberg

---

*Unless otherwise indicated, all dollar amounts in this chapter and in Chapters 15, 16 and 17 are in U.S. dollars.

Kravis Roberts & Co. had dropped $5.4 billion to take over Beatrice. The year before, Mobil had spent $5.7 billion for Superior Oil, Texaco had purchased Getty Oil for $10.1 billion and Chevron had bought Gulf for a stunning $13.2 billion. This was the environment that Robert Campeau entered, and this was the game he wanted to play. By early 1986 he had just about settled on Allied Stores Corp.

Allied, based in Manhattan, was the eleventh-largest general merchandiser in the United States. Incorporated in 1928, it owned almost 700 department and specialty stores in forty-six states, the District of Columbia and Japan. Best known among its twenty-four divisions were Brooks Brothers, the fashionable men's clothing chain, and Ann Taylor, the equally fashionable chain of clothing stores for women. Among the other divisions were New England's Jordan Marsh, The Bon in the Pacific northwest, Stern's in New Jersey, Pennsylvania and on Long Island, Florida's Maas Brothers, Joske's of Texas and Garfinckel's in Washington, D.C. Allied's assets were almost $3 billion, more than double Campeau Corp.'s, and its sales and revenues were running at $4.2 billion a year.

Campeau envisioned a wonderful marriage of retailing and real estate. Individual shopping centers were difficult either to obtain or to develop in the United States. Allied already owned several, and its stores were major tenants in many others. And anchor tenants usually could become part owners in the centers where they were located. There was also the potential of bringing Allied stores into shopping centers Campeau might develop.

"It was the vision that the complement of retail and real estate was the way to go," says Allen Finkelson, the New York merger lawyer Campeau retained to assist him. "The vision was in Allied."

In late March, Campeau formed a partnership with a Canadian company known as Perez Capital Corp. in which Campeau Corp. held 90 percent, and began buying up shares of Allied, which they code named Express so as not to tip their hand. By the end of the summer, he owned almost 2.1 million shares, or some 4 percent, of Express, having purchased the shares at an average $46.61 each. So far, no one outside a select few knew what was happening.

By late July, Campeau had assembled a team of key strategists and was operating from a fortieth-floor suite at the prestigious Waldorf Towers. The team included Finkelson, who worked for the law firm of Cravath, Swaine & Moore, Ronald Tysoe, a Campeau vice-president, and James Roddy, who in 1985 had replaced Don Carroll as executive vice-president of finance. (Carroll had become executive vice-president of corporate development.)

On August 1, Bob Campeau visited an unsuspecting Thomas Macioce, chairman and chief executive of Allied Stores, himself no stranger to the takeover game. Just a few years earlier, he had engineered the hostile takeover of Garfinckel's, Brooks Brothers, Miller & Rhoads for $225 million to propel Allied into the specialty store business. At the age of sixty-seven, Macioce was, like Bob Campeau, a man who had worked himself up from very humble beginnings. The son of an immigrant barber, he had been raised in the low-income district of East Harlem in New York. But unlike Campeau, he had gone through college, graduating from Columbia University School of Law, and he was a veteran of the corporate boardroom, having held executive positions at three companies.

Macioce had barely heard of the Canadian developer the day Campeau walked into Allied's head office at 1114 Avenue of the Americas. But it didn't matter to him whether your name was Campeau or Rockefeller. What mattered was your money, and whether you had the stuff to stay in the game. Which is not to say that Thomas Macioce necessarily liked Robert Campeau, but he did not dislike him because of who he was. And it is not to say that Macioce found Campeau any more a welcome guest than Kenneth White of Royal Trustco had in 1980. But he had no personal ax to grind.

Macioce listened as Campeau outlined what he had in mind. He had already bought up 4 percent and wanted to talk about acquiring the company.

"I've got the highest regard for Allied management," Campeau said, " and if there is an acquisition, you could expect that the management, consistent with our philosophy at Campeau, would get 15 percent equity participation."

It was obvious that Campeau was not a man to mince words. "Give me two weeks to think about it," Macioce said. "Then we can talk again."

They met again two weeks later. This time Macioce was joined by his senior vice-president, Benjamin Frank, and Campeau was accompanied by Ronald Tysoe. Campeau handed Macioce pro-forma financial projections relating to a takeover.

Macioce suggested another approach. Forget about a complete takeover and consider a real estate deal, perhaps involving Allied's five shopping centers in Washington, Massachusetts and New Jersey. Macioce was stalling, evidently seeking time to learn the full extent of Campeau's game plan and devise a strategy to fend him off. "I'll think about that," Campeau told him, and a third meeting was scheduled for three days later.

When the four men met again, Campeau, repeating that he still wanted to acquire the company, agreed to talk about the shopping centers. Furthermore, he indicated to Macioce, he would still hold on to his shares even if a shopping center deal were reached. During the week, Allied gave Campeau the financial information on the shopping centers.

Campeau met Macioce yet again about a week later. He had reviewed the information and was prepared to talk. But he wanted a fast deal. So they decided the two sides should agree quickly on a projected 1986 cash flow figure for the shopping centers and meet again to discuss price based on whatever they came up with. The next day their deputies, Tysoe and Frank, met alone and agreed on a cash flow figure of $23 million.

Campeau and Macioce held a final session a few days after that. Campeau warned the Allied chairman that he would end the talks if they did not reach a deal quickly.

"And if we can't do that," he added, "I want to talk about an acquisition." His offer was $300 million for the five shopping centers, and he gave Macioce a letter of intent.

"Three-hundred and *fifty* million might be acceptable," Macioce said. "I'll call you tomorrow."

Macioce phoned the next day and told him the offer was unacceptable and he was not prepared to continue talking. Macioce saw no sense in stalling any longer. It was time to get rid of his Canadian suitor.

One day later, on September 4, Campeau delivered a letter to Macioce outlining the terms of his proposed takeover. He offered to pay $58 a share, 80 percent in cash and the rest in unspecified securities, or $2.98 billion, to shareholders for all of Allied's stock. He was proposing a "friendly" merger with the support of Allied's board of directors, similar to the proposition he had put to Kenneth White at their ill-fated meeting in 1980. If Allied did not support Campeau, and he proceeded regardless, it would be a hostile bid.

Campeau wrote: "We believe that this price, which is based upon our detailed review of publicly available information relating to Allied Stores, is fair and generous to your shareholders, even considering that the stock of Allied Stores has risen significantly over the last several months due in large part to recent merger activity in the retail industry." He also repeated that he was prepared to offer Allied management 15 percent of the surviving company and that he would honor employment contracts.

Citibank N.A. had committed $500 million to the bid and would lead the banking syndicate that would finance the offer. Campeau wanted Macioce's answer by 5 P.M. September 11, seven days away.

Wall Street was surprised when Campeau released a statement and a copy of his letter to Macioce to the media that day. Few had ever heard of Bob Campeau, but Allied stock rose by $10.75 on the New York Stock Exchange to $59.375 on speculation that the Canadian raider would be forced to pay more than he had offered.

One day before Campeau's deadline, Macioce invited

shopping center magnate Edward DeBartolo to dinner. DeBartolo was a powerful man, the largest shopping center developer and manager in the United States with fifty-one regional malls and fourteen strip plazas. As well, he personally owned the Pittsburgh Penguins hockey team, and his family owned the San Francisco 49ers football club. He had once offered $20 million to buy the Chicago White Sox baseball team, but eleven of the fourteen club owners in the American League voted down the sale.

DeBartolo was a friend of Macioce; like Campeau and Macioce, he had come from the ranks of the working poor. And many Allied stores were located in DeBartolo malls, a fact that made the two natural allies. Over dinner, Macioce told DeBartolo that Allied wanted to remain independent but that Campeau had come along. Might DeBartolo be interested in some association? DeBartolo was open to the idea, but there were no negotiations at this point.

On Campeau's deadline, Allied responded publicly to the Canadian developer, announcing that its board of directors was rejecting the offer as not in the best interests of its shareholders. By that time, the general consensus among financial analysts on Wall Street was that the Campeau bid was too low and he would have to go to about $65 or $66 if he hoped to succeed.

This was something he and his advisers had already accepted, but on the day after Allied's response, Campeau came out with a tender offer, bidding $58 a share in cash for up to 30 million shares, or 64 percent, of the stock. He was still trying to avoid a hostile takeover, saying in a letter to Macioce: "We would like to emphasize that it is our strong preference to enter into a friendly, negotiated transaction and ... should we be afforded an opportunity to negotiate and be provided with further information, we would be willing to consider an increase in our $58 per share price."

One of the architects of strategies such as this that would continue throughout the takeover attempt was Bruce Wasserstein of First Boston Corp., the sixth-largest investment house in the United States, who joined the team in September at

Allen Finkelson's suggestion. Wasserstein was known on Wall Street for his brilliance in orchestrating takeovers. He and Joseph Perella, as co-heads of First Boston's investment banking department, had helped seal some of the biggest deals in America. Wasserstein had been the strategist when General Motors bought Hughes Aircraft and when Texaco derailed Pennzoil's planned takeover of Getty Oil (which led to a $10-billion court judgment against Texaco). Wasserstein quickly became one of Campeau's key advisers as the takeover game continued.

While Campeau waited for some new move from Allied, DeBartolo and Macioce were talking. On September 15, DeBartolo proposed friendly negotiations toward an acquisition at $62 a share, all cash. While not rebuffing this potential white knight, the Allied chairman again told him that the company wanted to remain independent if possible.

A week later, Campeau phoned Macioce, trying to set up another meeting and telling him that he was willing to negotiate any aspect of a takeover. "I'm prepared to pay all cash in a friendly deal for all the shares," Campeau advised. "And I'm prepared to look at increasing the price."

Macioce agreed to meet the next day, at which time Campeau told him he had financing commitments for $700 million. Campeau was pressuring Macioce here by showing he could get financing for a hostile bid. Macioce replied that Campeau was short in his financing commitments, and Campeau responded that it would not be difficult to make up the difference. Macioce also asked Campeau if he was prepared to go to $60, and Campeau said no. "I'll discuss it with the board," Macioce said, but he apparently had no intention of doing so.

The following day, Allied sent a letter to its stockholders reporting that the board of directors was unanimous in rejecting Campeau's $58 offer as inadequate. Although Campeau met with Macioce two more times that week and indicated that he would be prepared now to go to $60 cash for all the shares, Macioce remained uninterested. His message to Campeau was, "Withdraw the offer."

So far, Macioce and Campeau had been playing a game that was leading to stalemate. Macioce had stalled, promising to consider and take up with his board the various Campeau proposals, meanwhile searching for a way to keep from being taken over. Now he discussed with DeBartolo the possibility of selling the shopping centers, thus making Allied much less attractive to Campeau. DeBartolo was interested but negotiations led nowhere.

On September 29, Campeau made one last attempt to get Macioce to budge, then jumped his bid to $66 in cash, or $2.69 billion, for 40.8 million shares, which would give him 80 percent of the company if successful. Campeau's offer constituted what is known as a two-tiered bid. Those who did not tender to the $66 cash offer (the front end) would be paid after Campeau gained control (at the back end) with high-risk, high-yielding preferred shares. While the face value of this back end was also $66, analysts put the market value at only about $45. Such a bid is coercive to stockholders because of the higher value on the front end. There is pressure to tender to ensure not being locked out of the higher cash portion and being left with the lesser-valued securities at the back end.

This ploy also put more pressure on Macioce. Campeau informed him that he was now willing to negotiate buying all the shares for cash at $63 each. He was still trying to get Allied to do a friendly deal.

Instead, a classic game of takeover chess ensued, with every Allied move being parried by Campeau. The first piece Macioce played was his white knight. Macioce met with DeBartolo and Paul Bilzerian, an investor from Florida, to talk about the possibility of forming a company that would make a friendly takeover of Allied. One week later, DeBartolo and Bilzerian formed ASC Acquisition Corp. — DeBartolo was in for 90 percent and Bilzerian for 10 percent.

On October 7, this white knight rode to the rescue with a bid of $67 a share, or $3.5 billion, in cash for all Allied stock in a tender offer. This was considerably better than Campeau's bid in that shareholders were being offered $1 a share more, and all in cash. The Allied board, having no friendly alternative, approved the DeBartolo proposal and recommended that shareholders tender. DeBartolo could be expected to retain Allied management, whereas Campeau and his plans were unknown quantities. Particularly now, after their resistance, Allied management could not be sure of keeping their jobs under Campeau ownership.

Under its deal with DeBartolo, Allied agreed to what are known as "breakup" fees, payments to ASC Acquisition of investment banking expenses and an amount equivalent to $1 a share if the bid failed. It is interesting to note that Richard Thomson's Toronto Dominion Bank agreed to help finance the DeBartolo offer.

Now it was Campeau's turn, and he attempted to regain lost ground. At least this time, unlike with Royal Trustco, he knew who he was dealing with. On October 10, he announced that he was pushing ahead with his $66-a-share offer, which was scheduled to expire that night, but he said he would, if successful, elect a new board of directors and declare a $2-a-share dividend. That would be increased to $3 if the breakup fee to DeBartolo was canceled. In effect, this creative strategy increased the value of his bid by a minimum $2 a share, making it more valuable to stockholders, many of whom tendered.

Campeau filed suit in Chancery Court of Delaware, where Allied was incorporated, in an attempt to kill the breakup fees, which he maintained marked a breach of Allied's responsibilities to its stockholders. He also announced that he would sue Allied in Federal District Court in New York, accusing the company of violating U.S. securities laws for not disclosing its negotiations with DeBartolo.

The same frantic day, as each side jockeyed for position, Allied went to court in New York, claiming that Campeau's proposal to declare a special dividend constituted an amended tender offer, which must, under U.S. securities laws, be held open for ten additional business days. The court issued a temporary restraining order prohibiting Campeau from buying any shares, but only for ten calendar days. Anyone who wanted to withdraw shares tendered to date could do so. In response,

Campeau extended his bid to midnight, October 24, four days after the court-ordered extension.

Still later in the day, Allied adopted what is known as a "poison pill," a defense aimed at fighting a corporate raider by making the company less attractive. There are many variations. In this case, the pill was designed to increase Allied's debt by allowing remaining stockholders to swap their shares for $67 in short-term interest-bearing notes if a hostile bidder such as Campeau gained more than 50 percent of the stock without offering all shareholders at least $67 a share in cash. Fifty percent was the poison pill's "trigger point," the percentage of stock that must be accumulated by a raider for the defense to kick in. The pill would not take effect if the bidder proposed acquiring all shares for a least $67 in cash each, thus protecting shareholders on the back end of any deal. The additional debt it would bring apparently worried Campeau's bankers, threatening his financing commitments.

Poison pills have been adopted by several hundred companies in the United States. By early 1989, only one Canadian company, Campeau's old employer, Inco, had adopted such a defense, and it did so amid much controversy. Poison pills rarely end up stopping a takeover. More often they work to bring a hostile bidder to the bargaining table and increase the amount paid to shareholders in a negotiated settlement. In a 1986 study of thirty companies that actually used their poison pills, the Securities and Exchange Commission in the United States found a poison pill defense often acted to reduce the value of a company's stock. Fourteen of the 30 companies studied used the pills successfully to block takeovers, but their average stock value fell 17 percent within six months of the takeover battles.

In response to the Allied poison pill, Campeau went to court seeking to have it invalidated.

Then, on October 21, he sweetened the back end of his bid by boosting the securities component and thus raising its total value while making his offer less coercive. It is difficult to value an offer such as this because of the uncertainty of the value of the stock portion. In such deals, financial analysts and arbitrageurs, professional traders who speculate for profit during a takeover, calculate what is known as the "blended value," the per-share worth of a bid when the two parts are mixed together; in this case it was based on an estimate of what the stock portion was worth. Arbitrageurs put the blended value of the new Campeau bid at between $67 and $68 a share, at least equal to, and possibly better than, the DeBartolo offer.

On October 23, a day before his bid was to expire, Campeau's court attempt to kill the poison pill was denied. That night he told his people that he was prepared to walk away from the bid. Campeau, Finkelson, Wasserstein and others involved in the takeover met through the night in a smoke-filled conference room on the forty-second floor of the First Boston offices. At 8:51 A.M. October 24, the meeting ended and Campeau announced he was terminating his offer, seemingly admitting defeat. But just twenty-seven minutes later, Bob Campeau took part in the largest single block trade in U.S. history and scooped up control of Allied Stores Corp.

A third party had entered the picture. For several days, Jefferies & Co., a Los Angeles securities firm specializing in trading over the counter, or the so-called third market, had been assembling a huge block of Allied shares, primarily from many arbitrageurs. And it was Boyd Jefferies, known for trading big blocks of stock, who came to Bob Campeau's rescue. As the Allied fight was drawing to a close, the Jefferies people had asked some of the arbitrageurs holding large blocks if they wanted protection by, in effect, joining a group. By the time Campeau withdrew his bid, Jefferies had assembled a block of almost 30 million Allied shares.

Lawyer Allen Finkelson recalls that the Jefferies people had been calling the Campeau and DeBartolo teams during the previous week, asking both sides if they wanted to buy. However, neither could purchase the stock during the period of their tender offers without violating U.S. securities laws. And to withdraw their offers and buy the stock would have been extremely risky. The Campeau people were not sure Jefferies really had enough stock, or that he would not try to auction it if they pulled their bid and tried to buy it. In addition, there was always the possibility that a court would decide the Jefferies block had been purchased too soon after the bid was pulled and prevent the sale from going through.

Once the poison pill had been upheld, and Campeau realized he had little chance of succeeding, dealing with Jefferies was a risk worth taking. So when the L.A. trader's people called, shortly after Campeau announced he was pulling his bid, a deal was quickly made. There were no negotiations; Campeau offered $67 a share and Jefferies accepted. He had until the following Friday, October 31, to pay for the stock.

In what is known as a "street sweep," Campeau bought from Jefferies a block of 25.8 million Allied shares, roughly 48 percent of the company, with $1.8 billion in a bridge loan from First Boston. (It was the first time First Boston had helped finance a hostile takeover, and Citibank later agreed to put up about half the money.) Coupled with what he already held, the Jefferies block gave Campeau 52 percent — majority control — of Allied Stores. "It was a bold and innovative move," Macioce later said of the purchase.

Buying the shares, however, was still financially risky, a sign of just how badly Campeau wanted the company. There was no question that Allied would in desperation challenge the deal in court, and there were no assurances that the court would not rule that the block had been purchased too soon after the bid had been withdrawn. And if the court decided that Campeau could not vote the stock, he would be unable to repay First Boston except by selling the shares, possibly to DeBartolo.

Even though Campeau had now tied up more than 50 percent of Allied stock, the poison pill would not be triggered until he paid for the Jefferies block. So this gave him until the following Friday to consolidate his position. He was now in an excellent bargaining position. His opponents knew that once he had actually paid for the stock, he would be the majority owner of Allied, poison pill or not. With the First Boston bridge loan, his financing was far more secure than it had been when the poison pill first loomed, and the prospect of it being triggered was much less daunting.

Allied and DeBartolo immediately went to court seeking an order to halt any immediate takeover. The question here was whether Campeau had the *right* to own the shares. Allied alleged that what Campeau's team had done amounted to an illegal tender offer that violated the 1934 Securities Exchange Act; they claimed that Campeau had arranged for Jefferies to assemble a share block before the tender offer was withdrawn. Campeau lawyer Ronald Rolfe tried to turn the tables, arguing in court that Campeau Corp. now controlled the company. Gesturing toward Allied's lawyer, he said, "They are acting as outlaw directors."

Judge Pierre Leval issued a temporary restraining order barring Campeau from consummating the purchase or voting the Allied stock. He also approved a $5-million bond to be posted by Allied should the order harm Campeau Corp., and he ordered both sides to appear at a hearing on October 31, the day Campeau was to close the deal on the Jefferies block. But two days before the hearing, the court amended its order when Campeau's lawyers argued that he should be allowed to pay for the stock before the payment period expired. Campeau was given permission to consummate the purchase but not vote the stock.

During one court appearance, when Macioce's deposition was being taken, Campeau's lawyer asked him to stop by and see Bob, who was in a nearby room. Macioce agreed.

"Hello," he told his adversary.

"These are busy days," Bob remarked.

"Oh, not really," Macioce replied nonchalantly. "I've been watching television, popping chocolates in my mouth."

Campeau now owned 52 percent of Allied and held the upper hand. Allied could not count on winning its court case, so it opened negotiations with the Campeau team on October 30.

There was still the question of DeBartolo, however, who decided to make a last attempt to acquire Allied despite the change of heart by its directors. On Friday, October 31, in a letter to an Allied board meeting, he offered a cash-and-securities deal worth $70 a share. DeBartolo must still have been holding out hope that the court would force Campeau to divest the Jefferies block. Allied and DeBartolo representatives met during the day to discuss the proposal. Then, DeBartolo suddenly called a halt.

He had decided instead to negotiate with Campeau, who now appeared clearly in control. Campeau sealed the matter by agreeing that Allied, which he would soon own, would pay DeBartolo the originally agreed-to breakup fees, amounting to $116.3 million. In addition, he granted DeBartolo right of first refusal on certain Allied properties and operations should they be put up for sale, and agreed to bring him in as a partner in any new Allied shopping centers. Suddenly Campeau's adversary had become his ally.

The Campeau and Allied teams reached a negotiated settlement. Campeau agreed to pay remaining stockholders $69 a share in cash and securities, bringing the total cost of the deal to $3.5 billion. The full cost of the takeover, including expenses and assumption of existing Allied debt, was about $4.3 billion, making it the largest acquisition by a Canadian in the United States. As part of the deal, Macioce would become chairman of the Campeau Corp. board, a sign of just what a skilled negotiator Macioce was. Campeau, who would remain chief executive, later offered board seats to Bruce Wasserstein, who did not accept, and Allen Finkelson, who did. The deal was done on the same day the Jefferies sale was set to close, and thus the poison pill was never triggered.

With their agreement signed, Macioce invited Campeau and Finkelson to dine at the exclusive Sky Club atop the PanAm building in downtown Manhattan. It was a very civilized conclusion to what had been a bitter fight, a prime example of how quickly enemies can become friends – if the price is right. Over dinner, the men spoke of the future, replayed events of the last several weeks and rehearsed what they would say two days later when they publicly announced the deal. Perhaps Macioce even persuaded himself that he could happily work for this gutsy Canadian builder.

At about 11:30 that night, Bob called Ilse, who was on a trip in Germany. Although it was 5:30 A.M. in Europe, Ilse probably did not mind. This was one of the high points in her husband's life and she surely celebrated the victory with him. (Ilse was later put on the Campeau Corp. board of directors.)

It seems that everyone was happy with the final deal. Macioce managed to get $2 a share more for the remaining stockholders than did the arbitrageurs who sold through Jefferies. Without the Jefferies block, Campeau might not have won, but Macioce was not sour. "I think everybody was working for their own side. The arbitrageurs were working for them and Mr. Campeau was working for Mr. Campeau and I was working for Mr. Allied." He opted for a deal, he says, because "my stockholders were being protected and I was getting a fair value for the company, and, number two, my employees were going to be protected."

Bruce Wasserstein's stature was enhanced still further as a result of his key role in plotting the Campeau strategy. He had also moved First Boston in an important new direction by putting up the bridge loan that allowed Campeau to buy the Jefferies block. Says Finkelson: "That deal couldn't have happened without First Boston kind of ponying up the money and without Wasserstein's decision to get into merchant banking."

Robert Campeau had won for himself a large piece of the U.S. retailing industry and had finally achieved the status of big-time corporate raider he had sought since going after Markborough Properties thirteen years earlier. He had come to Wall Street an unknown and emerged a victor; now his name would be mentioned alongside those of Carl Icahn and T. Boone Pickens. And he had changed the takeover game when he bypassed the tender process to buy the Jefferies block using borrowed money from an investment bank. Within days, takeover specialists in the United States were saying Campeau had paved the way for similar such deals. Boasted Wasserstein: "This is the dawn of a new era of merchant banking."

Campeau may have made his mark on Wall Street, but he had also entered an industry about which he knew little, and he had saddled himself with heavy debt in the process. The full ramifications of his takeover still are not known, and will not be for some time.

Although Edward DeBartolo had not won control of Allied, he had made some good money for his trouble. As well, he would soon forge a strong and fruitful relationship with his one-time adversary. The shift in their relationship began almost immediately. In order to complete the Allied purchase by the end of 1986 to save money before new U.S. tax laws came into effect, Campeau went to DeBartolo for additional financing. The Youngstown shopping mall developer provided him with a $150-million loan and in exchange took an option to acquire 35 percent of Allied. (Under the deal, DeBartolo could have acquired the 35 percent by paying $60 million and adding in the loan money for a total $210 million.) This gave Campeau enough money to pay remaining shareholders in cash, which he ultimately did.

Just how good a deal Campeau had made would be determined by how quickly he could reduce the debt incurred in the takeover. This is the key to a successful leveraged buyout. His bank agreements required payments of $300 million by June 30, 1987, an aggregate $500 million by December 31, 1987, and the remainder by the end of 1988. Campeau also planned to refinance mortgaged real estate to meet an additional $608 million in bank payments by the end of 1988.

His first move, in early January 1987, was to sell off the five Allied shopping centers to DeBartolo for $400 million. Campeau retained an option to buy back half-interest for $200 million; The properties were valuable assets and sure sources of income.

A few days later, he set about to break up Allied, announcing plans to sell sixteen of its twenty-four divisions to raise $1.1 billion. Once the selloff was complete, Campeau would be left with about 270 stores of the almost 700 he started with. Of Allied's seventeen department store chains, he wanted to dump the least profitable: Joske's, Block's, Cain-Sloan, Dey's Donaldson's, Herpolsheimer's, Heer's, Miller's, Miller & Rhoads and both Pomeroy's divisions. He would hold on to Stern's and The Bon while merging Maas Brothers with Jordan

Marsh–Florida and Read's with Jordan Marsh–New England. Of the seven specialty store divisions, he earmarked for sale Bonwit Teller, Garfinckel's, Catherine's, Plymouth Shops and Jerry Leonard. Brooks Brothers and Ann Taylor were the only specialty units to be kept.

Campeau was following a well-developed formula: sell off weaker divisions, retain the most profitable. The divisions he was selling had accounted for 38.4 percent of Allied sales in 1985 but only about 11.8 percent of profits. The stores he would keep represented a little over half of Allied's total square footage, but generated 61.6 percent of sales and 88.2 percent of store profit.

Within one week of the announcement of the breakup, and just twelve days after becoming Campeau Corp.'s chairman, Macioce quit. He will not say why he left. Perhaps he found his golden deal was not so golden. Possibly he learned that he could not work with Bob Campeau. Macioce knew this industry well; Campeau did not, yet he wanted to run the retailing operations as he saw fit, setting the stage for conflict with the former Allied chairman. As well, Macioce's original Allied Stores would be nothing like it was after Campeau finished dismembering the company and slashing costs. Perhaps Macioce decided he wanted no part of the new company. Campeau took back the post of company chairman while also becoming interim Allied chairman.

The divestiture program moved forward quickly while Campeau raised money on other fronts. In March, he put out a three-part security issue — notes, unsecured bonds and Allied preferred shares — that raised $1.5 billion, $100 million more than expected because of high investor interest. This windfall enabled Campeau to repay First Boston. Also in March, Campeau sold half interest in his still-under-construction Scotia Plaza to the Reichmanns' Olympia & York for $198 million. This move sparked speculation in the financial community that he could not handle the massive debt.

Campeau moved far faster than anyone had expected. The divestiture program was completed by the summer, more than a year ahead of schedule. In August, Campeau bought out

DeBartolo's option to take 35 percent of Allied, paying back the full DeBartolo loan by the end of the year. He also refinanced all existing bank debt, and the original loans from the Citibank syndicate were repaid.

In November 1987, Campeau brought Robert Morosky into the Allied organization. Morosky, who had spent 15 years with The Limited, a retail chain, was to be the retailing general directing the show for Campeau. Because he was such a skilled retailer, his presence alone brought stability. He was responsible for eliminating about 4 percent of the 50,000 employees in the Allied group and cutting costs dramatically.

In late December 1987, with Allied behind him, Campeau wrote in a document to shareholders: "The company has also been reviewing opportunities to increase its business through the acquisition of other companies in North America or their assets. In [my] view, the recent decline in the stock market presents the company with attractive acquisition possibilities. Should the company proceed with any one of these acquisitions, the company or a subsidiary would incur substantial debt and risk ... it may be appropriate for the company to move quickly."

In fact, Campeau was already deep into the planning stages of his next assault on the U.S. retailing industry.

15 / Project Rose

"Hell, I'm going to get the company."
— Robert Campeau

BOB CAMPEAU WAS still in the midst of restructuring Allied Stores when in August 1987 he approached Bruce Wasserstein and the other First Boston advisers and gave them a list of other retailers he wanted to study. Over the next several weeks the First Boston team began developing ideas, studying the details and running the numbers. They soon settled on their target — Federated Department Stores Inc., in Cincinnati, Ohio, but incorporated in the state of Delaware — and began plotting strategy. As with the Allied bid, secrecy was of the utmost at this point, and as with Allied, a code name was used. The First Boston people called the dossier Project Rose, after Pete Rose, the legendary baseball player and manager of the Cincinnati Reds. The name was appropriate. Pete Rose is renowned for his competitive drive. So is Robert Campeau.

Federated Department Stores was a good fit with Allied. It held an attractive core group of department stores, many prime undervalued properties and several noncore businesses that could be dumped to help pay for the takeover. The Federated portfolio included almost 700 stores in thirty-six states bringing in about $11 billion a year in sales. It was the fifth-largest retailer and second-largest department store group in the United States, rich in assets with franchises throughout the nation. And it owned Bloomingdale's, the chic New York department store.

Federated was also steeped in history, which must have appealed to Campeau. It had been formed in 1929 by the merger of three family-owned companies, Abraham & Straus of Brooklyn, Filene's of Boston and Lazarus of Columbus, Ohio. Bloomingdale's joined shortly afterward. Nine of Federated's fifteen divisions were more than a century old, and its stores were household names: Abraham & Straus, Foley's of Houston, I. Magnin in San Francisco, Rich's in Atlanta, Burdines of Miami, Bullock's/Bullock Wilshire in Los Angeles. And of course everyone knew Bloomingdale's, a trend-setter whose flagship store at 59th and Lexington draws crowds of tourists and native New Yorkers alike. Founded in 1872 by Lyman and Joseph Bloomingdale, in 1987 there were sixteen stores in a national chain, with annual sales in excess of $1 billion.

Not only was Federated a juicy plum; it was ripe for the plucking. At Federated's helm was Howard Goldfeder, who had been chairman for seven years. A former coat buyer for Bloomingdale's, the sixty-one-year-old had a reputation as a tough manager. Yet he and his management team had failed to concentrate on the large company's core department store business, and that side had suffered. Its operating profit had increased less than 17 percent from 1981 to 1987, and its profits as a percentage of sales had fallen from 3.7 percent to less than 3 percent. As a result, its stock price was depressed and its flank was open to Bob Campeau.

Initially, the First Boston strategists figured Campeau could sell four Federated divisions — Ralphs, Gold Circle, MainStreet and The Children's Place — to help finance the takeover. Like the Allied takeover, this would be a leveraged buyout using some of the assets to help pay for the acquisition. The assets targeted were not among Federated's core department store businesses. Ralphs, for example, was a grocery chain; The Children's Place was a specialty store division selling children's clothes.

Bruce Wasserstein, Allen Finkelson and the rest of the strategy team never set a target price for the stock. First Boston believed the cost of a takeover would run to about $70 a share (in August 1987, Federated stock was trading in the $58 range), but Campeau felt the stock market was about to turn and he could get the stock for less. Events soon supported his conviction: when on October 19, 1987, the market crashed, the value of Federated shares plunged from $47 to $39. Federated stock continued to slide after the crash, hitting a low of $29 before settling in the $33 range.

The conditions were now right for Campeau to make his first move. On October 28, he quietly began buying Federated stock, eventually taking up 400,200 shares. During November, December and early January, the takeover team planned, gathered information and prepared the necessary documents. Campeau wanted to move before stock prices recovered and before the state of Delaware enacted tough new anti-takeover legislation. It was not clear to Campeau's lawyers whether the legislation would be retroactive to cover bids already in progress; they hoped to beat it by launching their bid before the legislation was signed into law. But they would be ready to immediately challenge the Delaware legislation in court.

In mid-January 1988, about two weeks before Campeau went public with his takeover plans, New York real estate magnate Donald Trump sought clearance under U.S. anti-trust laws to buy at least $15 million of Federated stock and, depending on market conditions, possibly up to 15 percent. There were allegations at the time that Trump was after what is known as "greenmail," payments a takeover target makes to a corporate raider to back off, though Campeau never believed he was moving for a takeover. Trump made no further moves, eventually selling his stock while the Campeau bid was in progress. Trump's actions, however, pushed the market value of Federated stock to about $37. With the Delaware legislation nearing passage, it was time to move.

There were to be no friendly advances to Federated before the bid, as there had been to Allied. Reasonably certain that Federated's board of directors would resist, Campeau chose to act aggressively from the beginning. On January 25, a half-page notice of a tender offer appeared in the *New York Times*, advising that CRTF Corp., a subsidiary of Campeau Corp., was bidding $47 a share — or $4.2 billion — for all outstanding shares of Federated Department Stores Inc. The bid was to expire at midnight, February 22 and was conditional on obtaining majority control.

The bid was also conditional on approval of the Federated board of directors and invalidation of a poison pill that had been adopted by Federated in January 1986 after widespread rumors on Wall Street that it was a takeover target. The first pill's trigger point, where the defense kicked in, was 50 percent, later reduced to 30 percent. After Trump's January announcement, it had been reduced again, to 15 percent. The poison pill was designed to ensure that any unwanted takeover would be prohibitively expensive. If a raider acquired 15 percent or more of Federated stock without the blessing of the board of directors, stockholders would be able to buy newly issued shares at half price, thus diluting ownership and devaluing the raider's shares.

The same day the ad appeared, Campeau sent a letter to chairman Howard Goldfeder saying he was prepared to up the bid in a negotiated deal. In it he warned Goldfeder not to try to block stockholder consideration of the offer or enter into other agreements without allowing him a fair opportunity to compete. "While we desire to enter into a friendly, negotiated merger agreement, we have been advised that our most prudent course is to commence a tender offer," Campeau wrote. "Therefore, Campeau Corporation today is commencing an all cash tender offer for all outstanding shares of Common Stock of Federated at a price of $47 per share. That price, determined after a review of publicly available information, represents a premium of about 37 percent over the price at which the Federated shares were trading prior to the recent takeover-related activity in the stock. We are available to meet promptly with you and Federated's Board of Directors to discuss all aspects of our offer and to answer any questions you may have. Your Board should be aware that we are prepared immediately to enter into negotiations with respect to all aspects of our offer, including price."

Federated immediately advised its shareholders to do nothing until it discussed what had happened with its financial advisers. There were concerns at Federated headquarters, though none of the executives was particularly surprised by the bid. "I think if it were 1976, it would have been a great shock because of what the business world was like in 1976," says Federated senior vice-president Thomas Cody. "I think in 1988 it's part of doing business, that those things happen. I mean, it wasn't like something that could never have happened suddenly happening."

Bob Campeau was no longer an unknown quantity, and Wall Street bet on a major fight that would spell big profits. Investors began buying shares in a spree that pushed the value of Federated stock to above Campeau's offering price of $47. The stock had closed the previous Friday at $35.875, and Campeau's announcement sent it soaring to $49 on the New York Stock Exchange. The bid price of $47 was not taken seriously by anyone, including Campeau. It was an opening shot only, meant to set the game in motion. (He still thought he could buy the company for less than the $70 per share his advisers predicted.)

Campeau wasted no time in moving on the legal front. On January 25, just after launching the bid, his lawyers sued Federated in federal court in New York, seeking to invalidate the poison pill, which would become an increasingly important element over the course of the fight. The suit was based on the premise that the poison pill was so structured as to give Federated stockholders, the company's owners, no chance to decide whether or not to accept an offer that might be in their best interests and that its main effect was to protect or "entrench" the Federated management and board of directors. By using this takeover defense, the corporation's directors were in breach of their fiduciary duties, their responsibility to protect their shareholders' best interests.

To bolster his case, Campeau cited Federated's "grossly excessive" golden parachutes, contracts that provide handsome benefits to executives who lose their jobs after a takeover. The parachutes granted the top Federated executives lump-sum payments equal to 120 percent of their current salaries for a three-year period, less the time an executive remained employed after a change in ownership. These benefits were payable, under certain circumstances, even if an executive quit. In addition, an executive compensation plan allowed for stock credits to immediately be converted to cash on a change of control. According to Campeau's suit, "the overall effect of the anti-takeover measures adopted by Federated . . . is to deter any takeover not welcomed by the Board by requiring a potential acquiror to incur staggering monetary penalties."

The phone rang early the next day in Campeau's suite at the Waldorf. It was a United Press International reporter calling from Toronto, surprised to get Campeau on the first try. He wanted to know what Campeau planned and whether he would break up Federated as he had Allied, a subject of widespread speculation.

"Mr. Campeau, you surprised everyone again," the reporter said.

"It's only you guys who are surprised," Campeau responded.

During the conversation Campeau admitted that he eventually would merge Federated and Allied but denied that he planned a major sale of Federated assets. At this point, he planned to shed only a few Federated divisions.

"Obviously this is not a company that has a lot of divisions to be sold. We've made our decision to buy Federated to further our retail business."

The reporter asked Campeau about the betting among Wall Street securities analysts that a bidding contest could push the price to at least $55 a share, possibly $60 if a full-scale bidding war erupted. The response was typical Campeau. "The analysts are not bidding. We have an offer there and the offer is there."

While Campeau was speaking to the reporter, Federated chairman Howard Goldfeder, in his Cincinnati office, was taking a call from New York. Edward Finkelstein, the chairman of R.H. Macy & Co., or Macy's, one of America's best-known department store chains, had phoned to offer his advice, one retailer to another, on what Federated might do to repel a takeover. It was a friendly chat. Clearly it was in Macy's interests to see Allied and Federated, two of its major competitors, kept in separate hands.

Later in the day, Federated made its first move on the legal front, filing a suit in Ohio. Since Federated was headquartered in Cincinnati, the company claimed protection under Ohio's Takeover Act. One of the most restrictive in the country, this act allowed companies to adopt poison pills and gave boards of directors a large say in whether to accept or reject takeover offers. Federated's suit sought a declaration that the Takeover Act was constitutional and applicable in the Campeau bid, and asked for a preliminary ruling that would block Campeau from taking any legal action related to the act in any forum other than the court in question. It was a clear signal that Federated was prepared to fight.

Late the same day, Ohio Judge Lewis Williams granted Federated a temporary restraining order preventing Campeau from challenging the statute in any other court.

On the New York Stock Exchange at the close of January 26 trading, Federated stock was at $50.625, a rise of $1.625 from the previous day.

The opening shots having been fired, the pace of activities now slowed. The Campeau team had a strategy to play out, but Federated was scrambling to put a defense in place. Campeau's deadline was more than three weeks away.

In Ohio, Federated management wasted little time in moving behind the scenes. Soon after the Campeau bid was launched, Federated's legal department retained lawyers John Chester and Roderick Willcox of the Chester, Hoffman and Willcox firm in Columbus to act for the company on all legal matters in the state of Ohio pertaining to the takeover attempt. Chester and Willcox had been doing takeover-related work since the 1960s and, coincidentally, had represented several Canadian companies. Their knowledge of Canadian law would come in handy as they pursued a strategy of developing new anti-takeover legislation for Ohio.

They decided on a two-pronged legislative attack, based partly on the fact that Campeau Corp. was a foreign company, and drafted two proposed pieces of legislation designed to repel

Campeau and protect Federated. The first would extend an existing law applying to Ohio corporations such as Federated, whose corporate home and principal state of business was Ohio but whose legal homes were in other states. This existing law required a shareholders' vote before a purchaser could acquire 20 percent or more of the corporation.

The second bill was original and was inspired by Canada's foreign investment review policy, under which the federal government is authorized to study and approve or reject sizable corporate acquisitions by non-Canadians. "We were familiar with what Canada did and thought, why don't we do what Canada does?" Willcox recalls. "The idea of structuring something in view of the Canadian foreign investment review seemed like a good idea."

This new bill would force foreign companies engaged in a takeover in Ohio to jump through a seemingly endless series of regulatory hoops and effectively bar any unfriendly attempt at a leveraged buyout. No foreign company would be allowed to acquire an Ohio corporation without the support of its board of directors until Ohio's Department of Development approved the takeover on the basis of whether the state would be hurt.

While Chester and Willcox were drafting these two pieces of legislation, Federated's corporate officers prepared the political ground. The main target of their lobbying effort was Senator Stanley Aronoff, president protem of the Ohio Senate and one of the most powerful Republicans in the state. Aronoff was a good choice as the politician to be approached. He was a powerful senator who had received substantial backing from business interests in Ohio, including Federated people. Aronoff's election campaign committee received twenty-eight donations, amounting to about $4,700, from Federated executives and employees.

Federated vice-president and secretary Boris Auerbach and two executives visited Aronoff at his office, explained what was happening and that the company was attempting to resist the Canadian takeover. They raised the issue of possible state legislation and scheduled a meeting between Aronoff and the lawyers Chester and Willcox. One of their key arguments was the potential loss of jobs in Ohio.

Chester and Willcox then met with the senator, outlined the proposed pieces of legislation and asked whether he would introduce the bills. "We simply explained the intent of the legislation, and explained why we wanted it and why we thought it was good not only for Federated but for the state of Ohio," recalls Chester. "We felt it would protect all the corporations who have corporate headquarters in Ohio but are incorporated in Delaware."

Aronoff was receptive, and when he sounded out his colleagues, both Democrat and Republican, he found, in his words, "a general support for trying to, at least at the outset, retain the Ohio image, Ohio presence, since rumors were flying around all over the place at that stage." Among the rumors was the suggestion that Campeau was going to move corporate headquarters to New York. This would mean lost tax revenues as well as lost jobs.

The senator would ultimately introduce both bills, but the second one was amended in committee to contain a sunset provision under which it would automatically expire in July. This was a law tailor-made to protect Federated.

While Federated was still pursuing its Ohio strategy, Campeau called an extraordinary meeting in Manhattan. Early in the afternoon of February 2, he met Paul Reichmann and Edward DeBartolo in his suite at the Waldorf for preliminary talks aimed at getting their help in financing his takeover bid. It was testimony to Campeau's adaptability as well as his success. After all, Paul Reichmann had helped block his takeover of Royal Trustco and DeBartolo was the white knight who had tried to thwart his assault on Allied. Each man brought with him a team of advisers and Campeau met with each group separately. "Those were not meetings where all three groups sat around talking to each other," says one of the men involved. "Those were Bob first with one and then with the other. They happened to be crossing paths. They all may have sat in a room at one point for a little bit, but they were basically separate discussions. They were more exploratory than anything else."

An incredible amount of money was represented in Campeau's suite that day. At one point during the meetings he phoned Tom Hayes, president of The May Department Stores of St. Louis, the largest department store group in the United States, to discuss the possibility of selling some of Federated's assets. Hayes was interested and joined the high-powered allies Campeau was lining up early in his quest. The talks with Reichmann and DeBartolo would continue for about a week, but would ultimately lead to a deal. And Hayes would promise $1.5 billion in return for two Federated divisions.

Later that day, Campeau removed from his offer the condition that a takeover first be approved by the Federated board of directors. He would put his offer to shareholders alone: the bid was now fully hostile. Though the board's approval would have helped, he did not need it; in the end, shareholders decide whether to tender. Campeau had known before he launched the bid that Federated's board would fight; this was simply adding pressure. And he could not be accused of not having sought the board's co-operation. It is safe to assume that the condition for board approval had been originally included with the intention of removing it several days later.

The Campeau team was also hearing rumors on the street that Federated was considering a wide range of defenses to make the company unattractive, including the possibility of declaring an extraordinary cash dividend of as much as $45 a share, which would saddle the company with a huge additional debt. There was also talk that the retailer was planning to sell certain unspecified assets, attractive parts of the business, in a defense known as the scorched-earth technique whose aim is the same as a poison pill. Campeau warned Goldfeder in a letter against any such moves. But there was not much he could do about them. Although costly to Federated, they were legal.

February 2 was also the day Delaware signed into law the bill to restrict hostile takeovers. The new statute was retroactive to December 23, thus encompassing Campeau's bid. Within hours, Campeau filed suit in New York challenging the legislation. Black & Decker Corp., a large powertool manufacturer based in Hunt Valley, Maryland, and then in the midst of a $1.8-billion takeover bid for American Standard Co. of New York, also filed suit, in federal court in Wilmington, Delaware.

The Delaware bill stirred controversy across the United States because of the number of corporations that made Delaware their legal home, including about 56 percent of the Fortune 500 companies and 45 percent of the companies listed on the New York Stock Exchange. The state, which had special tax rules and was liberal where companies were concerned, brought in some 17 percent of its income through corporate franchise taxes and fees. There had been threats of companies leaving the state if the statute was not enacted.

The legislation was designed to protect Delaware-chartered companies by blocking hostile takeovers for three years after a raider acquired 15 percent or more of the target stock, except in a case where the raider was able to acquire 85 percent in the same transaction. Since it is virtually impossible to obtain 85 percent of a company's stock if management is opposed, the statute in effect gave entrenched managements veto power over hostile takeovers. This denial of shareholder rights was the crux of Campeau's lawyers' argument. There was one escape clause, however: takeover offers were exempt if a white knight became involved.

Campeau's lawyers challenged the Delaware legislation on the basis that it conflicted with federal securities law, particularly the Williams Act of 1965. They said: "The Williams Act reflects the intent of Congress that, when an interstate offer is made for the shares of a publicly held corporation, its success or failure should be left to the free and informed judgment of the shareholders of that corporation."

(The Securities and Exchange Commission, in a separate suit brought in April, supported Campeau's position, saying Congress had intended a system of regulation that would allow shareholders a fair opportunity to assess the merits of a bid and that the major result of the Delaware statute was to disenfranchise shareholders. But by then Campeau's takeover fight was over.)

February 2 had certainly turned out to be an eventful day, but it was not over yet. Bruce Wasserstein announced that he was quitting First Boston to form a new merchant banking firm with his colleague Joseph Perella. This news, combined with the events in Delaware, caused jitters in the market, raising doubts over whether Campeau could now succeed. Federated stock fell by $2.50 to $51.25 on the New York exchange.

Campeau was unperturbed. The next morning he told a Toronto-based reporter that Wasserstein's departure would not hurt his efforts and that while he would retain the services of First Boston, he would also continue to consult Wasserstein. "Bruce is a very capable person, almost a genius," Campeau said. "First Boston will always remain our banker but we will use the services of Bruce Wasserstein from time to time." Indeed, Wasserstein continued to play a key role and the Federated deal turned out to be the first major success for his fledgling company.

On Thursday, February 4, Campeau increased the pressure on Federated by offering to increase his bid to $61 a share, or a total $5.5 billion, but only if Federated's board accepted by 5 P.M. the coming Saturday. Accompanying his new bid was a letter to the Federated board expressing Campeau's disappointment that the directors were not willing to meet. Wrote Campeau: "We are prepared to make a presentation directly to the Federated board, demonstrating our ability to finance the transaction, including our ability to commit in excess of $1 billion of equity." He did not, however, cancel the $47-a-share tender offer. That would remain in effect, along with its February 22 deadline. In the event of a friendly deal, the price could be raised accordingly.

Wall Street analysts believed the $61 offer was in the range of fair value, never thinking the bidding eventually would go as high as it did. They knew, though, that Federated would not accept the new offer and would continue to resist until there was no way out.

The new bid pushed Federated stock $1 higher, to $52.25.

At this point it appeared that Campeau was bidding against only himself, upping the ante in the face of phantoms. In fact, the increase to $61 was part of an overall strategy to block any defensive move. His advisers would gauge the marketplace and decide the level to which he had to go to pre-empt any defensive move. Now they were concerned that Federated might be able to structure a plan under which it would take on debt to pay stockholders a special dividend of as much as $60 a share. Not that there was anything definitive on which to base that estimate — this game was more an art than a science.

The same day, Ohio's Senator Aronoff sponsored and introduced the two protective bills in the state senate. The next day in Cincinnati, U.S. District Judge Carl Rubin upheld Ohio's existing takeover law as constitutional and denied a Campeau request for a preliminary injunction.

But pressure was also mounting on Federated, and on Friday the company finally responded to Campeau's Saturday deadline on the $61 offer. In a public statement the company accused Campeau of launching a "grossly inadequate" bid designed to capitalize on depressed postcrash stock prices. It rejected the standing $47 bid and said it would consider the second offer, of $61, only when Campeau could prove he could finance it. And that was doubtful because it appeared that its poison pill and the new Delaware statute impeded his ability to secure money. Federated said its board viewed the offer "as an opportunistic attempt . . . to acquire the company's shares at a price which contains an illusory premium but which in reality falls significantly short of the underlying value of the company." The Saturday deadline passed without further response from Federated.

The scene temporarily shifted to Toronto, where on February 9 Campeau hosted a ceremony to mark the topping off of Scotia Plaza, which now towered sixty-eight storeys over downtown. But the two journalists who met him on the summit had no interest in the event at hand and every interest in getting him to talk about Federated. Campeau was upbeat, showing his determination and his never-ending belief in his inability to fail.

"Mr. Campeau, the analysts say the ball's in your court," one of the reporters said.

"And we'll play it," Campeau responded. "Hell, I'm going to get the company."

The reporters dogged Campeau, continuing the questions in both French and English. Campeau suddenly announced, on the spot, that despite the fact that his Saturday deadline had passed, he was extending the $61 offer but that it was still contingent on a negotiated, or friendly, deal with Federated.

Was he ready to go higher? asked Gary Regenstreif of the Reuters news agency.

No, Campeau responded, it would be too expensive.

Regenstreif rushed back to his office and sent on the Reuters financial wire what is known as a flash, a brief item advising that Campeau had said he would not raise his bid. The Reuters wire feeds to stockbrokers, banks and investment dealers, and Campeau's comments had an immediate and major effect on the market. Before it closed, Federated's stock plunged $1.25 to $57.875.

While Campeau was celebrating at Scotia Plaza, he was under attack in Columbus, the capital of Ohio, where the debate raged in the senate over the two anti-takeover bills Senator Aronoff had introduced. Aronoff warned his colleagues that it was doubtful Campeau would leave Federated's headquarters in Cincinnati if he took control. He reminded the senate that Federated paid $25 million in taxes and that its payroll amounted to $237 million, $76.9 million of which would disappear if the Canadian takeover succeeded. At least 3,500 jobs disappeared after Campeau's Allied takeover, he told his fellow legislators, and Federated would be dismembered just as Allied had been. "This is corporate war and we have an obligation to protect Ohio companies," Aronoff said.

Senator Paul Pfeifer was not so sure. He cited the pending Canada-U.S. free trade agreement, under which trade barriers were to be dismantled rather than erected, and said he was concerned that the Ohio legislation would be found unconstitutional. Then Senator Michael White, a Cleveland Democrat, got into the act, calling Campeau executives "corporate barbarians" engaging in "economic decapitation." And so it went. In the end the senate voted 25 to 5 to pass the two pieces of legislation and sent them to the House for approval.

The day after the senate vote, the U.S. Federal Trade Commission, which reviews mergers and acquisitions, decided not to challenge Campeau's bid on anti-trust grounds.

The same day, Campeau's negotiations with DeBartolo and the Reichmanns finally bore fruit, yielding some of the financing he needed for a successful $61-a-share offer. A friendly agreement with Federated now seemed possible, and financial analysts began to speculate on the possibility of a meeting between Federated and Campeau executives. But they were off base; all but a handful underestimated Federated's determination to resist.

The deal with DeBartolo was for a $480-million loan at 9 percent a year. The agreement included the formation of a Campeau-DeBartolo partnership to develop real estate in the United States that would involve Allied stores and possibly Federated stores.

The Reichmann deal was far more dramatic. Reichmann-owned Olympia & York agreed to pay $260 million for Campeau Corp. debentures — unsecured bonds or a form of IOU. But these were convertible at a later date to subordinate voting shares in Campeau Corp. Along with other clauses in the agreement, the deal had the potential to reduce Campeau's voting rights to less than 50 percent in his own company. (As it was, his control fell from 76 percent to about 54 percent because of the deal, while the Reichmanns boosted their stake in Campeau Corp. from 11 percent to about 22 percent.) Campeau's willingness to trade away his voting rights, even after the painful experience with Power Corp., showed just how fierce was his determination to win Federated.

Campeau now had more financing in place to help back up his $61 bid. (Each time he upped the ante he had to find more money.) In addition to DeBartolo and the Reichmanns, the Bank of Montreal and Security Pacific National Bank committed money. (Campeau also had arranged a $100-million bridge loan from First Boston because of the possibility that the money from his deal with the Reichmanns would not be in hand in time.)

On Thursday, February 11, the Ohio House voted 70 to 21 to approve the bill that virtually barred an unfriendly takeover of Federated until that July. (The amendment to the existing takeover bill had been rejected by the House rules committee as unconstitutional.) The following day, Governor Richard Celeste signed the Ohio legislation into law, warning that the state would "take whatever action is necessary to prevent the loss of jobs in the Cincinnati area."

That same Friday, amid rumors that high-powered New York merchant banking firm Kohlberg Kravis Roberts & Co. was trying to arrange a friendly leveraged buyout of Federated, Campeau warned in a letter that his company "will not stand by while Federated enters into unlawful schemes to deprive stockholders of the best price." He promptly threatened KKR & Co. with a lawsuit and raised his bid to $5.9 billion, or $66 a share in a friendly deal, in an attempt to undermine any possible leveraged buyout in the range of $65 a share. But rumors of other friendly mergers continued to fly.

What Campeau could not possibly have heard through the Wall Street rumor mill was that Macy's chief Ed Finkelstein had again phoned Federated's Howard Goldfeder. This time he was not offering advice; he was proposing some type of joint venture between the two retailing giants. This led to a Macy's proposal for a friendly merger and a request for access to confidential business information about the company. Federated agreed, and Macy's signed a confidentiality agreement allowing it to review Federated's own numbers. So while Campeau moved forward, thinking he was still the only contender, Macy's executives pored over internal Federated documents and the board of directors discussed the possibility of making a competing bid for Federated.

At Federated head office in Cincinnati, employees had begun sporting buttons depicting a red maple leaf and the word

Campeau with a slash across it in the universal "No" sign. The company was not about to give in.

On Tuesday, February 16, four days after Campeau raised his bid, the Federated board met all day in New York to consider its response. The result was predictable. It declared that Campeau's ability to finance the deal remained questionable and that it had authorized negotiations with other parties. In rejecting Campeau's latest bid, Federated countered with an ambitious defense. The company would sell more than half its stores, divesting most of its non-department store holdings, and if necessary issue preferred shares. (Preferred shares generally are nonvoting, but have preference over common stock in the payment of dividends and in cases of liquidation. A preferred share issue allows a company to raise funds without changing the existing voting power.) With the money this raised, it intended to buy back more than half its common stock. However, most analysts agreed that the plan would not work because a sale of assets could not have netted the money needed to finance a stock buyback, and a sufficiently large issue of preferred stock to raise additional funds was very risky. The Federated directors were likely bluffing to a large extent and stalling for time; perhaps they truly believed their defense was workable.

In response to this latest Federated rejection, Campeau arranged further financing from the Bank of Montreal and Banque Paribas. As well, First Boston now agreed to commit $900 million in bridge financing. Campeau was, piece by piece, putting together the massive amounts necessary to fund his bid. A number of lenders, though, refused to fund a hostile takeover.

Campeau's takeover battle, now three and a half weeks old, had been attracting a lot of attention in the press and among U.S. politicians. On February 17, Representative Thomas Luken, chairman of the congressional subcommittee that oversees the Federal Trade Commission, called a hearing to study what he said was the commission's failure to thoroughly investigate Campeau's bid. The commission, however, had already allowed Campeau to proceed and there was little the politician could do. It appeared to be more an opportunity to let off steam and possibly score some political points.

The hearing was stormy, with dire talk of job cuts and injustice. Among those who testified was Howard Metzenbaum, the abrasive Democratic senator from Ohio and the chairman of the senate anti-trust committee. He worried about unemployment and higher prices resulting from reduced competition, saying the proposed acquisition raised serious anti-trust concerns. Then he took a swing at Campeau and Canada by way of the Canada-U.S. free trade deal, the final draft of which included a provision allowing Canada to review potential U.S. takeovers. "In principle, I do not object to foreign companies investing in this country," he said. "However, if the tables were turned, and Federated attempted to take over Campeau, the Canadian government could block the attempt. That's not equitable, it's not free trade, and it's not fair."

But Bob Campeau was not worrying about the complaints of politicians. He was preparing to raise the pressure another notch. At this point he was operating on two levels. On one level was his latest offer of $66 a share in a negotiated deal. On the other level was his initial tender offer of $47 a share, which still stood. On Wednesday, February 17, he raised this tender offer to shareholders to $5.5 billion, or $61 a share, and extended the deadline. Stockholders could now get $61 apiece for their shares — $47 had never been a serious bid — whether or not the Federated board of directors approved. Yet all involved knew that having offered $66, Campeau could not end with a $61 offer.

In Cincinnati, just ten days after the Ohio anti-takeover bill was signed into law, U.S. District Judge Carl Rubin ruled that the legislation was unconstitutional. Federated officials did not appeal the decision. Their Ohio strategy had come to naught.

Now, although the Campeau forces did not know it, Macy's resurfaced as a potential white knight. Macy's executives secretly proposed to Federated that they make a competing bid

of $50 in cash and $11 in stock. But Federated could not take
this seriously. The face value of the Macy's bid was $61, while
Campeau's was $66. As well, Campeau was offering all cash,
and Macy's was offering a less attractive package with stock as
a component. At this point, Macy's did not feel it could go
higher and eclipse the Campeau offer.

Meanwhile, Campeau was still under pressure to prove he
could fully finance a deal, despite the money he already had in
hand. So he began moving his chessmen, sacrificing one
valuable piece for something he wanted more. In this case, the
pawn would be Brooks Brothers, his most prized acquisition in
the Allied deal. Campeau already knew exactly who the buyer
would be.

Earlier in the year, First Boston had introduced Campeau
to Lord Rayner, chairman of Marks and Spencer, the huge
British department store chain famous for moderately priced
quality woolens, underwear and food. The two men met to
discuss the possibility of Marks and Spencer investing in
Campeau Corp. Incidental to that meeting, Rayner had
expressed a strong interest in acquiring Brooks Brothers, but
Campeau had told him the chain was not for sale. Rayner had
been informed in advance of the move on Federated, and Marks
and Spencer agreed it would not, unless Campeau approved,
acquire any of Federated's shares or assets.

On February 22, Campeau called Rayner in London to let
him know that Brooks Brothers was now for sale. Late that
night he arrived in London aboard the Gulfstream III jet he
had acquired in the Allied deal. Allan Ruchman, First Boston's
investment banking director, had arrived the previous day and
begun negotiations. The next day talks continued at Campeau's hotel suite at the Ritz. Within about an hour, the two
sides had the basis for a deal. Marks and Spencer had agreed to
meet Campeau's main condition, that Brooks Brothers would
be sold only if he succeeded with Federated. At a meeting the
next day, the Marks and Spencer board approved the basic
deal: if Campeau acquired Federated, he would sell Brooks
Brothers for $770 million. Then, while Ruchman and
executives of Marks and Spencer caught the Concorde to New

York to complete the details, Campeau headed to Germany for a vacation. Everything was finally falling into place. Campeau knew when he left for Germany that the pressure on Federated would now become intense and that his troops could move in for the kill.

In New York on February 25, Campeau's public relations firm announced that Brooks Brothers would be sold to Marks and Spencer if Campeau acquired Federated. At the same time, the tender offer was sweetened from $61 to $66 a share, or $5.9 billion, making the direct offer to shareholders equal to his existing offer to Federated. A negotiated deal was no longer a condition for stockholders receiving $66 a share.

Federated was already under considerable pressure from shareholders who had begun filing lawsuits against the board of directors for ignoring the Campeau bid, a not unusual development during takeover battles in the United States. More important, big institutional shareholders, such as pension funds, were urging the company to act. They were concerned that Federated, in an attempt to make a deal with a friendly party, could agree to an offer that was not all cash. Federated could have now tried to rely on the poison pill or the Delaware anti-takeover legislation, but did not.

Campeau's gamble succeeded. Now that he had cemented much of his financing with the Brooks Brothers gambit, and with his boosted tender offer to shareholders, Federated finally came to the bargaining table. Its investment bankers phoned Bruce Wasserstein at about 5 P.M., offering to talk if Campeau would consider increasing his offer to $6.1 billion, or $68 a share. Campeau was reached in Germany for his authorization and negotiations began in New York.

By the next day, the day the Campeau bid was due to expire, the two sides had agreed on the price of $68. Other details would be negotiated over the weekend and the deal could go to the Federated board for approval Monday morning. At long last, it appeared Campeau had won.

16 / At All Costs

"We're both lucky to get out of this alive."
— Edward Finkelstein

ON MONDAY, FEBRUARY 29, it was easy to look back and see that Federated had been buying time over the weekend, searching for any way out, no matter how remote, and that the Campeau negotiators hadn't realized it. They were too busy completing the negotiations with Federated so that a deal would be ready to be signed and put to the Federated board of directors for approval on Monday morning. So sure was the Campeau team of the deal that it had even met on the Sunday night with a potential buyer for Federated's Ralphs supermarket chain.

What Campeau and his men didn't know was that at the eleventh hour Federated had started a second set of negotiations, while continuing to behave as if the deal with Campeau was done. On Sunday morning, Ira Millstein, a lawyer representing Macy's, placed a call to an investment banker working with Federated. Millstein's message was simple: Macy's wanted to make another bid for Federated. They had run their numbers again and decided they could do considerably better than the $61 cash-and-securities bid of several days earlier.

"Are you *serious*?" the banker asked.

"Come on," Millstein said. "We're serious! We've got an offer to make. Look, can you come in, we'll sit down, we'll go over it."

It took some convincing, but finally the investment banker

agreed to pass on the message. By Sunday afternoon, the Federated people and the Macy's people had started to work.

On Monday, Federated announced that it had another bidder and that the deal with Campeau was on hold. It did not, at first, disclose the identity of the white knight, only that there had been a last-minute offer. This was what Federated had been searching for, and it wasn't hard to figure out that Campeau's deal was doomed.

When Federated announced that it had a white knight, the Campeau negotiators were stunned and relayed the news to an astonished Campeau, who was still in Germany. Said securities analyst Monroe Greenstein of Bear, Stearns & Co. of New York: "Campeau must be in shock today. He's in for big money already." Having worked so hard for a full month, playing the game perfectly all the way along, the Campeau team seemed suddenly to have lost it. At first, the Campeau people spent hours tracking down the identity of their mysterious adversary. By late in the day, they determined it was likely Macy's.

A Macy's-Federated merger would indeed be something. Macy's would own the three largest department stores in New York City: its own flagship Macy's, the world's largest department store on a full block in downtown Manhattan, along with Federated's flagship Bloomingdale's and Abraham & Straus operations.

Macy's was already America's tenth-largest retailer with almost 100 stores in fourteen states that brought in more than $5 billion in sales annually. Macy's chairman Edward Finkelstein, who had an ego the size of Bob Campeau's, had only two years earlier taken the company private in a $3.5 billion buyout. The immediate sentiment in the U.S. financial community was that Campeau could not possibly stand up to this opposition, a feeling obviously shared by Finkelstein. He underestimated Bob Campeau.

Late Monday night, Federated's public relations people started phoning reporters across North America to outline the possible deal they had with Macy's. It was a combined cash-and-securities bid quite different from Campeau's all-cash tender offer, but was a two-tiered bid similar to what Campeau had made in his initial attempts to win Allied Stores. It was set to expire April 4, three weeks after Campeau's last tender offer. The front end of the bid consisted of $73.80 a share for about 80 percent of Federated's stock. The back end, the securities portion, proposed swapping the remaining 20 percent of the stock for shares that would equal 40 percent of the stock in a merged Macy's-Federated, whose board would include major representation from the Federated board. (It was assumed that Campeau was going to rout the Federated directors if he won.) Because it was two-tiered, shareholders were under pressure to tender to ensure they got the higher cash portion of the deal rather than the poorer securities in the second step.

Like many two-tiered cash and securities bids, this was difficult to value because of the uncertain stock component. When arbitrageurs calculated the blended value — the mix of the two tiers — the Macy's bid did not hold up well. The apparent face value was about $6.6 billion, but by the time arbitrageurs had gone through the proposal, they had put a value on the offer of between $66 a share, or $5.9 billion, and $69 a share, or $6.2 billion, slightly less or just about equal to Campeau's all-cash bid. (In addition, arbitrageurs prefer all-cash bids.) In its deal with Macy's, Federated also agreed to pay up to $45 million for Macy's legal and other fees if the bid failed for reasons other than those related to financing.

From Campeau's point of view, there was only one good thing about the Macy's white knight bid. It meant the Delaware anti-takeover legislation no longer applied.

The Campeau team now scrambled to recover the advantage. The following day, Tuesday, March 1, Campeau responded in a public announcement, saying that the Macy's proposal was a "front-end loaded, illusory offer designed to mislead individual shareholders." He maintained that his bid was better but said he too was prepared to structure a two-tiered deal if that was what Federated wanted. Meanwhile, Campeau negotiators raised the possibility of boosting their bid to $69.50 a share in cash from the $68 they had agreed to on the previous Friday. And they tried to ease fears of the economic impact on Federated's home base, saying Campeau would move Allied's headquarters from New York to Cincinnati and combine management there. If Macy's won, it was safe to assume that it would move the head office to New York.

Federated replied that it was studying both offers, though it was obvious to all observers that Macy's was the choice.

By the end of trading on this hectic Tuesday, Federated stock was up $1.25 to $67.75 on the New York Stock Exchange.

Macy's next move, the next day, was to amend its bid slightly, boosting the front end to $74.50 from the original $73.80. Even though this bid was not clearly superior to Campeau's, to no one's surprise Macy's now signed a definitive merger agreement with Federated. The blended value of the Federated offer was put at between $67 a share, or $6 billion, and $70 a share, or $6.3 billion, compared to Campeau's proposed $68.

Clearly, Macy's and Federated believed Campeau was defeated. But neither knew just who they were dealing with. Eight years had passed since Royal Trustco, and Bob Campeau had learned a lot. His advisers were among the best in the country. He played a far tougher game now, he was far more sophisticated at it, and he was determined not to be defeated again. Only hours after the Macy's-Federated deal was signed, Campeau decided he, too, could play the Macy's game and countered with a two-tiered bid of his own, but still all cash — $75 each for 70.5 million shares on the front end and, in a merger that would follow, $44 on the back. The bid, which Campeau was treating as a revised version of his existing offer, would expire at midnight March 15, well before the Macy's bid. The blended value was $68 a share, no more than his last offer but $1 more than the lowest value put on the Macy's bid. This could be seen as even more coercive than the Macy's offer. While the value of the stock portion of the Macy's bid was uncertain, the values of both components of the Campeau offer were clear. Thus, if shareholders did not tender to the $75 front end and Campeau won, they could be left with just $44 on the back end.

Then Campeau went to court to challenge Federated's agreement to pay the $45 million in Macy's expenses, saying he would raise the back end of his deal by $2.20 if his lawsuit succeeded.

Meanwhile, arbitrageurs kept picking up Federated stock in anticipation of an all-out bidding war. At this stage, they were still inclined to tender to Campeau's all cash deal, if he succeeded in invalidating the Federated poison pill, which had not been ruled on in court. (In fact, the only role the poison pill had played so far was to indicate to Campeau just how serious their opposition to him was.) Macy's was under pressure to disclose more details of its bid, in particular to put a value on the stock portion.

On Thursday morning, Campeau took a call from a Toronto-based reporter who asked him how he felt about the Macy's-Federated deal.

"It's so unfair what they have done," Campeau told him, only a hint of anger in his voice. "The courts will turn them down."

Would he consider backing down?

"We're not giving up the fight."

By now Campeau had returned to New York from Germany and immediately threw himself into the fight. He knew he needed more money if he was to remain in the bidding, so he began talking again to Tom Hayes of The May Department Stores Co., who had a vested interest in stopping Macy's from growing larger. On the afternoon of Friday, March 4, he arranged to sell Federated's Filene's and Foley's divisions to The May for up to $1.5 billion if his takeover was successful. Foley's, a thirty-eight-store chain based in Houston, was one of Federated's strongest divisions, with annual sales of about $1.1 billion. Boston-based Filene's, an eighteen-store chain, had sales of about $390 million. The battle lines were drawn: Campeau, the Reichmanns, DeBartolo and The May against the combined forces of Macy's and Federated.

The following Tuesday, March 8, Macy's attempted to stall Campeau's bid and so gain a big advantage. It filed a suit alleging that his restructured offer really amounted to a new deal under securities laws and thus must be held open for at least twenty business days in order to allow shareholders to study the proposal. That would mean Campeau's bid could not expire on March 15, as planned. Timing really was crucial here because the bid that expired first was difficult for shareholders to resist in a two-tiered situation. Anyone who waited to tender to the second bid risked ending up with the lesser-valued back end of the first bid if it succeeded.

As the cost of Campeau's bid rose, so, too, did the number of assets of the takeover target he would have to shed in order to finance the buyout. So he had to reconsider what he would now divest of Federated if he won. When he first launched the bid, he had planned to sell the Ralphs grocery chain, the twenty-outlet MainStreet division in Illinois, the 191-store Children's Place in New Jersey and the seventy-six-unit Gold Circle chain in Worthington. He had just agreed to sell Foley's and Filene's to The May. Now, he would probably also have to sell the twenty-two-outlet Filene's Basement and, possibly, the twenty-five-store I. Magnin chain based in San Francisco, as well as the six-store Goldsmith's chain of Memphis. Combined, these divisions had sales of almost $5.5 billion. If he won, he would be left with Bloomingdale's, Abraham & Straus, Bullock's/Bullock Wilshire and a few other choice divisions. The plum was shrinking.

The day after taking Campeau's raised bid to court, Macy's disclosed that it had cut a side deal with Federated to pay hundreds of its employees cash for their stock while remaining stockholders would receive the standing two-tiered bid. There was no real advantage to this for Macy's, other than perhaps winning favor with the Federated employees. It was a far more lucrative deal than Macy's had offered Federated's other shareholders. In the event, it backfired. Arbitrageurs and institutional shareholders, such as the New York State Teachers Retirement System, which represents a teachers' pension fund and held about 665,600 shares, were outraged.

By Thursday, March 10, Campeau had clearly regained the upper hand with his revised bid. He had lined up more financing as well, from Citibank and the New York branch of Sumitomo Bank Ltd. Arbitrageurs were planning to tender to him and some brokerage houses were also advising their clients to sell to Campeau. But this recommendation still hinged on the court case involving the poison pill, which was scheduled to be heard the following Monday.

On Sunday, March 12, Campeau extended his deadline for three days, to March 18.

On Monday, under pressure because of the superior Campeau deal, Macy's increased the cash portion of its bid from $74.50 to $77.35 and modified the back end slightly. But the arbitrageurs, who by now held an estimated 40 percent of the Federated shares, did not see it as a clearly better offer because it still had an uncertain stock component. They put the blended value at about $69 a share, or $6.3 billion. And Federated stock was still trading at $66 on the New York Stock Exchange, indicating that the market did not think much of the new Macy's bid.

Macy's now struck another side deal with Federated, this time for some insurance if its bid failed. Under the agreement Federated granted Macy's an option to buy its I. Magnin chain for not less than $150 million and its twenty-nine-store Bullock's/Bullock Wilshire (based in Los Angeles) for not less than $800 million.

Campeau was furious. He ordered his public relations people to call the *New York Times* and the *Wall Street Journal* to set up interviews at the Waldorf. His advisers, worried because of Campeau's unpredictability when roused, tried to cancel, but it was too late. *Wall Street Journal* reporter Bryan Burrough and Isadore Barmash of the *New York Times* were already on their way.

At the interview Campeau was in vintage form as he dissected the two bids for the reporters, explaining why his was clearly superior, and promising he would not sit idly by while Federated agreed to sell I. Magnin and Bullock's if their deal fell apart.

"We're going to sue their whole board if that takes place," he vowed. The Macy's offer was a charade. There was no pressure on him, he said.

"My bid's for a hell of a lot more money," he fumed. "We're not boosting anything."

Late that same Monday in Federal District Court in Manhattan, Judge Leonard Sand began hearing arguments about the validity of Federated's poison pill. In a preliminary decision he ruled that both bids were to remain in effect for at least three business days after he ruled on Campeau's poison pill suit. That meant Campeau's offer could still expire first, leaving him with the upper hand.

Judge Sand was also hearing a second argument, the one concerning Macy's attempt to force Campeau to extend his bid on the basis that it amounted to a new, not an amended, offer. The Securities and Exchange Commission filed a brief with the court supporting Campeau's position, saying his restructured bid amounted to an amended offer, not a new offer as Macy's claimed. But the commission also argued that he still did not have all his financing in place and recommended that he be forced to keep the bid open for five days from the date of disclosing final and full financing arrangements.

On Friday, March 18, the same day Judge Sand was to rule, Campeau ignored his advisers' advice and took out full-page advertisements in the *Wall Street Journal* and the *New York Times*. The ads were in the form of a 1,200-word open letter, signed by him, to the Federated board of directors. The letter said in part, "Judge Leonard Sand, in hearing the case Monday, seemed to be concerned with protecting the small shareholders. I agree with him. I do not like a two-tier offer. That's playing the arbitrageur game. Monday, Macy's played this game again. However, I want you and the world to know that this is not my game — that I am responding to Federated and Macy's game — and I think it should be stopped. We want to appeal to your sense of justice."

Judge Sand's ruling was not what Campeau wanted to hear. The judge refused to invalidate the poison pill, which was a major setback. He ordered Campeau to extend his bid until the following Friday, March 25, before which he would have to fully disclose that he had met financing requirements. But he denied the motion by Macy's, whose bid expired April 4, that Campeau's revised bid be treated as a new offer. Campeau's time advantage over Macy's was thus narrowed, but his bid would still expire first.

Campeau now seemed powerless to stop the poison pill. But on Monday, March 21, Campeau lawyers returned to Sand's court with a compromise. Campeau would extend his bid to expire on the *same day* as the Macy's offer if the poison pill was invalidated. That would allow shareholders to judge both proposals on their merits. Sand denied the application. Arbitrageurs sat back, expecting Campeau to boost the front end of his bid to bring the blended value to at least $70 a share, or about $6.3 billion.

On Tuesday, March 22, Campeau brought the front end of his bid up to $82 and lowered the back end to $37 from $44. This pumped the blended value of his offer to $73 a share, or $6.54 billion, far surpassing what anyone had expected. With the back end lowered, there was even more pressure on stockholders to tender rather than be left with the second tier. Campeau also extended his offer to midnight, April 4, the same expiry as the Macy's bid. Pressure was on Macy's to do something.

Two days later, the entire game changed when Federated decided that, despite its merger agreement with Macy's, it would let Finkelstein and Campeau each sit down and bargain. While Federated still clearly preferred Macy's, it had a legal responsibility to its stockholders to get the best value for their shares. In addition, Federated's preoccupation with the takeover fight was starting to cause its business to suffer.

The company sent letters to Campeau and Macy's, asking each to submit a sealed bid with its best offer, which would be studied at a board meeting on Wednesday, March 30. Both Campeau and Macy's chief Ed Finkelstein were invited to address the meeting. As part of this new process the rivals were required to give the winning proposal a head start by agreeing to a provision under which the losing bidder would either end his tender offer or extend it by thirty business days. Because an amended offer must, under U.S. securities laws, be extended only ten days, that would have given the winning bid a twenty-day advantage. The Federated board also promised to either kill or modify the poison pill to allow the winning bid to get to shareholders unimpeded by the takeover defense. Finally, it asked Macy's to allow Federated to back out of their agreement if Campeau's bid was found to be superior, but left intact the Macy's option to buy I. Magnin and Bullock's in the event its bid failed.

The Federated directors had given much thought to this complex new bidding procedure, but even after two months they still had not figured out Bob Campeau. He, of course, said no, and he didn't stop there. Describing the Federated proposal for sealed bids as "unlawful and designed to ensure that stockholders not be given the opportunity to evaluate the competing bids," he went back to Judge Leonard Sand to challenge the procedure and try again to invalidate the poison pill. Sand took no action on either issue. But while in court, Campeau's lawyer asked whether Federated would consider a bid that did not meet its terms. After a short recess, the Federated lawyer said that a bid would indeed be studied if submitted, whether or not Campeau met the terms of the letter. If Federated was prepared to study both offers, the poison pill would not be invoked and, in theory, would no longer be a roadblock.

Jaded Wall Street had seen nothing like the next two days. An investment community that thrived on corporate raids watched in amazement as two players waged a colossal battle of egos, playing with billions of dollars and thousands of jobs.

Throughout Wednesday, March 30, the Federated board was closeted in the law offices of Skadden, Arps, Slate, Meagher & Flom at 919 Third Avenue in Manhattan as they considered new bids from both sides. Ed Finkelstein appeared for Macy's, Bruce Wasserstein for Campeau.

Among Campeau's proposals: entering into an agreement under which Campeau would purchase up to 90 percent of the shares in a tender offer at $74 each, and the remainder in a subsequent merger, also at $74; entering into an agreement under which Campeau would offer $74 a share for all stock in one stage.

Campeau's bids, each worth $6.63 billion in total, also provided that a regular 37-cent-a-share dividend be paid to stockholders. So his bid could be considered to be worth as much as $74.37 a share.

Since entering the fight, the Macy's team had been perplexed by Campeau. Not that they had underestimated his persistence, but they did underestimate his ability to raise more financing. Every time the Macy's people raised their bid, they thought Campeau would be tapped out. Such was the case again this day. Not knowing what Campeau had offered, Macy's submitted a sealed bid that proposed buying 80 percent of the shares at $77.35 each. In a subsequent merger, the remaining 20 percent would be traded for up to 36 percent of stock in a Macy's-Federated Inc. on the basis of about five common shares for one Federated share. But shareholders could instead choose to take $60 in cash in the second step, for the first time placing a value on the stock portion of the Macy's deal. There was no provision for a dividend.

The blended value of the Macy's bid was about $73.88 a share, 12 cents less than what Campeau had offered in his $74 bid. When Campeau's 37-cent dividend was added in, the Macy's bid was 49 cents shy.

Federated told the Campeau team that its bid was superior, and negotiations began. By Thursday morning, they had reached terms of a definitive agreement that would go to the Federated board, in a telephone conference call, within hours.

But Finkelstein was not prepared to let the matter rest there. He spoke to the Federated directors by phone, angrily arguing that he should have the opportunity to put in another bid. Macy's had played by Federated's rules, he pointed out. Campeau had not. He reminded them that Federated had broken the agreement between the two companies and that this could be seen as a breach of contract.

Federated allowed Finkelstein to put in another bid. He came back with a $6.73 billion offer, increasing the front end cash portion of the night before to $78.92. The blended value of the new offer was $75.14. The 37-cent dividend was included, in effect making the bid worth $75.51, better in straight money terms than Campeau's.

Federated could have ended the battle here, but decided instead to let it run another day, extending bidding until 8 A.M. on Good Friday, April 1. They were gambling that they could get even more money out of either Finkelstein or Campeau.

Meanwhile, the Campeau and Macy's teams were negotiating behind the scenes, trying to reach an agreement between themselves, yet these back-channel talks had so far yielded nothing. That Thursday afternoon another meeting took place with the Macy's people, this one at lawyer Ira Millstein's office. After two hours, Campeau's negotiators, Wasserstein and Finkelson, were no closer to an agreement, but they did learn for the first time that Macy's, too, had been signing agreements to dispose of Federated divisions if it succeeded in the bid. It had agreed with various companies to sell the Lazarus and Goldsmith's chains for about $1 billion, the Foley's division for about $870 million and the Ralphs supermarket chain for $1.1 billion.

Finkelson and Wasserstein realized that there was no way Macy's could win Federated if it wanted a negotiated settlement with Campeau, and at this point a settlement would be less costly than continuing the bidding and would leave both sides with something. Considering what the Macy's executives had already presold, there would have been little left once they agreed to sell to Campeau the divisions he would demand in return for pulling out of the contest. Campeau would not have withdrawn without a promise that he could have Bloomingdale's and other choice pieces of the Federated operations. The negotiations were stalemated by the fact that Macy's and Finkelstein refused to admit defeat.

Before leaving, a frustrated Allen Finkelson spoke by telephone to Campeau to let him know what was happening.

"Nothing," was Finkelson's terse summary.

"Look, I think the only way for me to do this is to meet Ed Finkelstein face to face," Campeau replied.

A meeting was arranged at Finkelstein's townhouse for seven that evening.

At a strategy session at Campeau's headquarters at the Waldorf, it was decided that only Finkelson and Campeau would go to this pivotal meeting. The Campeau team believed then, and Finkelson still says, that everybody knew where the discussions were heading — toward Macy's backing out. The question that remained was what it would take to get Finkelstein to walk away. Macy's, on the other hand, maintains that Finkelstein went into the meeting still believing he could win Federated in a settlement. But the evidence is on Campeau's side. Macy's had, after all, already agreed to sell four Federated divisions. To have given Campeau several other divisions would have meant the almost complete dismemberment of Federated. For all its trouble, Macy's would have ended up with very little.

"They were posturing," says Finkelson. "The facts are that they knew that they were going to go away because us going away was no longer an option for them. So I don't care what they said. What they said was a ritualistic mating dance. The bottom line was, what was it going to cost for them to go away. Period."

It was a clear and crisp evening when Campeau and Finkelson arrived at Finkelstein's two-storey graystone townhouse on East 77th Street on Manhattan's exclusive Upper East Side. They approached the elegant Romanesque facade with its forbidding iron grilles across the doors and windows of the bottom floor and were promptly ushered inside. There Finkelstein, in a business suit, greeted Campeau, who was dressed casually in slacks and a sweater. The rest of the Macy's team, including lawyer Millstein, were already there. The tension must have been almost palpable; so much was riding on the next few hours.

After a few opening pleasantries, Campeau and Finkelstein met alone in the living room for half an hour while the others waited downstairs in the recreation room. Finkelstein told Campeau that, in return for backing out, he wanted Bullock's, I. Magnin and Rich's and the expenses he had incurred in this bidding war. Campeau talked him down to two divisions — Bullock's and I. Magnin — that would be sold to Macy's if a deal could in fact be reached. Campeau had already planned to sell I. Magnin, so would be losing little. Bullock's, though, was valuable property. It was indeed a concession for him to give it up.

Campeau then went to confer alone with Finkelson, while Finkelstein consulted Millstein. When the meeting resumed, all four men were present and ready to bargain to final terms. They sat around the spacious living room and bartered, rising occasionally for a soft drink. Campeau at times lectured Finkelstein, one of America's premier retailers, on retailing. Jumping up and down, he emphasized his points by stabbing his finger in the air, as he had done at Ottawa city hall so many years ago. Upstairs, Finkelstein's wife popped her head out of the bedroom a couple of times to listen to what was happening. Eventually, the four men narrowed the sale price of the two divisions, but they were still far apart on the amount of money that would be paid to cover the expenses that Macy's had incurred. The struggle was at a crucial point now and a deal could stand or fall on the next several minutes. Campeau and Finkelstein said they had gone as far as they could. Perhaps there would be no agreement tonight.

But the two deputies, Finkelson and Millstein, thought the two chairmen were at least within range of a settlement and that the negotiations should not fall apart now, when they were so close. They felt the answer lay in separating these two determined men.

"Millstein and I decided to try and hammer it out," recalls Finkelson. "We decided it was silly to fall apart over where they then were, which was obviously close enough for both of us to feel that."

So Campeau and Finkelstein went to separate rooms, Campeau to the kitchen and Finkelstein downstairs to the recreation room. Then Millstein and Finkelson shuttled back and forth between the two principals, meeting briefly in the living room or another midway point to discuss various proposals. How much for this? How much for that? "We weren't together very long," says Finkelson. "We'd kind of meet, chat for about two seconds and then go back to our principals."

During this shuttle phase, the two sides negotiated first the price Macy's would pay for the two Federated divisions, and then the amount of money that would go to cover the Macy's expenses. After about an hour, they had a deal.

In the end, Macy's agreed to withdraw from the bidding in return for the right to purchase Bullock's and I. Magnin for $1.1 billion. Campeau agreed that Federated would pay $60 million to Macy's to cover its expenses. Said Ed Finkelstein a couple of days later: "We're both lucky to get out of this alive."

Finkelstein, who had anticipated a deal, brought out a bottle of Dom Perignon '82 he had put on ice. Even Campeau, who did not drink much alcohol, raised his glass, savoring this moment. Not the best champagne, he would later recall, but not bad at all.

17 / The Best Revenge

"I like to take risks."

— Robert Campeau

THE DAY AFTER HIS meeting with the chairman of Macy's, Campeau left New York to spend a few days relaxing at his house in Florida. Lawyers for both sides had worked through the night to complete the paperwork, and while Campeau's plane was in the air the Federated board of directors was digesting the details of what had happened. Because of the private deal between Campeau and Finkelstein, the Federated directors really had no choice now but to accept a new Campeau bid of $73.50 a share, or $6.6 billion, less than Campeau had offered in the last rounds of bidding but $500 million more than the $68 per share on the table when Macy's stepped in at the last minute to block his bid. Federated's board of directors approved it that day.

With the deal to buy Bullock's, Macy's obtained what it had long sought, a major presence in southern California. And Campeau achieved his goal of becoming a major force in the U.S. department store and shopping center sectors.

This had been one of the most bitter and complex corporate takeover battles in U.S. history, involving politicians in Washington, Delaware and Ohio. Even the Canada-U.S. free trade deal had been questioned. It involved armies of bankers and lawyers and some of the major corporate players in the United States, Canada and even overseas: Federated, Macy's,

The May, Marks and Spencer, the Reichmanns, DeBartolo. Bob Campeau does nothing in a small way.

The deal was the fifth-largest corporate takeover in history, and the biggest ever not involving an oil company. The total cost to Campeau: $8.8 billion, when all expenses, including the fees for lawyers and investment bankers (an estimated $200 million), were included. Millions of dollars had to be paid to the Federated executives who would now leave the company with their golden parachutes intact. Chairman Howard Goldfeder, who soon quit, was entitled to almost $7 million and president Norman Matthews to almost $3 million. With the $2.1 billion debt outstanding from the Allied takeover, Campeau was in hook for a total of about $10 billion.

It would take several weeks for Campeau to fully put together the final financing package and complete the tender offer. In order to do this, he borrowed about $6.75 billion from a wide array of international banks, including Citibank, Sumitomo Bank, Sanwa Bank, Nippon Credit Bank, the Bank of Tokyo Trust, the Fuji Bank, Arab Bank and Hypo Bank. Bridge financing came from First Boston, PaineWebber Group and Dillon Read Interfunding, and equity committed in connection with the takeover came from the Bank of Montreal, Banque Paribas, the Reichmanns and Edward DeBartolo.

Three days after his victory, Bob Campeau strode into the Bloomingdale's in Fort Lauderdale, picked up a pay phone and called the *Wall Street Journal*. His strategists had asked him to speak to the *Journal* and the *New York Times* to get certain facts out quickly to the financial community. But he could not resist the theatrical gesture of conducting the interview from one of his stores, and, being Bob Campeau, could not refrain from a little boasting. With the din of cash registers in the background, he told the *Journal* reporter: "Entrepreneurship demands taking risks for gain and I have done that all my life. I like to take risks."

To the *Journal* and *New York Times* reporters he explained his plans as newly crowned king of America's department store industry. Perhaps he would expand Bloomingdale's across the

United States, maybe even into Canada. At that moment, he might have been wondering what Richard Thomson, Ken White and their friends who had prevented him from winning Royal Trustco would think of *that*. This was indeed the best revenge.

A couple of days later, Campeau returned to New York and met reporters at a crowded news conference at the Waldorf. Beside him sat Robert Morosky, president of Allied and designated as the chief executive of Allied-Federated. Campeau explained that his immediate plans were to cut his $8.8 billion of Federated debt in half by selling $4.4 billion of assets, including those earmarked for Macy's and The May. Slapping his hand on the table, he explained to the 150 reporters, photographers and television cameramen how he could pay the interest on his massive debt and, based on estimates of Federated's earnings, still come out way ahead. A newspaper report said his face at that moment resembled that of a Roman legionnaire. And indeed, one of the New York television reporters told viewers, "He came. He saw. He conquered."

Federated stores were spread across the United States, and most of the reporters wanted to know how the deal would affect jobs in their communities. Though he did not answer their questions specifically, Campeau did not mince words. He said his philosophy was that companies could not "survive and compete by keeping jobs and jobs and jobs. It is much better to save ninety-five jobs than trying to keep 100 and go below the ledger." And comparing the U.S. business climate to that in Canada, he said: "I like the way things are done down here."

Campeau knew he had a lot of work to do and set about getting to know the company he was buying and dismembering. He immediately toured the operations across the United States and began selling off pieces of the once large Federated empire. Because of the escalation in the bidding war, he was starting with far less than he had originally envisioned. Filene's and Foley's were sold to The May; I. Magnin and Bullock's to Macy's. Over the next several months, he sold off Federated's Gold Circle, Filene's Basement, MainStreet and The Children's

Place and shut down five of the Stern's department stores in the Philadelphia and southern New Jersey areas. The sales of all the units brought in about $3.2 billion. He had also had to give up Brooks Brothers to Marks and Spencer. Another $430 million came from the sale of Allied's fashionable Ann Taylor chain.

When it was all over, Campeau was left with slightly more than 260 department stores and 135 grocery outlets — out of more than 1,300 in the original Allied and Federated portfolios — in nine divisions. Many of the ones that remain, such as Abraham & Straus and Bloomingdale's, are prime retailers, but financial analysts who follow the retail business in the United States still expected he would be forced to sell more, perhaps individual units, perhaps whole chains such as Abraham & Straus or Lazarus. It depended on whether he ran into trouble trying to service the $10 billion in debt from his two takeovers.

The retailing industry in the United States was hurting, threatening Campeau's new empire even as it was born. Edward Finkelstein said after the deal was reached that he backed off partly because he had doubts about being able to turn Federated around in the current retail environment. "I'm very pleased I don't have to deal with it and he does," the Macy's chairman said. As well, there had long been the feeling that the United States was "overstored." Campeau was not concerned: "I think it is in certain areas, but there is room for growth in some areas."

With store sales soft industry-wide, Campeau moved quickly to streamline operations. By the summer of 1988, the estimates were that of the 9,000 people who had lost their jobs in retailing, employees of Federated accounted for about 3,500. Twelve hundred people were thrown out of work in the Lazarus chain, almost 800 at Abraham & Straus, 600 at Goldsmith's, 320 at Burdines, 250 at Rich's and almost 245 at Bloomingdale's.

The effects of Campeau's cutbacks were soon evident, particularly at Bloomingdale's, which just before Christmas 1988 offered sales for several days on selected merchandise.

Customers complained about longer than normal lineups and fewer sales people at the store. Said the *Wall Street Journal*: "Once-tony Bloomingdale's suddenly looks like a bargain basement . . . the fashionable and the famous apparently are snubbing it for Bergdorf Goodman Inc. and even R.H. Macy Co." A cartoon in *The New Yorker* magazine showed two women strolling down the aisle of a department store, one saying, "Whenever someone scoffs at dreaming the impossible dream I tell them to think of Bloomingdale's — the way it was long, long ago and the way it is now." The publicity got so bad — in particular, a highly negative article in the *Wall Street Journal* — that in early January 1989 Campeau took out advertisements in several North American newspapers, in the form of an open letter to his employees, citing his achievements in cutting costs and debt and increasing operating profits at his stores.

Not long after the Federated takeover, Campeau ran into his first financing trouble as he was preparing a $1.15 billion offering of Federated "junk bonds," so called because they are high yielding but also high risk. The offering was to provide long-term financing for the Federated takeover, paying off the $1.1 billion bridge loan from First Boston, PaineWebber and Dillon, Read that was used to complete the acquisition. Campeau was forced to delay pricing the issue because investors were shunning the bonds. Part of the trouble was related to the man himself. Said Cricket Barlow, a New York bond trader: "People are concerned about the retail industry and they're also concerned that Campeau is in a bit over his head. He's a real estate person taking over a retail company." In late October 1988, Campeau sweetened the terms, offering far higher interest rates, and cut the size of the bond issue to $750 million to attract investors.

The market jitters were not solely related to Campeau's inexperience as a retailer. By 1989, corporate debt levels in the United States had soared to such heights that investors were increasingly wary. Several buyouts — the $24.9-billion buyout of RJR Nabisco, for example — prompted concerns over a glut of bond issues to finance debt, something Campeau could not have anticipated when he bought Federated.

To make matters worse, Robert Morosky, whom Campeau had hired to run the retailing empire after the Allied takeover, had quit in May, just after the Federated deal. The bankers who had put up the money for the Federated takeover had been calmed by the presence of this seasoned and respected retailer. The problem was Campeau's unwillingness to let Morosky run the show. Morosky says Campeau reneged on a promise to name him chief executive of Allied-Federated, deciding he wanted to keep the job for himself. And, says Morosky, "I decided that there wasn't room for two bosses." Yet soon after Morosky left, Campeau named John Burden, the former vice-chairman of Federated, as chairman and chief executive for the combined operation. Said Morosky: "Mr. Campeau's actions will prove the title ineffective. Mr. Campeau will be somewhat active as he was in the past, so I think it's probably a title that was demanded by John."

Campeau had made his name in the United States with the Allied takeover; the Federated deal catapulted him into the limelight. Suddenly, Robert Campeau was a man about town. In September 1988, Bloomingdale's chairman, Marvin Traub, invited about 250 people, among the elite of New York City, to meet his new boss at a reception at the Egyptian temple in the Metropolitan Museum of Art. Cosmetics queen Estée Lauder and fashion designers Liz Claiborne and Ralph Lauren were among those who showed up for the party. Said the *New York Times* the following day: "Everybody loves Campeau." To celebrate Ilse's birthday, Campeau threw a small party at Le Train Blue restaurant at Bloomingdale's in Manhattan, complete with Petrossian caviar. And the cover story of the *New York Times Magazine* in July 1988 was on Bob Campeau, under the headline "The Man Who Bought Bloomingdale's." The entire front cover of the magazine was taken up by a photograph of Bob and Ilse sitting out front of the Bridle Path home with their two dogs. One month later, *Fortune* magazine featured Campeau. The story carried a photograph of an

American flag superimposed over part of his body. Campeau was also the cover story in the October 1988 issue of *Business Month* magazine.

The takeovers made Bob Campeau a bigger celebrity back home, as well. He was invited to a dinner Conrad Black hosted for British Prime Minister Margaret Thatcher at the exclusive Toronto Club. And Bob and Ilse began attending other celebrity events around Toronto. *Chatelaine* magazine named him one of Canada's ten sexiest men.

But along with the fame came questions that were not so pleasant to answer. As North American journalists delved deeper and deeper into Bob Campeau's past, they soon discovered that he had had two children with Ilse while still married to Clauda. When these stories appeared, they caused even more heartache in an already torn family. Campeau was particularly furious over a *Toronto Star* article that quoted Rachelle as disclosing the history of his relationship with Ilse. After it appeared, he cut his first child out of his life, saying: "I'll probably never speak to her again."

This was only the latest in a continuing tale of family strife, much of which centered around Bob's attempts to retain control of the shares in the family trust estates. In the summer of 1987, Bob's youngest son, Danny, sued his father in the Supreme Court of Ontario over an attempt to reorganize the estate. Court documents filed by Danny said Bob had wanted to trade the Campeau Corp. common shares for preferred shares in a private company that he controlled. Danny did not proceed with the case and was made a Campeau Corp. director. The company also began funding his fledgling racing career. In July 1986, he had graduated from the Spenard-David Racing School, and soon after being made a director took a three-year leave from Campeau Corp. to compete on Europe's Formula Three racing circuit.

Several months after Danny's lawsuit, it was his older brother Jacques's turn. Bob sued in the Supreme Court of Ontario, trying to halt the transfer of Jacques's shares from the original trust until it was ensured that they would remain part of a unified family voting block. (Jacques would turn thirty-five in December 1987.) Bob disclosed in the court documents that he had been negotiating with each of the children involved to ensure the preservation of the family's control of the company. Bob said he was concerned that Jacques might try to sell the shares before his now-estranged wife, Carolyn, whom he had married in 1985, and their daughter could make claim. By the time Jacques separated from Carolyn, his shares were worth more than $36 million.

In early March 1988, Jacques filed a statement of defense and counterclaim, which said his father's claims were "embarrassing, frivolous, vexatious, irrelevant." The document added: "Robert Campeau has neither met nor sought to meet Jacques Campeau's wife or child and is using them as pawns in his dispute with his son Jacques. The plaintiff is attempting to cloak this ill usage of Jacques Campeau's wife and child in the respectable mantle of paternal and grandfatherly concern, but in reality the only concern the plaintiff has in these claims is the benefit he will derive from delaying the proper distribution of Trust Property to Jacques Campeau, which delay assists the plaintiff in maintaining his control over Campeau Corporation."

Another trust was also in dispute. In 1979, Bob had set up a "son's trust" for Jacques, Danny, Bobby, Jr., and Jan Paul. He then added Rachelle and Giselle. In the midst of the Federated bid, Jacques sued over this trust, saying his father was seeking the power to determine the amount that would go to each child.

The disputes over the shares and the divisions within the family soon made it into the newspapers. In the April 8, 1988, edition of the *Financial Post*, Danny pleaded for unity: "It's better the family discusses things and goes to the board with one voice. Whether our father is there or not, we should say there has been an agreement and this is the way it's going to be." Jacques, who had spoken to his father only rarely over the previous six years, responded twelve days later in *The Globe and Mail*: "It's pretty easy to side with my father when you're

the heir apparent. My own brother has not spoken with me for
about three months. All of a sudden he pleads for unity in a
newspaper."

Then, in September 1988, Bob sued Rachelle seeking a
declaration by the court that the shares she had received from
the trust estate were subject to a unified family voting control
block. He asked the court for an order blocking Rachelle from
selling the shares, and an order that he had the right to vote the
stock, or, in the alternative, damages of $50 million (Canadian).
The court cases with Jacques and Rachelle were crucial to Bob
maintaining majority control of Campeau Corp. Bob and the
family trusts together controlled about 54 percent, and Bob's
personal voting stake could fall below 50 percent if Jacques and
Rachelle were allowed to vote independently. (There were no
such problems with the children of his second family. Bobby,
Jr. was now working for his father's company, Giselle was
trying to decide whether to become a lawyer and Jan Paul was
behaving like a normal teenager, becoming an expert trick
bicycle rider and playing electric guitar.)

As of June 1989, the lawsuits are not yet resolved.

After the Federated deal, the Reichmanns held 22 percent
of Campeau Corp. They then proceeded to buy more Campeau
Corp. shares, as well as debentures that could be converted into
stock. By the end of December 1988, they had increased their
holdings in Campeau Corp. to more than 25 percent. If Bob
Campeau was worried that he had left his flank open to the
Reichmanns, he put on a brave face: "It's a free country, it's
quite all right with me. I think they're very good shareholders."

Should Campeau run into severe trouble maintaining the
U.S. retailing operations, however, the Reichmanns could move
in to take control. Or they could help Campeau take his
company private while taking the U.S. retailing operations
public to raise equity. (When Campeau Corp. became owner of
Allied and Federated, the U.S. companies were delisted because
no stock was in the hands of the public.)

Whatever the fate of the Federated takeover, Bob Campeau
has already dramatically altered the U.S. retailing industry. He

has taken two large companies and broken them up, retaining only some of the best divisions. And if the grand vision behind his takeover succeeds, he will be not only a giant retailer but one of the biggest shopping mall developers in the United States as well. Long ago, he saw the potential of owning both the shopping malls and the retailing outfits they contained. Any malls he now develops will be the favored choice for an Allied or Federated store, stores that other developers covet as anchor tenants. "This gives enormous anxiety to the shopping mall people who compete with Campeau," says Edward Finkelstein of Macy's. Add to this Campeau's relationship with Edward DeBartolo, who now owns a 7.5 percent stake in Federated, and you have a potential powerhouse that could blow the competition out of the water. DeBartolo and Campeau have already revealed plans to build between fifty and a hundred shopping malls over twelve years. That level of shopping mall development is unprecedented in the United States, and it seems unlikely that they will achieve that goal. Whatever they build, they are all but guaranteed a Bloomingdale's or a Burdines as an anchor tenant. Nevertheless, none of this will be possible unless Campeau can keep his new retail empire afloat.

As this book goes to press, Campeau's debt is still so huge that there are fears his empire could crumble in the event of a recession, overwhelmed by the amount of money needed just to service his debt. Campeau Corp. itself has recently admitted as much: "As a result of the increased level of debt and the related principal and interest obligations, the company may be less able than it has been to meet its obligations in the event of a downturn in its business or the economy or any increase in competitive pressure especially through price pressure by less highly leveraged competitors ... In order to generate funds sufficient to make all its interest payments and to make principal payments and necessary capital expenditures, the company will have to improve its results." By late 1988, analysts were labelling Campeau stock a high-risk investment because of the company's high degree of leverage.

Whatever happens to Allied-Federated, Campeau will have

personally done very well. He is now being paid an annual after-tax salary of $1 million by Federated and Allied. He also arranged a $5-million interest-free loan from Campeau Corp. secured by Allied-Federated. Should Campeau die or suffer some form of long-term disability before repayment, Allied and Federated would be liable for the loan. Campeau personally is wealthy enough to weather any financial storm.

The company's latest financial reports, for 1988, showed Campeau Corp. lost $34 million, a large improvement over 1987's $196-million loss. On the face of it, the financial picture was improving. His 1988 losses would have been dramatically poorer but for the money earned on the sale of Brooks Brothers to Marks and Spencer and the selling off of some real estate assets. Campeau's operating profit almost doubled to $881 million, but most of that was lost in the increase in financing costs, which in 1988 were $877 million. Allied Stores lost $161 million, and Federated lost $158 million. The retail revenues were consistent with what was happening elsewhere in the industry. The difference was that the rest of the industry was not carrying Campeau Corp.'s debt, now at more than $7.8 billion.

In the spring of 1989, forty years after he started to build houses, Bob Campeau transformed Campeau Corp. into purely a holding company overseeing the retail subsidiaries, Federated, Allied and the Ralphs grocery chain, as well as two real estate groups, one in Canada and one in the United States. The transformation signaled his increasing focus on the U.S. market and the company's diversification.

At the same time, James Roddy, who had replaced David King as president less than a year earlier, resigned his post, apparently because he did not approve of Campeau's plans to raise new financing through special mortgages and retire large chunks of his debt. Within the last two years, Campeau had lost in his senior ranks Allied's Thomas Macioce, his retailing lieutenant, Robert Morosky, deputy chairman, David King, financial wizard Don Carroll and now Roddy, who had been instrumental in the takeovers.

Through all the changes, Bob Campeau remained *le chef* of

a company whose assets had reached $14.3 billion and whose annual revenues were now $8.7 billion. In place of the close-knit group of French Canadians who took the company through its first decades was a group of aggressive businessmen who could put together multibillion-dollar deals on Wall Street. Bob Campeau has come a long way from his days of hauling lumber and heaving sacks of potatoes. The men who helped him build his company are all dead or long retired, yet he goes on with seemingly undiminished energy. And love him or hate him, no one forgets him. In that respect, he has indeed emulated the heroes he admires.

Says his old competitor Bill Teron: "His compulsiveness is so complete and his confidence in his own ability is such that he says 'I've been right all the time and therefore I'm going to be right again.' It's kind of a blind spot. I hope he makes it."

Ilse's older sister Hilde: "I think I would prefer [Bob and Ilse] if they had less money, if they were more down-to-earth. You know, money does certain things to people. They're not the same people I used to know. She used to tell her children money is the root of all evil, and it was something the family always believed in. And whether one likes it or not, money does change people very often. It makes them more selfish, self-centered, and they live in a different world."

Alban Cadieux: "There aren't many men like Bob. He's a good man and he can move things."

Jacques: "Sure, I wish we could be a normal family. I don't have a father and my daughter doesn't have a grandfather. I don't get invited to his fishing camp in the summer or to the benefit dinner at Bloomingdale's. I'm not part of any of it. I'm not dying to be part of it, mind you, but I always thought my whole life would be with him and I've resigned myself that it won't be."

Father Ovila: "I think he's a kind of genius. He sees things that other people don't, and you may be completely against him when he wants this and that and the other thing, but after a while you have to admit he was right. And it could be that he has a role to play – I hope he has a role to play – in the expansion of the Kingdom of God. We have to have rich people;

we have to have good businessmen. In a country where there are no good businessmen, people are starving to death."

One of the original Twelve of the inner Campeau Corp. circle: "Eventually, all of us were not good enough. Maybe he was right. We didn't have the same vision. We didn't all want to conquer the world. Some of us were quite happy with what we had done, and we were quite proud of what we had done. He wasn't. There was never an end and there probably never will be for Bob. After Federated, it's going to be something else. He'll get restless. Why did Napoleon conquer one country after another? The way Bob sees himself, there is nothing that he couldn't do, he couldn't conquer. And he sincerely believes that to this day. Nothing will stop him."

APPENDIX

The Campeau-Power merger in November 1969 included the following financial details:

- Campeau Corp. exchanged 3.2 million of its common shares for 4.75 million shares, or 82.8 percent, of Canadian Interurban in a 7-for-10 share swap;
- Power obtained 2.65 million additional Campeau Corp. shares in exchange for 3.4 million Blue Bonnets common shares, 6,500 Show-Mart common shares, a $4.1 million 6.75 percent Show-Mart note, 300 Trans-Canada common shares and a $440,000, 7 percent Trans-Canada note;
- Bob Campeau sold Power 400,000 of his own common shares at $7.50 each;
- Campeau Corp. issued to Power 1 million Class B shares — each share carried warrants allowing purchases of an additional two shares in the same class — for $200,000;
- Power obtained a $6.4 million Campeau Corp. promissory note, bearing 6.63 percent annual interest, that was to be convertible at either company's option to 748,160 Campeau Corp. shares on what initially was a due date of December 31, 1974. In exchange, Campeau Corp. took an $859,358 note at 5.5 percent and $5.5 million note at 6.75 percent of Blue Bonnets. (In 1973, Power sold Campeau Corp.'s $6.4 million promissory notes to Quebec's Caisse de dépôt et placement for $12.4

million, reflecting discounted value and interest by the due date of December 31, 1982.)

Campeau Corp. issued a total 5.85 million common shares to Power, valued at $34.4 million, and 1 million of the Class B shares valued at $200,000. Campeau's personal sale of 400,000 shares brought the total cost to Power to $37.6 million.

Campeau Corp. later made a follow-up offer to remaining stockholders of Canadian Interurban, bringing its owner-ship up to 98.5 percent in a similar 7-for-10 share swap, and also increasing the number of Campeau Corp. shares outstanding.

Power ended up with 6.3 million common shares of Campeau Corp., or about 48.5 percent of that class, and all 1 million special Class B shares outstanding. In total, Power held just shy of 7.3 million share votes, or 52.2 percent of the almost 14 million votes in the Campeau Corp. structure.

The Class B shares carried one vote each, but a trigger was built in. If more Campeau Corp. shares were ever outstanding, for total voting rights of 14.6 million, those shares would have ten votes each. Otherwise, Power's control could have been reduced to a shade under 50 percent if Campeau Corp.'s total votes had ever reached 14.6 million.

If the 10-for-1 system had ever kicked in, Power would have owned 16.3 million votes of a total 24.6 million votes in Campeau Corp., or well above 50 percent.

The 1 million Class B shares issued to Power were placed in escrow for fifteen years. The agreement specified that Power would sell those shares to Campeau Corp. for cancellation under the following circumstances:
• If the total number of common shares held by Campeau, Clauda and the family trusts fell below 2 million, a level that would represent about 14.3 percent of the total votes of Campeau Corp.;
• If Power's holdings, with Campeau's consent, fell below 4.5 million shares at a price at least equal to the market price of the stock;
• If Power decided to sell all its Campeau Corp. common shares at prices not less than the going market price.

Power also agreed it would not dump more than 5,000 of its Campeau Corp. shares as long as Campeau, Clauda and the trusts continued to own at least 2 million shares, unless Power offered to buy from other stockholders a proportionate number of their shares.

NOTES

Direct quotes not attributed below or in the text itself are from interviews conducted by the authors.

Prologue
• The Bloomingdale's AIDS benefit story is based on the Canadian Broadcasting Corp.'s "Venture" and a New York Times Service article printed April 7, 1988, in the *Globe and Mail.*

Chapter 1
• Page 10, paragraph 4. Campeau quote is from Sheila McLeod Arnopoulos, *Voices from French Ontario* (Kingston and Montreal: McGill-Queens' University Press, 1982), p. 152.
• Page 11, paragraph 3. Campeau quote is from the *New York Times Magazine*, July 17, 1988, p. 20.

Chapter 3
• Page 34, paragraph 1. Campeau quote is from a Canadian Press report printed August 19, 1980, in the *Sudbury Star.*
• Page 35, paragraph 4. Rod McQueen, *The Moneyspinners* (Don Mills, Ont.: Totem Books, 1984), p. 43.
• Page 38, paragraph 8. Campeau quote is from *Executive* magazine, June 1982, p. 59.
• Page 45, paragraph 2 is based on Lionel Campeau, "Les Splendides Débuts de la Corporation Campeau" (unpublished memoirs of Lionel Campeau). Many of the specifics on building projects in Chapters 3

and 5 are from this source, as well as interviews with Lionel Campeau and other former employees of the company.

• Page 46, paragraph 2. Jean Paradis quote is from Susan Goldenberg, *Men of Property: The Canadian Developers Who Are Buying America* (Toronto: Personal Library,1981), p. 170.

Chapter 4

• Page 48, paragraph 2. Christmas season and the 1952 company party are based on Lionel Campeau, "Les Splendides Débuts de la Corporation Campeau."

• Page 52, paragraph 3. The Campeau reunion story is based on Lionel Campeau, "Les Splendides Débuts de la Corporation Campeau."

Chapter 5

• Page 59, paragraph 1. Quotes are from an interview with Joe Johnston and from Lionel Campeau, "Les Splendides Débuts de la Corporation Campeau."

• Page 64 paragraph 3. Campeau quote is from *Executive* magazine, June 1982, p. 59.

Chapter 6

• The encounters between Campeau and Charlotte Whitton throughout this chapter are based largely on articles printed in the *Ottawa Journal.*

• Page 73, paragraphs 3 and 4. Whitton and Campeau quotes are from a Canadian Press report printed August 19, 1980, in the *Sudbury Star.*

• Page 76, paragraph 2. Campeau quote is from *Toronto Life*, November 1975.

Chapter 7

• Page 93, paragraph 2. Jacques Campeau quote is from *The Globe and Mail*, April 20, 1988.

• Page 94, paragraph 4. Clauda and Campeau quotes are from a document filed in their divorce proceedings.

• Page 95, paragraph 5. Campeau quote is from Sheila McLeod Arnopoulos, *Voices from French Ontario*, p. 154.

Chapter 8

• The Place de Ville story is pieced together from Ontario Municipal Board files; *Ottawa Journal* articles; Campeau Corp. reports;

Douglas H. Fullerton's special 1974 government study on the National Capital, *The Capital of Canada: How Should It Be Governed?*; and Robert Collier, *Contemporary Cathedrals: Large-Scale Developments in Canadian Cities* (Montreal: Harvest House, 1974).

Chapter 9
• Page 119, paragraph 1. Campeau quote is from *The Globe and Mail*, June 20, 1975.
• Page 123, paragraph 2. Jean Paradis quote is from *Canadian Business* magazine, April 1982, p. 63.

Chapter 10
• Page 136, paragraph 1. Campeau quote is from Susan Goldenberg, *Men of Property: The Canadian Developers Who Are Buying America*, p. 163.
• Page 137, paragraph 1. Jean Marchand quote is from *The Globe and Mail*, January 5, 1979.
• Page 139, paragraph 4 and following. The events and negotiations leading up to government approval of Les Terrasses de la Chaudière are taken from *The Globe and Mail*, January 14, 1980, and the *Ottawa Citizen*, June 28, 1978.
• Page 141, paragraph 3. Raymond Affleck quote is from *The Globe and Mail*, January 5, 1979.
• Page 142, paragraph 4. Pierre Juneau letter is quoted in Susan Goldenberg, *Men of Property: The Canadian Developers Who Are Buying America*, p. 176.
• Page 143, paragraph 2. Douglas Fullerton quote is from a Canadian Press wire service report carried June 9, 1978, in *The Globe and Mail*.
• Page 143, paragraph 3. Lawsuit details are from the *Ottawa Citizen*, September 28, 1978, and November 18, 1978.
• Page 144, paragraph 3. Susan Goldenberg, *Men of Property: The Canadian Developers Who Are Buying America*, p. 177.
• Page 145, paragraph 4. Judd Buchanan quotes are from *The Globe and Mail*, January 5, 1979.
• Page 145, paragraph 5. First Campeau quote is from *The Globe and Mail*, January 5, 1979; second Campeau quote is from *Report on Business Magazine*, March 1987, p. 27.
• Page 147, paragraph 5. Details of the memo are from *The Globe and Mail*, January 29, 1985.

Chapter 11
- Page 161, paragraph 1. Campeau quote is from *The Globe and Mail*, August 2, 1984.
- Page 161, paragraph 4. David King quote is from Susan Goldenberg, *Men of Property: The Canadian Developers Who Are Buying America*, p. 171.
- Page 163, paragraph 2. The William Pershaw story is from the *Ottawa Citizen*, February 1, 1978.
- Page 164, paragraph 4. Jacques Campeau quote is from *The Globe and Mail*, April 20, 1988.

Chapter 12
- Page 176, paragraph 4, and following. The conversation between Campeau and Kenneth White is reconstructed from testimony to the Ontario Securities Commission in 1981. Virtually all conversations, and most of the recollections, in this chapter are from the OSC testimony.
- Page 182, paragraph 2. Campeau quote is from Sheila McLeod Arnopoulos, *Voices from French Ontario*, p. 154.
- Page 182, paragraph 3. Campeau quote is from Diane Francis, *Controlling Interest: Who Owns Canada?* (Toronto: Seal Books, 1987), p. 179.
- Page 182, paragraph 4. Kenneth White quote is from an interview.
- Page 184, paragraph 3. Ira Gluskin quote is from *Maclean's*, October 13, 1980, p. 46.
- Page 187, paragraph 3. Campeau quote is from *Report on Business Magazine*, March 1987, p. 30.
- Page 193, paragraph 3. Don Carroll quote is from *The Globe and Mail*, September 22, 1980.
- Page 196, paragraph 3. Campeau quote is from *Report on Business Magazine*, March 1987, p. 28.

Chapter 13
- Page 197, paragraph 1. Don Carroll quote is from Susan Goldenberg, *Men of Property: The Canadian Developers Who Are Buying America*, p. 188.
- Page 198, paragraph 5. Campeau quote is from *Executive* magazine, June 1982, p. 61.
- Page 199, paragraph 3. Campeau quote is from *Canadian Business* magazine, April 1982, p. 61.

• Page 208, paragraph 3. Campeau's remark to Richard Thomson is from *Report on Business Magazine*, March 1987, p. 30.

• Page 208, paragraph 4. Campeau quote is from *Report on Business Magazine*, March 1987, p. 30.

• Page 212, paragraph 1. Campeau quote is from *Report on Business Magazine*, March 1987, p. 28.

Chapter 14

• The Campeau-Macioce conversations in this chapter are, for the most part, reconstructed from an Allied Stores Corp. information statement to shareholders released after the deal with Campeau was reached.

• Page 229, paragraph 5. The Campeau-Macioce encounter is from an interview with Macioce.

• Page 231, paragraph 4. Bruce Wasserstein quote is from the *Wall Street Journal*, November 4, 1986.

• Page 234, paragraph 3. Campeau quote is from a December 31, 1987, offer-to-purchase document by a Campeau-owned numbered company seeking to buy subordinate voting shares and debentures of Campeau Corp.

Chapter 15

• Page 240, paragraph 2. The reporter was Michael Babad.

• Page 246, paragraph 3. The reporter was Michael Babad.

Chapter 16

• Page 259, paragraph 4. The reporter was Michael Babad.

• Page 262, paragraph 1. Campeau quote is from the *Wall Street Journal*, March 15, 1988.

• Page 269, paragraph 3. Ed Finkelstein quote is from the *Wall Street Journal*, April 4, 1988.

Chapter 17

• Page 271, paragraph 4. Campeau quote is from the *Wall Street Journal*, April 4, 1988.

• Page 273, paragraph 3. Ed Finkelstein quote is from the *Wall Street Journal*, April 4, 1988.

• Page 279, paragraph 1. Ed Finkelstein quote is from the *Wall Street Journal*, April 4, 1988.

• Page 281, paragraph 5. Jacques Campeau quote is from an article carried April 26, 1988, by the Southam news service.

BIBLIOGRAPHY

Amiel, Barbara. "Robert Campeau's Waterfront Memorial." *Toronto Life* (November 1975), pp. 48-52, 71.

Arnopoulos, Sheila McLeod. *Voices from French Ontario*. Kingston and Montreal: McGill-Queen's University Press, 1982.

Ballen, Kate. "Campeau Is on a Shopper's High." *Fortune* (15 August 1988), pp. 70-73.

Campeau Corp. Annual reports, 1968 – 87.

Campeau, Lionel. "Les Splendides Débuts de la Corporation Campeau." Unpublished memoirs.

Collier, Robert. *Contemporary Cathedrals: Large-Scale Developments in Canadian Cities*. Montreal: Harvest House, 1974.

Fleming, James. "Glory Days." *Report on Business Magazine* (July 1988), pp. 36-46.

Francis, Diane. *Controlling Interest: Who Owns Canada?* Toronto: Seal Books, 1987.

Fullerton, Douglas H. *The Capital of Canada: How Should It Be Governed?* Special government study on the National Capital, 1974.

Goldenberg, Susan. *Men of Property: The Canadian Developers Who Are Buying America.* Toronto: Personal Library, 1981.

Johnson, Arthur. "The Best Revenge." *Report on Business Magazine* (March 1987), pp. 22-31.

Lilley, Wayne. "Living Well is the Best Revenge." *Canadian Business* (April 1982), pp. 62-66.

Lorimer, James. *The Developers.* Toronto: James Lorimer & Company, 1978.

McQueen, Rod. *The Moneyspinners.* Don Mills: Totem Books, 1984.

Patton, Phil. "The Man Who Bought Bloomingdale's." *New York Times Magazine* (17 July 1988), pp. 16-20, 32, 51, 58, 61.

INDEX